New Views
of Tibetan Culture

New Views
of Tibetan Culture

edited by David Templeman

Monash University Press
Caulfield

Monash University Press
MAI, Building H
Monash University
Victoria 3145, Australia
www.monash.edu.au/mai

All Monash University Press publications are subject to double blind peer review

© Monash Asia Institute 2010
The authors retain ownership of intellectual property for their own chapters

National Library of Australia cataloguing-in-publication data:

Title: New views of Tibetan culture / edited by David Templeman.

ISBN: 9781876924775 (pbk.).

Series: Monash papers on Tibet ; 1.

Notes: Includes bibliographical references.

Subjects: Tibet (China)—Civilization.

Other Authors/Contributors:
             Templeman, David.

Dewey Number: 951.5

Cover design by Minnie Doron. Cover images of prayer flags and prayer wheels by Jenny Hall (jenny-hall.smugmug.com). Image of Tibetan children by Chris Dade (chrisdade.co.uk), and reproduced with permission of the Tibetan Children's Village.

To support the work of the Tibetan Children's Village in nurturing and educating destitute Tibetan children in exile, please visit www.tcv.org.in.

Printed by BPA Print Group, Melbourne, Australia - www.bpabooks.com

contents

	Contributors	vii
	Introduction *David Templeman*	1
Chapter one	Defining peripheral power: writing the history of the Kingdom of Lhathog, Eastern Tibet *Amy Holmes-Tagchungdarpa*	7
Chapter two	A window on Rebkong: architecture, technology and social change in Amdo Tibetan communities *Mark Stevenson*	21
Chapter three	Intersections of physical and spiritual powers *Kalzang Dorjee Bhutia*	43
Chapter four	Multiculturalism on the Tibetan border: the temple of Trilokināth in Lahul *Diana Cousens*	53
Chapter five	Ama Adhe, the voice that remembers *Isabella Ofner*	79
Chapter six	He who shall not be named: the Shugden taboo and Tibetan national identity in exile *Wokar Tso Rigumi*	93
Chapter seven	Tibetan clerical attitudes to armed conflict: the cases of Tāranātha and the 14th Dalai Lama *David Templeman*	103
Chapter eight	A modern portrait of a Tibetan incarnate *lama* *Gillian Tan*	123
Chapter nine	Laughing Vajra: the oucast clown, satirical guru and smiling Buddha in Milarepa's songs *Ruth Gamble*	137
	Glossary of Tibetan spelling	167
	Bibliography	175

contributors

Kalzang Dorjee Bhutia is a PhD candidate at Delhi University and an independent scholar. His research explores Sikkimese history and the relationship between religion and state as portrayed in Sikkimese and Tibetan literature between the 17th and 20th centuries. He is also interested in the role of treasure discoverers (tertön) in the development of Tibeto-Himalayan political and religious cultures.

Diana Cousens completed a PhD on the temple of Triloknath in Lahul at Monash University in 2008. Her study stemmed from a long-standing interest in self-arising sacred objects, which in turn came about as a result of extensive pilgrimage in India and elsewhere in the 1980s and 1990s. Diana's other research interests are in the treasure and visionary traditions of Tibetan Buddhism. She has made a practical contribution to the Buddhist community in Australia through an ongoing engagement in Buddhist palliative care and interfaith dialogue.

Ruth Gamble is completing a PhD on the travelling songs of the Third Karmapa at the Australian National University, where she also works as sessional lecturer and tutor. She is also involved in research projects on Tibetan women's oral traditions, and contemporary Tibetan literature. She has worked as a journalist in Melbourne and Japan, and as a Tibetan–English interpreter in Australia and India.

Amy Holmes-Tagchungdarpa is an assistant professor in the Department of History, University of Alabama. She completed her PhD at the Australian National University in 2008. Her current research focuses on the construction of authority and empiricism in the Tibetan cultural sphere through research on traditional genres of Tibetan historiographical and religious literature, particularly biographical and genealogical texts, and also the relationships between gender, sexuality and authority in the borderlands of Tibet.

Isabella Ofner is a PhD candidate in the Centre for Postcolonial Writing, School of English, Communication and Performance Studies at Monash University. She holds the position of Administrative Assistant at the Centre for Postcolonial Writing and is Managing Editor in Postcolonial Literature of Routledge's online Annotated Bibliography of Literary Studies. Her thesis explores Tibetan women's autobiographies within the discourses of diaspora and nationalism. She is also interested in researching the intersections of travel writing and political representation, diasporic literature as testimony, the discourse of literature and human rights, as well as contemporary Asian-Australian writing.

Wokar Tso Rigumi completed her degree in BA (Honours) in English Literature at Miranda House, University of Delhi. She has recently completed a Masters in Cultural Studies at RMIT University, Melbourne, on the hybridity of three Tibeto-Chinese writers of the 'root-seeking' literary generation in Tibet.

Mark Stevenson (PhD Melb, 2000) is an anthropologist and senior lecturer in Asian Studies at Victoria University, Melbourne. He has research interests in problems of social change, art and social space. He is currently exploring these problems in two separate fields: contemporary Tibetan communities, and late-imperial Chinese literature (1550–1911). His study of change, art and social space in Tibetan communities has been conducted primarily in Amdo Rebkong, and he has published papers on the recent history of painting in Rebkong, on the writing of the late Dondrup Gyel, and on the introduction of non-traditional art forms. He is currently developing a project on contemporary processes of culture contact and architectural changes that reflect shifts in social relations along the Sino–Tibetan interface.

Gillian Tan holds a PhD in anthropology from the University of Melbourne. Her thesis was titled *'Into the pass: perceptions of change and permanence on the Tibetan plateau'*. She has worked for a variety of international development organisations and lived in Tibet for a number of years. She conducted ethnographic fieldwork in Eastern Tibet (Khams) in 2006. In addition, she is co-founding Director of Rabsal, a Tibetan non-governmental organisation that uses multimedia technology to train young Tibetans in ethnographic and documentary film-making. At present she is a visiting scholar at the Collége de France, Paris.

David Templeman (PhD Monash 2009) has been for many years a translator of Tibetan historical texts. At present he is an Adjunct Research Fellow at Monash Asia Institute, Monash University, Melbourne. His interests are the religio-political nexus in 16–17th century Tibet and the dynamic of Tibetan exilic life. Currently he is researching the late phase (16–17th centuries) of Buddhism in India and the methods of its transfer to Tibet, as well as its reception there. He has published three translated works as well as many articles on a variety of Tibetan topics.

introduction

David Templeman

This book presents an overview of contemporary work in the field of Tibetan research in Australia. It is both encouraging and gratifying to see such innovation in the scholar's exploration of previously unexamined areas of Tibetan culture. Australian contributors to Tibetan studies appear to have consistently adopted unusual, and sometimes unique, approaches to their subject. At the same time they have managed to retain a high level of scholarly integrity. This has arisen largely because scholars of various Tibetan fields have normally been forced to work in isolation, and frequently within discipline areas only marginally connected with Tibetan studies. Tibetan language and culture has never been taught formally at Australian tertiary institutions, save as an adjunct to China studies or as occasional and sporadic lectures contained within the more general topic of 'Buddhism'. This has been the general rule with only three exceptions which I am aware of.[1]

Despite this lack of formal instruction young Australian scholars continue to pursue their research and to produce Tibetan studies in a variety of disciplines ranging from anthropology to literary theory. Many of these scholars bring to their work novel and unique perspectives not frequently encountered in contributions arising from more formal teaching situations.

The question must then be asked, 'If there are so few places in Australia for younger scholars to study Tibetan language, culture, history and so forth, where exactly do those who manage to study it in the academy get their grounding?'. It appears to be the case that many students engaged in Tibetan studies in Australia have been what might be referred to as 'self-starters'. That is, they have learned their particular skills independently of the academy, for example as translators for Lamas, through their work in the field for NGOs, or as private scholars with an abiding interest in the field. Such an overview holds true for the authors of many of the chapters in this modest collection. At least four of the contributors have entered the field having gained their considerable skills in precisely these types of extra-academic setting. Following from this, and to extend an observation concerning the new wave of Tibetan scholars made by Brandon Dotson (2009:x), the great majority of the contributors in this volume are Tibetan speakers and are able to move in a wide range of situations ranging from anthropological observation on the ground to specific problems of Tibetan modernity and other new fields of study.

One of the strengths of these chapters is their spirit of originality and their willingness to move beyond the traditional confines of 'Tibetan Studies', which in the past has often become simply a synonym for 'Buddhist Studies'. The chapters cover a variety of locations, times and approaches and retain a strong sense of being truly independent pieces of scholarship. The sometimes clearly individualistic approach may well be part of the spirit of the emerging Australian academic mood. This mood is one in which restrictions are only rarely placed on young scholars who for the most part, remain able to pursue their fields quite independently.

The work of Tibetanists such as Geoffrey Samuel, Toni Huber, Matthew Kapstein and Hildegard Diemberger appears to have informed much of the work of these younger scholars. The field of Tibetan studies seems to be no longer hemmed in by the extremes of a purely philological approach or the anthropological niceties of the endless emic / etic debate. These scholars demonstrate that for them at least, many of the previous restrictions that tended to curtail a free approach to inquiry are now considered quite passé. Along with this clear attitudinal change these scholars bring a broader armamentarium of skills to bear upon the discipline, demonstrating their acute awareness of the trajectory that Tibetan studies has taken internationally.

A certain sense of bravado is required for such an approach. It will be noted that this confidence is to be found in the work of these scholars in abundance. This observation is in no manner intended to imply that theirs is a foolhardy or unthinking approach. Rather, it suggests that the quite clear and defined boundaries that once held the discipline firmly within generally accepted confines, now seem to have been breached, revealing a wider and sometimes more productive horizon.

In chapter 1, Amy Holmes takes the reader to the isolated and little-known Lhathog region of Khams. She explores the nature of peripheral authority as exemplified in Lhathok through a reading of the largely unstudied text, the *Lha thog gdung rabs*. In particular, she focuses her discussion upon the fact that despite the sense of independence that the rulers of Lhathog felt from both the Tibetan Government of the Ganden Podrang and Chinese Imperial rule, the kings of Lhathok themselves were still preoccupied with a centralised (and to an extent, bureaucratised) system of authority. This point is used further to explore the nature of power in the region, and Holmes argues that the process of legitimation in peripheral areas of Tibet still required older, more powerful centralised imageries for their sense of legitimation.

In chapter 2, Mark Stevenson explores the introduction of new technology into the Tibetan social landscape. He uses the cultural artefact of the lattice window frame as the vehicle for his discussion. Noting the considerable social change that has occurred in Rebkong in Amdo, he identifies the window frame as a useful indicator of that change, and as the means by which the household can represent itself to the outside world. Moreover, Stevenson argues convincingly that the lattice window serves as a boundary marker to delineate the world of the private family from that of the public sphere. Not only does the window frame serve as a marker, but it also offers an outer indicator of the measure of economic success a family has developed—a sort of 'aesthetic public barometer' of one's achievements.

In chapter 3, Kalzang Dorjee Bhutia approaches a tendentious and difficult topic with grace and a broad sense of understanding. Primarily, his paper discusses the nature and significance of the 1712 donation by the ruler of Sikkim of vast estates to support the monastery of Pemayangtse. The chapter goes on to discuss the vexed issue of the now missing original donation document and the deleterious economic effects this has had on the monastery since the Indian annexation of Sikkim in 1975. But rather than lament the loss of the territory, Bhutia contextualises this difficult situation by exploring both the nature of the original donation itself and the various interpretations of it made by the British and the Indians. To their own advantage, both groups ignore the solemn and culturally important final few verses of the document, which stipulate that the ceding of the land to Pemayantse is beyond any revocation whatsoever. Bhutia concludes with an evocation of the positive mood evoked by the Treaty of Waitangi Tribunal in the 1970s in New Zealand as an example of a possible way out of the impasse that stalls Pemayangtse at present.

In chapter 4 Diana Cousens takes the reader to Lahul in the Western Himalayas where, at the temple of Triloknāth in the Chandrabhāga valley, there exists a mixture of local indigenous belief, as well as Hindu and Buddhist practice. Cousens records something of the complexity of the area and discusses the several overlapping accounts of the temple itself. But her primary focus is on what local people, and to a great extent, pilgrims from as far away as Ladakh and Central Tibet, believe to be the nature of the temple's focal image, said to have been a self-created image. For the Hindus the image represents Lord Śiva; for the Buddhists it is an image of Avalokiteśvara. The two are in agreement that it was spontaneously created. The chapter briefly explores the extent of overlap in the common site, such as Hindus revolving prayer wheels and Buddhists wearing blessed wrist bands, all of which contribute to what Cousens refers to as a sort of 'multiculturalism' in which several ostensibly variant communities are brought together by a common holy site and the veneration of a single image.

The current level of interest in modern Tibetan literature is reflected in chapter 5, in which Isabella Ofner discusses the means by which a sense of 'authenticity' may be conferred upon *testimonio* by Tibetan women writers. Ofner explores the various layers of expectation ('exotic commodification') that Western readers impose upon Tibetan *testimonio* literature and notes the various means by which our expectations and assumptions about what constitutes such writing may be effectively challenged. Writing about what is referred to as the 'vested interests of both the Tibetan community in exile and a sympathetic Western audience', she explores the interstices at which a more authentic and viable understanding might be reached. A particularly thorny issue is the tension between three agencies in such works: the Tibetan need for *testimonio* writing to work towards ultimate justice for the cause; the requirement for it to 'assume agency and thus to enter history'; and the sometimes diametrically opposed requirements of the publishers of such material, who frequently have quite different aims for such writing. Although the publishers might sympathise with the writer and her plight, their ostensible aim as 'wings' of Tibet support groups or of Dharma organisations is often directed primarily at their own needs. Such a tension then reflects in the editorship and ultimately the presentation and reception of the *testimonio* itself.

In chapter 6, Wokar Tso Rigumi presents the reader with a novel approach to the controversy of the Dalai Lama's attempt to encourage a unified image of Tibetans in exile by 'banning' of the worship of Dorje Shugden. She summarises the present state of the debate and then charts the deity Dorje Shugden in Tibetan cultural memory. While recognising that Dorje Shugden has a role outside that of Tibetan state formation, Rigumi suggests that he has now entered the realms of folk culture, sometimes attaining among Tibetan youth what she presents as an almost caricatured aspect, rather than the deadly serious image he presents to his worshippers and his opponents. Rigumi's chapter demonstrates how the controversy over Dorje Shugden has coagulated to become the alter-ego of a derivatively imagined Tibetan nation-in-exile.

I venture to discuss, in chapter 7, the problems experienced in the 17th and late 20th centuries when Buddhist prelates have been confronted with the realities of violence and warfare. The chapter opens with a case study of the 16–17th century Tibetan Lama Tāranātha, who was prelate to the ambitious and militaristic rulers of Tsang. Tāranātha seems to have been unable to criticise his patrons in a forthright manner for their precipitous behaviour, and it is suggested that he was unwilling to do so because he risked losing their valuable patronage. Tāranātha saw no conflict between his monastic rules and certain activities he was commanded to perform, such as blessing troops prior to battle. His advice on military matters was either non-committal, or avoided the issue entirely. The chapter then examines similar difficulties encountered by the present Dalai Lama in openly acknowledging the moral position of the Chuzhi Gangdrug, the so-called Tibetan guerrilla movement. Largely because of his monastic vows, the Dalai Lama feels unable to give open support for the Chuzhi Gangdrug's aims of defending both the land of Tibet and the Buddhist religion. This has led to the deeply felt but largely unchronicled disappointment of survivors and their relatives, many of whom feel utterly disenfranchised from the larger Tibetan body politic as a result.

In chapter 8 Gillian Tan allows the reader a precious glimpse into the life of a Tibetan Lama in the Minyag area of eastern Tibet. She describes in ethnographic terms the changes that have followed his building of a huge Golden *Stūpa* and the consequent attraction of a large number of student disciples. The chapter deals with the unique aspects of the Lama's activities and suggests that it is in fact as a result of his various successes that the Lama, Khenpo Dorje Tashi, might be what Weber refers to as a 'charismatic' person. The ethnographic description of various aspects of life in and around the Golden *Stūpa,* reveals precisely how inextricably linked his wide-ranging activities are, with not only a modernist approach to a practical Buddhism but to older, more traditional approaches to Buddhist development. Tan spent a considerable time living inside the *Stūpa* as part of the community of practitioners, and this adds to the description a sense of clear authenticity.

In chapter 9 Ruth Gamble presents a detailed overview of the role of humour, self-deprecation and wit in the so-called 'songs' of Milarepa. With judicious attention to the collection of the spontaneous songs as collected by the charismatic 'Mad *Yogi* of Tsang', she demonstrates how Milarepa not only drew on the traditions of the earlier Indian *siddhas*, the nonconformist saints who became a template for much Tibetan renunciate behaviour, but how he forged something uniquely Tibetan from those models. Gamble also locates the role of humour in the expression of religious experience and questions the rather more dour understanding of 'religious humour' that we in the West have become accustomed to. She suggests that, for Milarepa, humour was the very essence of how to express the nature of enlightenment itself.

Notes

1   The most notable exceptions to this have been Professor de Jong's post-graduate Buddhist studies programme at the Australian National University in the 1970s and 1980s and that of Mr Zahiruddin Ahmad, who taught a survey course in Tibetan culture in the mid-1970s at La Trobe University. More recently, a course on Tibetan culture has been taught every second year since 2000 by Dr Mark Stevenson at Victoria University, and appears to be very popular among undergraduates.

chapter one

Defining peripheral power: writing the history of the Kingdom of Lhathog, Eastern Tibet

Amy Holmes-Tagchungdarpa

Until 1959, the area known as historical Tibet encompassed myriad types of institutions and systems of authority. While there have been excellent academic overviews of some of these political systems, including those of monasteries and the estates of incarnations, and of large aristocratic estates related to religious families, such as those in Sakya, those of smaller units in peripheral areas ruled by leaders who gained legitimacy through being part of unbroken lines of hereditary authority remain largely unexplored. This chapter is part of wider movements in current scholarship that seek to expand upon knowledge of the peripheral border areas of Tibet by exploring traditional political systems through reference to a particular genre of literature known as a *gyalrab* (widely translated as a 'genealogy' or 'annals' of the ruling elite of a particular area). This chapter focuses on the historical development of the eastern Tibetan kingdom of Lhathog. Lhathog is a fascinating case study of a traditional Tibetan political system, as it remained largely isolated from the wider events around it and retained distinctive forms of social hierarchy. By the beginning of the twentieth century, Lhathog was one of only five political units in eastern Tibet that had a king (*gyalpo*) and an aristocratic family, even though most of the population were nomadic. The inhabitants of peripheral areas such as Lhathog appear to have had their own highly local forms of identification based on tribal and familial affiliations.

Looking at how two texts (that will be introduced below) represent the genealogy of the Lhathog kings, I explore the wider implications of *gyalrab* in the creation and consolidation of peripheral political units in Tibetan societies. Genealogies are often read only as lists of facts and sometimes serve as brief biographies of various leaders. However, the obsession that their authors often exhibit in the meticulous recording of events reveals that genealogies also function as statements of legitimation for alternative centres of power within the Tibetan cultural sphere, thereby outlining an alternative mode of remembering in Tibetan culture. These alternative centres of power can be considered as powerful on social, economic and spiritual levels, as well as on a political level. A mechanism often used in Tibetan genealogies, as in the genealogies of the kings of Lhathog, is the recounting of how a kingdom has descended from the lineage of the Yarlung kings, who were considered to be the earliest kings of Tibet. Considering Lhathog's apparent concern with emphasising and reinforcing its autonomy by recording it in text, textual content that traces the aristocracy's lineage back to the traditional original rulers of Central Tibet may at first appear strange. Why were the biographers of the Lhathog kings, centuries after the disappearance of the Yarlung dynasty, still preoccupied with centralised authority? I argue that this appearance is in no way contradictory and does not disrupt the validity of the genealogies of Lhathog as historical texts. I believe that the way in which genealogies and the information within them are received needs to be reconsidered. Rather than seeing the appearance of the Yarlung kings in the annals of Lhathog either as a kind of power-borrowing exercise on the part of a small kingdom or as a way that the Lhathog kings might establish themselves as holders of ancient authority in constrast to other newer groups, I regard it as an attempt to define Lhathog as a centre in its own right through the borrowing of figures from histories that are most often considered central in Tibetan imagination. This statement ultimately disrupts previous concepts of the idea of the centre and periphery in Tibetan societies, since this reading of a genealogy suggests that kingdoms and political unities such as Lhathog ultimately conceived of themselves as their own centres, even as other centres tried to define them as the periphery. The genealogies of Lhathog are fascinating documents whose contents outline historical incidents, interpersonal networks, marital affiliations and other forms of power creation that all established a unique sense of place and identity for Lhathog.

This chapter is intended to be construed as part of a wider attempt to problematise more generally the creation and interpretation of the reading of history in Tibetan societies. Rather than seeing smaller political players as being swept away by wider currents, I explore in this chapter the contents of a text that is emically recognised as being historical, in order to understand more about the internal categories of historical veracity that existed in Tibetan literature and about what they can tell us about power in traditional Tibetan societies. I also aim to suggest how peripheral areas of Tibet may be situated within the wider discourse of centre–periphery studies. This is an important exercise, as cultural Tibet was historically extremely diverse, providing many forms of political and social configurations for researchers to explore. The case of Lhathog suggests a configuration in which authority is redrawn in complex ways on local and national levels in Tibet and may perhaps be used to draw some of Tibet's peripheries into wider conversations about the nature of statecraft in borderland areas of Asia.[1]

My discussion is informed by two texts. Several annals have been written for the aristocracy of Lhathog, but in presenting the argument in this chapter I am focusing on two texts with very different backgrounds. The first was written by a Lhathog resident, Gyurmé Namgyal sometime in 1852 (LTDR1) and the second in 2005–06, by Lhathog-born Kathmandu resident, Tshompa Lo Washul Geleg (LTDR2). These texts are distinct because the authors were born at different times and wrote their works with different considerations in mind. Initially, I wondered if references to the Yarlung kings in the more recent text might have been influenced by the politics of Tibetan government-in-exile, which present Tibet as a historically coherent and unified nation, in the modern sense of the word, by emphasising links to central Tibet and by creating a coherent memory of Lhathog through textualisation and publication. It is interesting to consider the readers of the two texts and how this readership influences the presentation of events recorded within them. The 1852 text would most probably have been read by literate people in Lhathog. The 2006 text has a much wider potential audience—it was printed and distributed among Tibetan exiles in South Asia—and is more easily accessible, as it can be purchased at a number of public book stores in major centres of exile. It has some similarities with the earlier text by Gyurmé Namgyal. The coherence of certain parts of the 2006 narrative suggests strong oral traditions, although it also appears that the author of the 2006 text has certainly read the earlier text. The 1852 text refers more frequently to other written works and also emphasises the role of Buddhism as a tool for creating the legitimacy of the aristocracy, an emphasis that is not discussed further in this chapter.

'Constellations of power' in Tibetan societies: the centre and periphery of Tibetan politics

To begin with, an understanding of wider concepts of power and statehood in Tibetan societies is important to put Lhathog into a political context. Geoffrey Samuel (1982) has suggested that Tibet was by and large stateless in the pre-modern period, made up of decentralised powers. On different parts of the Tibetan plateau and in areas around it vastly different forms of political systems operated, including hereditary fiefdoms, monastic estates and nomadic tribes. No power ever became large enough to unite the many systems until the appearance of the Ganden Phodrang in the 17th century. This central government appeared initially with the establishment of the office of the Dalai Lama with the military support of the Dzungar Mongols in 1642. However, the real effects of the power of this regime on a local level were highly uneven in peripheral areas of the Tibetan cultural world. Reasons for this unevenness are complex and may have related as much to natural geographical boundaries as to differing localised cultural conceptions of power. Often the only real power that the central government had was to request taxes and tribute from smaller states.

Kham, the eastern part of Tibet, has been identified in many studies as an example of an area loosely defined by cultural links that distinguished it from central Tibet and other areas but containing a variety of political groups over which other powers had difficulty gaining centralised control. Many political groups, including the Ganden Phodrang after 1642 and the Qing dynasty, attempted on various occasions to create a sense of unity. The inhabitants of Kham and its geographical barriers contributed to the difficulty of maintaining control over the area and Kham was never unified independently of foreign intervention either. As Geoffrey Samuel (1995:61–3) has noted, much of Tibetan society before 1959 had no fixed centre of power. He has used Stanley Tambiah's concept of 'galactic polities' to describe different centres of power in Tibetan societies. Yudru Tsomu considers that to use Tambiah's theory alone to account for the complexity of political forms in Kham is insufficient. She suggests that the historical states within Kham could be called 'polities', allowing for the idea of an elastic relationship between two centres that have'... a system of moral and political economy in a limited sense which existed as an autonomous entity and without much interference from an external sovereign body' (Yudru 2006:28). The concept of an external sovereign power being present in pre-modern Kham is deeply problematic, as the idea of sovereignty implies a type of legitimate rule that did not exist, other than in the requesting of taxes and tributes mentioned above. Yudru Tsomu's conceptualisation accounts for the plurality of political forms in Kham and also recognises the theoretically autonomous nature of authority within many of these polities. These polities were managed by local leaders and, though they did have relationships with external political powers, they regarded themselves as autonomous. There were several forms of local leadership: the traditional aristocratic chieftains or kings (*gyalpo*); the hereditary lords (*depa*); the later *tu si* (local chiefs nominated by Chinese dynasties to reign loosely over frontier regions through whom they exercised indirect rule); and lamas who controlled monastic centres. While relations between states were often maintained through marital ties or other trading agreements (Yudru 2006:235), conflict between them was the norm. Societies in Kham had strong cultures of *machismo* and revenge, and disputes over land and wealth were frequent (Yudru 2006:235).

The geographically imposed isolation of different social groups in Kham did not mean that there were no organs of authority. William Coleman (2002:32) has identified four groups in Kham that had social authority: the local monasteries; the local leaders; the Qing officials; and the merchants in the area. He notes that none of these groups held absolute power. Drawing upon

Prasenjit Duara's framework of a 'cultural nexus of power', he concludes that it was their negotiation between one another that created authority. In Duara's words, 'the cultural nexus serves as a framework that structures access to power and resources in local society [and] also serves as the arena in which politics is contested and leadership developed in a society' (Duara 1998:15).

In this chapter, however, I want to move past the concept of a 'cultural nexus of power' to explore the types of localised powers that formed the nexus. Although Duara recognises that power is defined by local conditions, his framework does not account for the fluidity of local power. The study presented in this chapter is based upon the assumption of this fluidity and upon the idea that power shifts between different groups over time. Power does not necessarily rest only with groups. Other, more ambiguous forces may also be at play, including cultural ideologies such as religion. The term 'constellations' is used in this study because it encompasses the different forms and movements of power and acknowledges that power is not absolute or fixed. Constellations can be seen as groups of ideas that may be perceived to be related through sometimes tenuous themes, or as arrangements of parts or elements that are connected somehow. The primary meaning of the word 'constellation' relates to astronomy and the mapping of stars and their relationship to each other. In this study, the interplaying constellations of power in societies can be derived from themes common to all the definitions above. As Coleman and Yudru have both shown, authority in the peripheral areas of Tibet was often held by disparate parties that engaged in ongoing negotiation that tipped the balance of power between them in different instances. In my own research, the disparate groups and the ideological forces present on the periphery of Tibet are presented as constellations—shifting and fluid, but connected and, although plotable on a map, always prone to change.

As Yudru Tsomu has recently pointed out,

> ...too often traditional studies of the frontier emphasize the imperial state or centers of power as the sole historically-important actor in the relationship between the center and periphery, and, in doing so, they deny the local perspective and agency of the frontier societies by portraying them as passive objects and completely overlooking their initiatives as well as response to the hegemonic power of the center (Yudru 2006:3).

The frontier studied in this chapter is the religious one presented by geographically and socially independent communities, such as the kingdom of Lhathog. These communities were only partly related to a centre but observers have often over-emphasised this relationship. This has led to presentations of communities that deny their local perspective and agency, as Yudru notes in the passage cited above. The way to address this denial is to attempt to capture and present the voice of this frontier so that the localised events that took shape through the agency of those on the periphery are represented more evenly. Yudru continues: 'With this new emphasis on localised context, events unfold as dialogue and negotiation, rather than with a dominant centre and passive local' (Yudru 2006:3). This chapter only begins this process for the kingdom of Lhathog and I intend to draw out the voice of Lhathog further in future research. This chapter presents the thesis for this research and, hopefully, will encourage others conducting research into the history of peripheral areas in the Himalayas to look beyond convention in their use and interpretation of sources such as genealogies.

The genealogical genre in Tibetan literature

A means of access to the voice of the periphery are texts such as genealogies or annals, known as *gyalrab* or *dungrab*. These texts are often mined for historical information, but readers are often confronted with lists of names and dates rather than juicy stories and dismiss the mythical sections that relate the original appearance of the aristocracy of an area as fanciful. Rather than seeing these names and dates and myths as irrelevant, I believe that they are intended as proof of an internal form of historical recording and empiricism that outlines power relations. The details of marriages, for instance, provide fascinating suggestions of how small polities such as Lhathog reinforced their boundaries through interpersonal connections, and the information that links aristocrats to different monasteries as patrons or as monks reveals just how aristocrats reinforced their own authority. The mythical genealogies do not necessarily only represent wishful links to previous kings; they are also real indicators of how groups legitimated their triumphs over competing factions for power. The texts of *gyalrab* present, therefore, alternative histories that are internally legitimated within Tibetan societies and make political statements that reiterate the legitimacy of a ruling family over a particular area. Genealogies were written by the kings themselves and are found throughout Tibet and, although they are highly localised in their content, they tend to adhere to a particular structural norm that ratifies them as part of a coherent literary genre and affords them culturally imbued power.

Lhathog as a physical space: representations of Lhathog in the genealogies

In order to support this interpretation of genealogies as political histories and manifestos that define boundaries of polities, I will discuss representations of Lhathog found in the texts mentioned earlier, which are among the few surviving textual sources about the kingdom, all of which support in some way claims of Lhathog's isolation and autonomy. Nestled in the heartland of Khampa culture,

Lhathog has been largely ignored in accounts of Khampa regional politics. The only Western traveller who wrote of his experience there, British consular official Eric Teichman, visited during the battles between the Chinese Republican forces and the representative of the Lhasa government, the Kalön Lama, in 1918. He made only the brief comment that 'Crossing the Lazhi La we passed from Chamdo territory into Hlato (Chinese Nato), a small native State constituting a narrow wedge between De-ge and Chamdo' (Teichman 2000 [1922]:156).

Though a number of foreigners passed through Kham—Lhathog appears on their maps west of the Yangtze River—during this period,none actually described Lhathog. Perhaps because it was small, Lhathog was often considered to be part of the neighbouring kingdom of Chamdo, as noted in several Lhasa reports. Lhathog thus appears to be precisely the kind of peripheral power described by Yudru Tsomu; its voice, therefore, is largely unheard.

The Kingdom of Lhathog was surrounded by several major powers in Khampa politics. To the north was the kingdom of Nangchen, ruled by a *gyalpo*; to the east was the kingdom of Dégé, also ruled by a *gyalpo*; to the southwest was the polity of Chamdo, ruled by a *lama*; and to the south was the kingdom of Beri, ruled by a *gyalpo*. Further south were the monastic polities of Drakyab and Markham (Teichman 2000 [1922]:3–5).

Lhathog was divided into three parts: Upper Lhathog (Lhathog tö), Lower Lhathog (Lhathog may), and Drugu (GGLG 1988:474), which are separated by high mountains and deep ravines. The fertility of its land and its extreme altitude meant that Lhathog was appropriate for nomadic pastoralist inhabitants. The land of Lhathog has been described in the 2006 text as being full of 'lung pa mdzes shing yid du 'ong ba/ sa gshin pa/ gter kha du mas phyug pa/ rtsa' shing sogs yul gzhan las lhag pa'i 'bel pa yod pa sogs la brten/ [beautiful, charming valleys with good soil, rich in minerals, with herbal trees and so on that surpass any others in the region in their abundance]' (LTDR2:7)

The history of Lhathog as presented in the genealogies

The exact date of human settlement of Lhathog is unknown. According to the first text about Lhathog by Gyurmé Namgyal (LTDR1:2), the name 'Lhathog' is derived from a story about the beginning of the Lhathog aristocracy. The Kings of Lhathog trace their lineage back to the original Tibetan kings in the Yarlung valley. The history of the imperial kings begins with an individual named Nyatri Tsenpo, who is said to have descended from the heavens of luminous gods to rule Tibet (LTDR1:2). He and the kings who came after him remained connected to heaven through a 'rope of light' which they used to return to heaven after their rule ended. However, at some point, one king's rope of light was broken after a dispute and afterwards the kings of Tibet became mortal. The Yarlung dynasty moved to Lhasa sometime in the sixth century and the kings who ruled over Lhasa became immortalised again in history through their role in bringing Buddhism to Tibet in the seventh century. During the ninth century Tibetan imperial rule disintegrated because of internal factionalism which led to a dark period of political fragmentation. The dark period gave way to a renaissance in Tibetan culture in the 11th and 12th centuries, when Buddhism was again diffused through Tibet and political authority was determined through alliances between monastic groups and various Mongol clans (Diemberger 2007:29–31).

The disintegration of Tibetan imperial rule did not mean that mythic memory of the early kings was wiped out. Many fiefdoms in Tibet claimed to be the descendants of the original Tibetan imperial family (Diemberger 2007:34) and Lhathog was one of the many small polities in Tibet that shaped a distinct authority from the legitimacy sanctioned by imperial ties. In Lhathog's oral tradition, the last of the 28 imperial kings, King Lhathothori Nyen Tsen, is held to be an emanation of the Buddhist primordial deity Kuntuzangpo. He had three sons, the oldest of whom became become ruler of Tibet and the youngest, known as Lhatsen, was sent to the realm of Dokham where he subjugated two districts, including the area Drugu Ladrag. So that the lineage of the first king would be remembered, Lhatsen named his kingdom Lhathog, a shortened form of his father's name, Lhathothori Nyen Tsen (LTDR2:7–9).

The story relates that when Lhatsen arrived, 'sbra gur la brten nas bzhugs gnas chags [a tent became his abode]' (LTDR2:8), suggesting a long history of nomadism in the area, as Lhathog was presumably a predominantly nomadic pastoralist area when the story took its present form. Robert Ekvall has written about the challenges of establishing authority over nomadic groups:

> Nomadic pastoralist communities have in many areas become identified with administrative districts of the central Tibetan government, yet the tribe, as a district and very early unit of political power, with varying degrees of autonomy and quasi, or real, independence, is the principal power entity. Pridefully, it has its own name, identity, and a strong sense of its rights, maintained by both force and evasive mobility. In some areas under pressure, it may retain little more than a name and vestigial powers; elsewhere it is a strong organization. (Ekvall 1968:29)

Despite the apparently autonomous nature of nomadic groups, the genealogical records portray that the inhabitants of Lhathog all recognised the authority of the king. This portrayal leads to a consolidated and unproblematised depiction of Lhathog's history, which is also found elsewhere in the genealogy. The genealogies do record that the rulers managed to retain their land through a series of skilful negotiations. A significant way for rulers of small polities to protect themselves was through marriage alliances. Both genealogical texts recount in great detail the marriage alliances between the kings of Lhathog and other neighbouring districts (for example, LTDR1:57–8).

Lhathog had other methods for protecting its borders. The nomadic inhabitants of the kingdom also formed a strong defence against attack. Oral sources tell of occasions when Lhathog and its neighbour Beri staved off the attack of the Lhasa government.[2] In 1751 they, along with the 39 Hor tribes,[3] were put under the supervision of the Chinese-appointed *amban* (Yudru 2006:39). During the ascendancy of Gonpo Namgyal, Lhathog was among the polities harassed by Gonpo's troops and may have been partially invaded.[4]

A crucial form of legitimacy for the continued rule of the Lhathog kings that has often been overlooked was the association between them and religious leaders within Lhathog, a point emphasised in both of the genealogies. Links with the Drukpa Kagyü were particularly close. This is recorded in episodes in *The Annals of Drugu* (GGLG) that mention extravagant gifts to religious hierarchs (for example, GGLG:477–8). Close relationships between religious hierarchs and the Lhathog aristocracy are also memorialised in oral tradition. One well-known example tells of how the second Drugu Chögyal incarnation was given a large area of land around Lhadag Pema Yang Dzong to build Drugu monastery and affiliated retreat centres, following his performance of a marriage ceremony for the Lhathog king and his new bride (Teichman 2000 [1922]:156n2).[5]

These early structures of authority, both imagined and exercised, persisted into the 20th century. Lhathog was one of the five polities within Kham that was ruled by kings in the early 20th century (Teichman 2000 [1922]:156), but the nomadic pastoralist population were largely autonomous in their daily lives. Following his brief visit in 1918, Eric Teichman noted that Lhathog had a population of 'only some 550 families' (Teichman 2000 [1922]: 156) in the area, who were mostly nomadic.[6] There is little information available to suggest what role, if any, Lhathog may have taken in the wider political events leading up to the change in government in Tibet in the 1950s. Yudru Tsomu has noted that indigenous rulers, such as the kings, tended to be highly selective in their involvement in wider politics, which meant that their relationships with larger sources of power were ambiguous. This does not mean that the kings of Lhathog did not collaborate with other authority groups. The lack of information about their collaboration, other than the mentions of marriage alliances, could be read as a desire for nostalgia on the part of the genealogies' authors. This nostalgia supports images of Lhathog as a unique and powerful place in its own right, which has been disrupted by the forces of modernity but which remains in its portrayal by the genealogists a place outside time and the forces of external authority.

There are unfortunately no anthropological accounts of the realities of life for nomads in Lhathog to help us understand the everyday dynamics of Lhathog and the genealogical texts include little information of this type. Literature about the kingdoms around Lhathog, such as Dégé (for example, Thargyal 2007) and further afield in Amdo to the north (for example, Ekvall 1964, 1968), tends to present images of nomadic life in different parts of the Tibetan cultural world that differ widely. While many accounts, such as Ekvall's, have depicted nomadic societies as egalitarian and imbued with independence, Rinzin Thargyal's recent study of Dégé suggests that nomadic hierarchies are not straightforward or easy to generalise and that some of these depictions are based more on romantic nostalgia than reality. For instance, Thargyal writes that it is misleading to call all relationships between lords (*pön*) and dependants (*korpo*) feudal, as Tibetan case studies are devoid of many of the characteristics of feudalism (Thargyal 2007:19). Thargyal has identified an important contractual interrelationship in his depiction of Dégé nomadic groups in the early 20th century (Thargyal 2007:20). In this contract, both the ruler and his subjects had power, as their relationship was symbiotic: the ruler represented subjects in dealings with other states, but if he did not serve his subjects appropriately these subjects could easily rise up against him and, since they had the appropriate force to protect the borders, this endowed them with leverage. This contractuality suggests that relationships and hierarchies in nomadic kingdoms were negotiable and to some extent fluid, much like the other forms of power that are explored in this study. Yudru Tsomu supports this idea:

> The relations among the indigenous polities in Kham were governed by a complex network of ties of various kinds. Some of them formed alliances through mutual agreements, and others were frequently involved in armed conflicts over territories, subjects and property. In order to expand his power and curb the threat posed by other regional powers, an ambitious ruler would always win over the powerful neighboring rulers, either by entering into marriage alliances or establishing neighbourly and friendly relations with them (Yudru 2006:66).

The promulgation of a strong, localised identity was supported by the autonomy of the lives of nomads in Lhathog and by the fact that the population was small (Yudru 2006:51–2). The genealogies of the Lhathog kings, which stretched back to imperial times, endowed the social structure of Lhathog with a legitimacy that was developed in local politics through the development of a unique political system headed by the king. The legitimacy of the system was enhanced with supernatural support as well as local support, as the genealogies are full of references to the Lhathog kings as generous patrons of Buddhism and of images of the Lhathog kings wielding Buddhist ideas as political philosophy. The portrayal of the local rulers as patrons of religion was an important and recurring trope in the genealogical genre, as it endowed the kings with an aura of sanctity and concern for their people's wellbeing that extended as far as the celestial realms. Moreover, they extended their support to more localised forms of religion and local leaders exerted great effort not to upset the local deities in ways that might disadvantage the populace on a mundane level through adhering to a strict calendar of propitiation as well as avoiding actions that would be interpreted as unmeritorious. The portrayal of this behaviour was an important method used by writers of genealogies to present their kings as just rulers in the classical Buddhist sense as well as in the local sense and, thereby, to create a positive image for the people of Lhathog to aspire to, in contrast with the behaviour of more mischievous rulers of neighbouring areas. These images may have also consolidated a strong ideology of loyalty and perhaps fear, as the Lhathog kings became elevated from the contemporary human realm to the realms of the distant past where kings possessed supernatural powers and might still wield the favour of the local deities against any local miscreants.

The idealised depiction of the kings of Lhathog as just Buddhist rulers has persisted in the imagination of the inhabitants of Lhathog until the present and has remained an important political mechanism that inspires loyalty and a social signifier that connotes authority. The more recent genealogy published in 2006 (LTDR2) suggests that the stories of Lhathog remain important for Tibetan communities in exile in South Asia and in other countries. The interest shown in Lhathog in publications in the People's Republic of China also suggests continuing interest among Tibetans within Tibet. It is difficult to know how much access the current inhabitants of Lhathog have to this newer information as that part of Tibet remains a closed area. Perhaps the oral traditions that formed the original texture of the annals remain strong and may have become even stronger as symbols of localised identity for Lhathog pa in the face of colonisation and globalisation.

Centre and periphery in the Lhathog *gyalrab*s: resisting simplistic presentations of Tibetan history

The persistence of remembering links to the Yarlung dynasty and alliances with the surrounding kingdoms of Kham does have interesting implications for understanding the significance of genealogies of the kingdom of Lhathog. The genealogies' depiction of Lhathog as forming a distinct, autonomous polity in Kham prior to 1959 and the details they record about how the aristocracy represented their legitimacy have interesting implications for wider interpretations of Tibetan political history. Significantly, source materials from other political units in the Himalayas also mention links to the Yarlung dynasty. As Matthew Kapstein has pointed out, in the formation of mini-states that took place following the disintegration of the Yarlung dynasty, many groups claimed links to the original kings in an effort to create an aura of legitimacy (Kapstein 2006:89–90). We can speculate that Lhathog was yet another of these polities.

While Lhathog was a peripheral area, in the collective imagination of the authors of our genealogies, it was its own centre. The genealogies have their own version of centres of power in Tibet through their recording of peripheral definitions of power. The presence of the Yarlung kings, for instance, is not a debt to be repaid by Lhathog to central Tibet, but is rather a means of creating a culturally recognised starting point for the community of Lhathog which would have cultural resonance elsewhere in the Tibetan world and would at the same time reinforce the distinctiveness of Lhathog as a political power in its negotiation with different constellations of authority. The constellations of social, economic and, to some extent, spiritual power that were negotiated in the creation of a viable political system are laid out in the genealogies of the aristocrats of Lhathog in a way that validates their right to rule and acts simultaneously as a political manifesto and a history for the kingdom of Lhathog. The inclusion of particular information in the genealogies that consolidates Lhathog's depiction as neutral and autonomous are problematic and appears to be more based in nostalgia than reality should not be dismissed. Instead, these techniques should be recognised as part of a wider mode of veracity in Tibetan historiographical literature that favours particular forms of authority as being crucial to the legitimacy of peripheral political units. This information makes the division of Tibetan polities in the centre and the periphery problematic, for it suggests that the genre of the *gyalrab*, often penned by members of the community that it concerns, ultimately places its centre of focus as a centre on its own. Therefore, the internal categories of veracity presented by genealogies disrupt the almost simplistic divisions of central and peripheral authority in a way that confuses conventional ideas of the purpose of a historical document such as a genealogy by infusing it with a powerful, localised memory of a centre. The kingdoms of Kham and other polities in Tibet were neither totally peripheral nor totally central and existed in a space somewhere between. Their political systems, functioning as they did in different ways in different circumstances, were fluid within different historical contexts and conditions. The implications of such a reading of texts such as genealogies could be extensive in considering the formation and consolidation of societies throughout the Tibetan cultural world. Texts such as the genealogies are ultimately subjective narratives of history, yet they remain ultimately objective, empirical and true for the writer and for the writer's partial audience—the inhabitants of a place that exists physically, in the case of Lhathog in eastern Tibet, and in the imagination of the inhabitants of those places, as in the imagination of those who identify as inhabitants of Lhathog.

Conclusion: Power in Tibet

This chapter has sought to use the genealogies of the aristocracy of Lhathog as a means of understanding more about the nature of power in Tibet. While the voices presented in these genealogies are the 'voices of the frontier' defined by Yudru Tsomu which defy depictions of the periphery of Tibetan societies as being without agency in the wider currents of history, they also present an alternative way to write and understand history as a political tool to create physical and imaginative boundaries around a place. The borrowing of power from wider Tibetan cultural narratives, such as that of the Yarlung kings, in the depiction of the origin of genealogies in small polities such as Lhathog was not one-sided and did not leave the creators of the genealogies in debt to those wider narratives. Instead, these widely recognised images were revitalised in their re-imagining in the genealogies and created the opportunities for a multitude of centres. Genealogies of peripheral powers also problematise the important dichotomy of Tibetan societies between centre and periphery by introducing local depictions of a place as its own centre, as they present unique modes of remembering and internal concepts of evidentiary authority. Thus, considerations of genealogies of kingdoms such as Lhathog, which are not acknowledged in many histories that are concerned only with centres, are crucial to understanding the wider currents and constellations of power in Tibetan societies.

Notes

1 Scott (2009) provides a recent and powerful argument for how this may be done in Southeast Asia.
2 Gru gu chos rgyal rin po che the 8th, personal communication, December 2006.
3 These tribes were ruled by internal leaders, were nomadic and were largely autonomous.
4 Tashi Tsering (1985:196–214) claims that Lhathog was invaded and taken into the territory of Mgon po rnam rgyal. Yudru (2006:xiv), however, locates Lhathog within the boundaries of harassed, yet uninvaded states.
5 Gru gu chos rgyal rin po che the 8th, personal communication, December 2006.
6 It is not clear how Teichman reached this number; although it is not verifiable, it remains useful as an estimate of the population size.

chapter two

A window on Rebkong: architecture, technology and social change in Amdo Tibetan communities

Mark Stevenson

It is not the aim of the project I am introducing here to question the introduction of modern technology into Tibetan social landscapes—it is difficult to say how the current interface of Tibetan village and town with technology could be otherwise. Nor is it a critique of technology or development—new approaches to window frames have hardly been directed by anyone. The project is, on the other hand, concerned with how technology and artefacts enter into and participate in social life and thus become tools for social analysis.

It is possible to read changes in the material environments constructed by people and see in those changes new forms of social relationship. A window might not leap out as the most obvious index of social change, and certainly a single window will not tell us very much. But a series of windows, or even a series of windows over time and/or through a territorial arc, might just have some important things to reveal to us. In some ways this is a very 1980s approach, from the time that Bruno Latour was just entering the technology and society scene.[1] Nevertheless, it happens to be the approach that best suits what I have been observing in Tibetan communities since 1990—a busy experimentation in domestic and monastery architecture, especially windows. Having been half aware of these changes for a decade and a half, a couple of years ago I stopped and started to take a closer look.

Places and styles

I have been visiting the Tibetan tribal territory of Rebkong since 1990, when I began my dissertation fieldwork. Located on the eastern edge of Qinghai province, Rebkong lies within the Malho (Huangnan) Tibetan Autonomous Prefecture, corresponding roughly with Tongren and Zêkog counties. It lies just 60 kilometres northwest of the renowned Amdo[2] monastic centre of Labrang (although the bus trip is quite circuitous) and about 125 kilometres (190 kilometres by road) south of the provincial capital, Xining. I arrived, on my first visit, wanting to discover what had happened to the local tradition of *tangka* painting after 1949; in retrospect it is nice to reflect that one of the first things I got involved in was painting the front of a friend's house, including its lattice windows.

In 1990 it seemed that all the monks at Rongwo Monastery, the major Gelug monastic centre in Rebkong, were building and decorating their new quarters. My friend Sherab was just moving out of temporary lodgings in the court of the monastery's Assembly Hall and into his new house. 'Didn't you say you were interested in painting?' he said, 'Take this and help,' handing me a paintbrush. After a couple of afternoons applying coats of paint to the front wall, I graduated to the intricacies of colouring his window lattices.

Along with most of the other monasteries in the same valley, Rongwo Monastery suffered extensive destruction in 1958 during a series of campaigns to suppress Tibetan uprisings. Less than a decade later, the events of the Cultural Revolution (1966–76) ensured that Rongwo and surrounding monasteries were active only sporadically until they were officially re-opened in 1980 (Pu Wencheng 1990:432–3). For most of that 20-year period Rongwo was used as a depot for the prefectural government. When I first visited in 1990 a number of temples and colleges were being rebuilt and monks were pulling down the barrack-style buildings which had until then signified what can only be described as an occupation within the monastery perimeter. Dropping in on Sherab again a few months later, I found he had bought ten large sheets of window glass. 'Isn't that a lot of glass for just your house?' I asked. 'It was cheap,' replied Sherab, 'and if I have any left over someone will always buy it.' 'Can you go and buy a glass-cutter?' he asked, 'And make sure you get one with a real diamond.' 'Do you know what you are doing?' I asked. I had previously helped as he installed electrical wiring and that experience didn't leave me overconfident. 'Sure, the Chinese carpenters showed me how to do it,' he said. His previous quarters, indeed all the homes in his home village, had paper-backed lattice windows, or *drama*. Glass was an exciting new option, and resourcefulness was a point of pride for the Tibetan men and women I was getting to know. Decked out in his robe, an *ad hoc* apron and leather gloves, Sherab measured out a pane to fit into his window, picked up the cutter, flexed his arm and…zzzzup, crack, tinkle, tinkle. 'I shouldn't have bought this cheap Shaanxi glass,' said Sherab. How many times were those sounds of unruly glass repeated over the day? In the end the stack of ten sheets turned out to be barely enough, and one or two panes had to be fitted together from more than one piece of class, leaving cracks that allowed warm air to escape from his rooms. I had not had home renovations in mind when my fieldwork commenced, but the friendship Sherab and I forged out of these small adversities later opened up opportunities for me to meet *tangka* painters. But that is another story; now I am back where I began—working on windows.

In 2001, back in Qinghai once again, still trying to learn Amdo Tibetan, one of my teachers at the Nationalities University happened to start talking about windows (I was the only student in the 'class'). Initially he had merely intended expanding my vocabulary, but what he had to say drew my attention to the importance of Tibetan window lattice designs—something so obvious and so prevalent that I had not previously stopped to consider their significance, despite my early experiences painting them. I even thought he suggested that their designs were passed down in the family. 'Wow, something like a tartan or cloth weave from eastern Indonesia,' I wondered.

Later, in January 2006, I had an opportunity to go back to Amdo and, starting in the Tibetan monastery towns of Hezuo (Tsö, Gtsos in Tibetan) and Labrang in Gansu Province, I made a rough photographic survey of windows in homes and temples wherever I could find them. Then, back in Rebkong, I was able to do some quick interviews and to observe what old friends were doing with their windows. Like a lot of Rebkong Tibetans, many Amdowas had new and ornate windows, and these are part of the account I am developing here.

Before moving on to look at how lattices and windows have changed in recent decades I need to make it clear just what these architectural features are. According to the *Art & Architecture Thesaurus Online*, (Getty 2009), lattices are 'networks of small light bars of wood, metal, or other material crossing at regular intervals, usually diagonally' and lattice windows in Amdo are window casements, crisscrossed with patterns of wooden bars and thus meet the primary requirements of this definition. In the first half of the 20th century, Daniel Sheets Dye[3] prepared notes and illustrations on almost 2,500 examples of 'Chinese lattice' (Dye 1949),[4] which he arranged into 26 styles (or 'groups') that span five broad types (or 'emphases'). Wooden lattice windows are something Amdowas both share and don't share with Han Chinese. Unlike the picture given by the Eurocentric definition above, they are based on a square orientation, rather than a diagonal one.[5]

Historically speaking, lattice windows have been a feature of domestic and temple architecture in both Tibetan and Han-Chinese cultures, but their styles were quite different. The main observable distinctions were a preference in Amdo for simple flat-sided bars and the absence of moulded (curved) bars and shapes, rendering the overall impression of the lattices in Amdo as highly geometrical. In Han-Chinese houses, lattice patterns were found in windows, doors, screens and balustrades; in Amdo, except in houses or other buildings built entirely from wood in the Chinese urban style, usually with two storeys,[6] lattices are limited very much to windows. Apart from the absence of moulding in the Tibetan windows, the main skills for making the windows were also the same, being the planning and measuring of the design and the cutting with a whipsaw, mortising and fitting of the bars as they were assembled into crisscrossing frames.

There were also differences in the way that window casements were fitted into the walls. In Chinese architecture, windows were usually fixed into openings in walls or were even integral parts of wooden wall construction. In Amdo there are examples of fitted casements, but there are also sliding and hinged (vertical or horizontal) casements (sashes). Sliding latticed casements slid horizontally on the internal side of the wall, sometimes accompanied by a wooden cover that slid on the external side of the wall. In larger households or in residential courtyards in monasteries, it is also not unusual to find latticed covers that slide on the outside of hinged lattice windows. In this last configuration, the intricately painted latticed covers are not backed by paper or any other material, which, given that the pair of covers are always open to the left and right of the window like framing wings, suggests that their purpose is purely ornamental. A comparison of these configurations suggests developments over time, sometimes in relation to culture contact, sometimes in relation to technological change and new materials. From my rudimentary survey in 2006, I suspect that adoption and adaptation is not unidirectional. For example, the Upper Erlang Temple Monastery (二郎庙上寺) at Hezuo, a Chinese Buddhist temple that has adopted daily smoke-offering rituals (*sang*) under Tibetan influence, had 'Tibetan'-style lattices on the doors of the main hall (see Plates 1–2).

Given that lattice patterns are made by itinerant carpenters who are not local, identifying styles associated with ethnic groups or regions is no simple matter. A number of noticeable features deserve comment. Han-Chinese lattices usually feature thinner bars in sparser patterns and are lacquered or painted on the outside in a single deep colour such as black or, more commonly, maroon. With copious use of moulded bends this graceful style, inspired by literati sensibilities, now has a long history in China proper ('inner-China', *neidi* in Chinese).[7] Tibetan lattices have thicker bars and are deeper, in denser patterns and either varicoloured (the most common combination being blue, yellow, green and red) or stained (see Plates 2–4). Moreover, while today most Tibetans in Amdo still live in a latticed world, most Han Chinese in Qinghai, or elsewhere for that matter, do not.

There is something about the screening effect of the lattice window that suggests a relation to the courtyard or other protected domestic spaces, including those found in palaces and monasteries, and this association holds for the Chinese *chuangling*, the Tibetan *drama*, the Kashmiri *panjira* (*pañjara* in Sanskrit), the *jali* of Indo-Islamic Architecture, or the *mashrabiyya* of the Arab world (see Dickie 1985:128–37; Frembgen 2005:133–48; Klimburg 2005:149–64). Leaving China proper aside, in the arid regions it has to do also with problems of controlling light, and a preference for a grill reticulating light would suggest strong sun and a lack of shade-giving vegetation, particularly in the winter. The grill allows light to enter, but cuts its intensity and, in effect, provides artificial shade. The same effect also allows interiors to share something of the airiness of the garden.[8] There can be no doubt that in these regions an aesthetic of reticulated line and light became an indispensible part of architectural design, punctuating the plainness of stone, earth or timber wall.

For Han Chinese the lattice is no longer associated with daily life, but rather with restaurants and other users of heritage décor. For sedentary Amdowas who have not moved into apartment blocks (still the majority by far), the lattice windows are more than just barrier and illumination, they remain, at several levels, a statement about the person owning the home. (This aspect of the windows is explored more fully below.) As new technology has been adopted and adapted, the articulation of statement, identity and status has undergone a number of shifts.

Stages of change

I have already alluded to several changes above. Much work needs to be done to record both the material of window styles in Amdo (if not all regions of China) and the intangible cultural heritage owned by carpenters and their customers, which is also in danger of disappearing. Further work should not be limited to preserving or salvaging knowledge of material culture; rather, far more could be learned from any study that attempts to identify change in windows over the last several centuries, particularly as panes of glass and metal hinges gradually became available. My aim here is much more modest, being simply to outline and analyse changes observed over the past 20 years, but I hope that the potential for studies of greater historical depth is also made clear through observation of contemporary change.

Returning to Sherab and the story of his new house, it is important to note again that his house took shape during a period of heightened rebuilding at Rongwo Monastery. Modest state funds had been allocated to Rongwo's opening and rebuilding in the early 1980s and local funds had also been accumulating so that rebuilding work could commence. In monasteries the major projects have been of two kinds, the rebuilding of temple buildings (*dükhang/lhakhang*) and the rebuilding or restoring of *labrang* mansions of senior *lama*s, with *tatsang* (colleges and their chapels and assembly halls) which represent an intermediate type. For the most part, the basis for this division has been their different materials; the temples have stamped earth (*gyang*) walls, wooden roofs and glazed tiles, whereas the large residential buildings are predominantly wood constructions, with wooden roofs and unglazed tiles. There have been similar rebuilding projects in Rongwo's subsidiary monasteries dotted throughout the Guchu valley.

Around the same time that the major restoration works were taking place, Rongwo's monks were also allocated land so thay they could build their own houses. The timing meant that they could employ the carpenters who were working on the larger projects or use their networks to bring in more carpenters, most of whom came from northern Sichuan and Linxia in nearby Gansu. Many lay households in nearby Saqi Dewa also took advantage of the presence of carpenters to commence renovations or add wings to their homes. As far as I can ascertain, it was around this time that a widespread conversion to lattice-with-glass windows took place in monasteries and villages, particularly in *tharwa*, which are villages attached to or adjacent to monasteries. (See Plates 5–6.) The introduction of glass occurred as if it was a natural choice, partly because glass was thought to offer superior insulation and illumination, and partly because it reflected a need to accommodate 'progress'. At the same time, economic and industrial change in western China through the 1990s ensured that panes of glass became readily available through state hardware wholesalers and private outlets in the county town.

It is not possible to arrange all of the developments in the rebuilding and restoration of Rongwo monasteries and villages along a single diachronic line, but the key role played by the monasteries in innovation is difficult to ignore. Monasteries have often been the source of architectural innovation, particularly in combining new and old materials in adaptations of traditional architectural forms. When we consider how monasteries were linked to extensive networks, including travel networks, in Tibet and beyond, this role is to be expected to a certain extent. It would appear, however, that two other elements shaped the role of monasteries in wider architectural change, both arising from the need to rebuild following the massive destruction inflicted in the late 1950s. The first is the prestige that surrounds the monasteries as sources of cultural leadership within their communities; the second, which is not unrelated to the first, is the money that has been made available for reconstruction. Another aspect of the role monasteries as innovators can be identified in their formal and informal relationships with local administration, and the privileged access to construction firms, craftsmen and materials, gained through those relationships. Monasteries, in short, engender major building projects. The combination of the prestige of monastic institutions and the commitment of local communities to maintain them ensures that monasteries become expressions of community pride, creating a general expectation that monasteries be showpieces of community success and prosperity.

As Tibetans rebuild or renovate, there has been continuous innovation, with each trend building on earlier changes and responding to new experiences and knowledge of practices elsewhere. As the number of households with television sets increased, so too did exposure to other, more powerful material cultures. Nevertheless, more local forms of contact still tended to dominate decision-making. By 1992, for example, the trend for converting verandahs into glassed-in sunrooms prevailed. The structures that resulted were made of the same materials (aluminium, lead, glass) that were appearing around the verandahs on multistorey apartment blocks in town and probably imitated them. The modifications to apartment blocks were, in turn, learned from Xining and beyond. At the same time, not a few well-connected Tibetan cadres had been allocated town residences as a result of initiatives originating in their work unit (*gongzuo danwei* in Chinese). Transferred and adapted to traditional monastic or domestic housing, the sunroom became a feature of considerable envy among monastic and lay households alike. I can remember Sherab taking me to visit a monk friend in 1995. He wanted to impress upon me the wonderful effect his friend had achieved by cementing the floor of the verandah and enclosing it within a canopy of glass. It was warm even in January, to the extent that they saved on heating fuel, and the reduction in dust meant that they could make the verandah a welcoming space with carpets and lounge suites. This particular friend of Sherab's had wall-to-wall display units-cum-bookshelves. Not only did the glass canopy provide modern comfort, it provided a living room, or parlour, where a socially mobile monk could express his personal sense of style. New technology was bringing new forms of self-expression.

Social space and ornamentation

The idea that a commonplace technology in the developed world reflects prestige in today's Tibetan communities should not be perceived as a form of 'talking down' Tibetan culture. The prestige of the new is always extended where there is an association with technology or new material, and the same extension of technology's prestige has been a feature of cultural change everywhere (although this process has been accelerated in the last 150 years). What I have also been observing, and want to describe now, is a parallel re-valorisation of Tibetan tradition in village architecture and what appear to be examples of the 'invention' of tradition. The retrospective examination of these two aspects of cultural change also reveals that something else was happening as these trends emerged in the early 1990s.

The arrival of something new always offers the opportunity to possess something before others possess it and, therefore, to have something others do not have; therein lies part of its distinction in Bourdieu's dual sense of differentiation in the economy of cultural goods and differentiation in social status (Bourdieu 1984). Old technology was not rejected in the architectural innovation I have been describing. The lattice window remained in some form and was never replaced by the total adoption of aluminium and glass, even though it might have been surrounded or enclosed by these (see Plates 7–8). The greatest change affecting the wooden lattice window may not be technological innovation, but shifts in social relations. To understand this we must first consider how window lattices have been made visible and to whom. Searching for answers to these questions also helps us understand why what seemed in 1992 to be an irreversible trend toward the use of manufactured products had reverted to an interest in wooden lattices ten years later.

No-one in a Tibetan village or in a Tibetan monastery in Amdo lives in a dwelling whose windows are immediately visible to the street, laneway, or alley. Like people all the way from southern Mongolia to Morocco[9], the dwellings of Amdo Tibetans are sheltered by earthen walls between two and a half and three metres high, which form a household compound (*gora*; *rakor*; *rawa*). Lattice windows, in spite of their ornamentation, are invisible to passers-by. At least that *would* be the case if Amdo Tibetans lived by the rules of the town or city, which they don't, because just about every passer-by is a potential visitor. If someone is home during the day the gate to the household compound is rarely locked, and there is a constant flow of neighbours coming in and out: the lattice windows are then visible in a special—I hesitate to write 'restricted'—way. The 'social identity' of lattice windows is thus to some extent delimited by the compound wall, but we must not ignore the fact that they look out onto a verandah (*khyamra*, or *yab*; *yangtai* in Chinese) (see Plate 4).

As any 'tour' of Amdo via Google Earth will show, the layout of Amdo village and monastery houses tends almost always to a southerly or south-easterly orientation, by which I mean the gate into the courtyard faces south.[10] Opening the gate, one immediately faces northward across the courtyard to the house, with its verandah, which also face south. In larger homes the house may be L-shaped, with one side of the L always facing south. (U-shaped configurations for house construction are rare in Rebkong.) The southern orientation is designed to take full advantage of the warmth of the sun and the verandah is used as a place to sit basking in the sun's warmth, saving on the use of fuel. During daylight hours, this is the usual place to share tea and bread with neighbours or guests and is a warm place to sit even when the air temperature has dropped to well below freezing. The southern orientation means that when visitors open the gate and enter the courtyard, the first thing that catches their eyes is the coloured window lattices on the house at the northern end of the compound. When they sit down on the verandah to have tea they sit directly under the lattices. Lattice, verandah and neighbours come together in the creation of a 'social space'.

The social space framed by lattice and verandah is a particular kind of focal point for socialisation. Sitting on a verandah a visitor receives hospitality but does not enter the house. This is not a highly conscious or fussed-over division compared to, say, the sharing of a single eating utensil (a taboo associated with considerable discomfit in Amdo). As should be expected, there is a certain intimacy of the household interior associated with direct kin and the home is not a place where regular neighbourly social exchange takes place after nightfall, although this has been changing somewhat with the introduction of television. Given the casual accessibility of domestic courtyards during the day, the verandah should be understood as a semi-public space. Once seated, the visitor can see about the courtyard, framed by the window lattices, and get a good idea of the wealth and management of the household by the height of the fuel piles and how free the well-swept ground is of debris. These are the material symbols through which a household communicates how well it is doing and 'who' they are, to which we should also add the window lattices themselves. But a difference also exists between lattice and fuel, for dung and firewood are the same in every house[11] and are mundane products of the daily cycle of production. Lattice windows depend on material wealth, but they can also, without overt ostentation, demonstrate other values such as taste, refinement or a respect for tradition.

What happens, then, when this half-outdoor, half-indoor, half-private, half public-space is covered in a glass canopy? Once behind the glass, effectively in a sunroom, is the visitor inside or outside? And does the significance of the lattice and the work of the carpenter change as a result? It would appear it does. One upland village household I know quite well, whose stylish lattice windows boasted the best glass and wood available, had undergone extensive renovation when I visited in 2006; its owner had added a glass and aluminium enclosure complete with sliding doors (see Plates 7–8). Visitors were left with a 60-centimetre cement border to sit on—barely enough room to sit cross-legged and not enough to comfortably lay out tea and bread. Work was continuing inside the house and it is likely a 'sitting-room' would eventually take shape behind the glass, needing only the purchase of a set of sofas. Crucially, the lattice windows, on which a lot of money was spent, were invisible behind the reflective glass screen that circled the eaves. The question of why the owner had spent so much money on something that was not openly visible had become something of an embarrassment, and the verandah had lost much of its former intimacy.

Experiments with architecture are risky and failures are embarrassing both because they disrupt aesthetic form and because of the outlays usually involved. I am increasingly convinced that this applies as much to the Tibetan world as it does in our own. Nevertheless, happily, people still engage in experiment. Wood and paper, wood and glass, aluminium and glass, new or old lattice patterns, non-lattice patterns, and sunroom or no sunroom are some of the dilemmas about which a series of different choices are being made. It was clear in 2006, however, that aluminium and glass were not going to replace wood and glass and that lattices were very much still in vogue (see Plates 9–10). It could even be said that lattices were a new vogue as the well-to-do began to see the expressive advantages wood had over more modern alternatives (see Plates 6, 11–12). A process of 'invention of tradition' had taken root, instituting a return to the 'prestige' of tradition, based upon the social capital of ornamentation and a craft aesthetic. Architecture was rapidly becoming a site for social competition. The house I have just described was renovated by an unmarried village teacher with a good state salary. He was keen to establish his status and receive recognition from the community, but at the same time unwilling to do so through participation in the activities of the village temple. The same prestige is also deployed in the use of ornate lattices in more public spaces, such as village temples or prayer halls (see Plates 13–14).

The story in upland villages is nothing compared to what is taking place in the villages situated down on the lush Guchu River floodplain, where one in every three households appears to be undergoing major renovations. In the lower villages, where the winter cold is not felt quite so keenly, the glassing in of verandah space remains rare. Here, in villages such as Wutun (Sengeshong in Tibetan) and Bao'an, in addition to the beautifully fine latticework, carpenters have been busy adding ornately carved eave overhangs or friezes (*draché*, literally, festoon, half-necklace, semi-drapeau[12]) to complement the windows (see Plates 11 and 13). These feature floral lacework surrounding motifs from Buddhist art, such as conch shells, *dharma* wheels, wish-fulfilling gems, jewel-spitting mongoose, lotus blooms, auspicious coins, dragon heads, the so-called 'Face of Glory' (*kīrtimukha* in Sanskrit, or *tsipatra* in Tibetan), snow lions, goldfish, fruit). I had not noticed any of these at all before 2006 and they are still limited to very well-off households, such as those of *tangka* painters, and temples.

In these floodplain villages there has also been a remarkable and more widespread trend for installing ornamental gateways, a trend not noted before 2006. In place of a gateway with a simple timber log lintel (*golay*), many villagers are now asking carpenters to construct finely carved lintel friezes or architraves (*gothö dzégyen*) over their courtyard gate (see Plates 15–16). Depending on the 'statement' desired, these are arranged in one, two or three horizontal layers, divided into three vertical panels and decorated with the same range of motifs used in the eave overhangs described above. Whether or not they are matched by similarly ornate lattices on the house beyond the gate, they represent a considerable outlay.

In line with the reading presented above, I interpret the recent appearance of friezes above courtyard gateways as indicating a shift in terms of social space. While the ornamentation above the domestic gate still serves much the same purpose as the lattice window, essentially making a statement about the household's social position, the social significance of repositioning that statement from well inside the family courtyard to its exterior— 'on the street', in urban terms (see Plate 15)—represents a shift that requires further investigation. My suspicion is that it signals a shift in village social relations and a renegotiation of the division between public and private space. This makes sense if we consider other changes occurring in village life, particularly new forms of social differentiation in terms of employment, income sources and income levels. As villagers have become increasingly self-conscious in relation to new forms of social difference, the meaning and boundary of domestic space has begun to change and may be becoming less open. As a consequence, a household's statement to village and neighbourhood about 'who they are' has had to move outside to the line that separates private 'property' (rather than simply 'dwelling') from public 'street'. It is interesting to reflect that one of the primary connotations of the Chinese term *menmei* (门楣, door lintel) is 'family status' and to compare it to the Tibetan term *thempa*, meaning both 'threshold' and 'rank'. I would not, however, like to read too much into this cultural link at this stage, especially considering that the Tibetan term for window lattice or latticework (alternatively *drawa* or *drama*) may be derived from the Sanskrit word *jāla*, meaning net or network, which is a suggestive metaphor for social relations.

Conclusion: shifting spaces of social identity

I have been suggesting that window lattices are one of the important vehicles through which a household presents itself to the outside world, particularly to other members of the village or neighbourhood. Lattices are able to do this because they are positioned on a boundary that defines the private and the public (a separation that needs to be handled carefully in cross-cultural research), while they also contribute to the definition of that boundary. Their significance for social space and social interaction ensures that villagers with little disposable income commit a significant investment in engaging skilled carpenters.

I have also argued that the factors shaping the social significance of architectural innovation—its social placement and prestige, its cultural-historical value, and the financial outlays involved in the employment of carpenters—must also apply to the 'newer' fashion for 'traditional' ornamental friezes over the entrance to the domestic courtyard. Given other changes in technology and social structure, the significance of all of the architectural elements discussed here is at present being renegotiated in relation to changing social and spatial relations. Whether it does so self-consciously or not, when a household decides to commission carpenters to work on its windows, eaves or gateways, it is participating in something of a social experiment. My working assumptions are that, while they do not speak of them in the same terms, households are actively interested in these dimensions of architecture and that changes they apply to architectural features will continue to serve as an index of social change.

Notes

Unless otherwise indicated all non-English terms are Tibetan. I would like to thank David Templeman for his advice during the preparation of this chapter for publication. I would also like to thank the Center for Chinese Studies, Taipei, for the opportunity to present an earlier version of this paper to their seminar, and to Victoria University for the period of sabbatical leave which allowed me to conduct fieldwork associated with this project. Any errors are, of course, mine alone.

1   Other work drawn upon in the approach used here includes that of Appadurai (1986), Marcus (1995), Latour & Weibel (2005) and Lefebvre (1991 [1974]).

2   Amdo (A mdo) is the Tibetan term for Tibet's northeastern territories, now distributed through eastern Qinghai, southern Gansu and northern Sichuan. Inhabitants of Amdo are referred to as Amdowas.

3   Dye (1884–1977) was a missionary who taught at West China Union University from 1910 to 1949 (see Dutton 1999:113–14).

4   Very little attention has been given to lattice windows in East Asia since Dye's publications, apart from the work of Yim Seock Jae (2005). There has recently been a small revival of interest in traditional lattice windows (*chuangling* in Chinese) in Chinese publications, for example the work of Fan Jialai (2005).

5   Eurocentric references still dominate English works on art and architecture, although the *Art & Architecture Thesaurus Online* (Getty 2009) is perhaps better than many other sources in recognising non-Western architectural traditions. Cowan and Smith

(1998:135) equate the 'lattice window' with the 'leaded light' window, made of glass and strips of lead to overcome the difficulty of making large sheets of glass, linking it with origins that are not valid in China. As is attested in Han dynasty funerary house models, the lattice window has a history that predates the use of pane glass in China by at least 2,000 years (see Dye 1949:31). Similar caveats must apply to most other non-Western traditions and care must also be taken in interpreting recent 'invented traditions'.

6   Some of the older wooden dormitory or mansion buildings still standing when I first visited Rongwo were similar to traditional wooden town houses, with roofs of simple *dougong* (Chinese) brackets and round clay tiles, found throughout Jiangsu and Zhejiang. This is not surprising given the ancient links between Rebkong and this area of China. In all likelihood, however, these were constructed during the Republican period in the first half of the 20th century.

7   This style, which could perhaps be called a Jiangnan or 'Lower Yangtze' style, is also found in what is left of older urban structures in Western China and in some rural domestic architecture. Outside of temple and urban architecture, however, the styles found in the north-west are less 'sophisticated' and have many similarities with styles favoured in Amdo, without the addition of colour.

8   Returning to China, I am reminded of some famous lines of the Song dynasty poet, Lin Bu (967–1028): 'Still bright when all the other blooms have faded,/ all the ardour of the garden yours alone./ Patches of shade crisscross on clear water,/ in the air, the moon at dusk, your soft perfume.// A frosted robin dives to perch and look,/ the butterfly is bound to lose his heart./ It's just as well a poet's here to share your life,/ there'll be no need for songs or wine for us tonight' (my translation). Here the airy crisscross effect is the natural shade of a small plum tree in Lin Bu's mountain garden. Of Lin Bu, a recluse at West Lake, it is said he planted plums to be his wives and fed cranes in lieu of having children. This poem is a serenade to one of his 'wives'.

9   Morocco provided the backdrops for Martin Scorsese's *Kundun* which depicts the early life of His Holiness the 14th Dalai Lama. The band of mountainous terrain from Mongolia to Morocco has an arid climate with severe winters, and one cannot help but be struck by the superficial similarity in dwellings in Amdo and in northern Iraq and Turkey, for example. High walls shelter their inhabitants from dust and cold winds, providing a welcoming space, home and protection.

10 In Google Earth, most villages appear as congregations of little open rectangular boxes, which are the walls to the courtyard (*rawa*). One (or two) side/s of the box will appear thicker (the roof of the house) and at the northern end of the rectangle. Located at the northern end of the compound, the house faces south.

11 Dung and firewood can often be spotted from outside the courtyard, where they are stored on the roof or porch.

12 'Semi-drapeau' is the translation David Templeman used in his unpublished *Biography of Kṛṣṇācārya/Kāṇha,* a translation of Kun dga' grol mchog's *Nag po spyod pa'i rtogs pa'i yal 'dab* (The Branches which Comprise the Realisation of Kṛṣṇācārya), where the word appears in relation to both architecture and ḍākinī apparel.

Plate 1. Lattice screen painted in the Tibetan style in Chinese monastery, Upper Erlang Temple Monastery, Tsö (Hezuo), Gansu Province. Chinese motifs (narcissus, plum blossom) appear above and below the latticed area

Plate 2. Painted lattice windows (drama) facing a verandah, monastic courtyard, Tsö (Hezuo) Monastery (Tsögon Geden Chöling), Gansu Province

Plate 3. Example of simplest style of lattice window, domestic Tibetan residence, Xiahe, Gansu Province. Latticed area is backed by paper and the upper panels open outward

Plate 4. Style of lattice commonly found in upland domestic dwellings in Tongren, Qinghai Province. Latticed area is backed by plastic and the upper windows open outward on brass hinges

Plate 5. Example of adoption of non-latticed window suited to pane glass, Xiahe, Gansu Province

Plate 6. Windows in new extension of domestic town residence, Saqi Village, Tongren, Qinghai Province

Plate 7. Unrenovated lattice window, upland Tibetan village, Tongren County, Qinghai Province. These are paper-backed and slide open along a track inside the wall. Note ends of old wall panels and windows stacked to the right of this window; these are from the renovated main wing of the same house (see Plate 8)

Plate 8. Renovated main wing of upland house (see Plate 7) and new glass-backed lattices, the home of a teacher in the village elementary school. The verandah is covered in a glass and aluminium shell that renders these ornate wooden windows invisible from the courtyard

Plate 9. Tibetan style lattices in abandoned house, Bao'an Township (Thowakya), Huangnan, Qinghai Province. Formerly occupied by a Han-Chinese family, this house is on the perimeter of the 'Wall Interior' Han-Chinese neighbourhood (Kharnang depa), where it is not unusual to find houses built along Tibetan lines

Plate 10. Wall panels and lattice window, Tibetan farmer's residence, Bao'an

Plate 11. Newly carved frieze (draché) under verandah eaves, house of a tangka painter, Upper Sengeshong Village (Sengeshong yago)

Plate 12. Newly fitted lattice windows under the eaves of the house depicted in Plate 11. The coats belong to the Sichuan carpenters

Plate 13. Eave friezes (draché) in the courtyard of the women's prayer hall (mani khang), Upper Sengeshong

Plate 14. Lattice windows in the same mani khang as in Plate 13

Plate 15. Domestic gateway in village lane, Bao'an Tibetan neighbourhood (Bökhor depa)

Plate 16. Central panel of lintel frieze, domestic gateway, Bao'an Tibetan neighbourhood

chapter three

Intersections of physical and spiritual powers

Kalzang Dorjee Bhutia

This chapter explores the intersections between temporal and spiritual powers in land ownership in Sikkim, (Denjong), through a case study of the history of the land holdings of Pemayangtse Monastery. Pemayangtse is a crucial site in the cultural heritage in Sikkim, as until 1975 it was the royal monastery of this Himalayan state. Until 1975, Sikkim was a nominally independent Vajrayāna Buddhist kingdom in the eastern Himalayas. Originally known as Demojong (the 'Land of Rice'), Sikkim was renowned as one of the 'hidden lands' of the eighth-century saint Guru Rinpoche's prophecies (BYGY1; BYGY2). Several ethnic groups inhabited Sikkim, including the Lepcha (known as Mön), the Lhopo and the Tshong, as well as hill ethnicities from Nepal, such as the Tamang, Sherpas and Nepalese Gurkhas. Sikkim was united and ruled by the Namgyal dynasty which commenced in 1642, when the first king was enthroned in west Sikkim by a group of travelling Tibetan religious figures headed by the visionary, Lhatsün Namka Jigmé (1597–1650/3?). This historical inception of the earthly kingdom of Demojong demonstrates and reinforces the early links between religious and political power in Sikkim, as religious figures initially gave legitimacy to the king.

Sikkim remained independent of Tibet and British India until a series of incidents in 1835 led the British East India Company to confiscate large tracts of land in the Darjeeling hills area (Bhutia 2009:21–2). While the British made political excuses to justify these actions, their ulterior motives were based around economic concerns; by consolidating their ownership of the Darjeeling hills, the Raj could also control the vast tea gardens that provided them with produce to export throughout the Western world and Asia. The takeover of Darjeeling gave the British an ideal holiday destination and respite from the sweltering heat of the Indian plains as well as a strategic major administrative location in the Northeast. While much research about Sikkim considers it to have been an uncolonised area in the Himalayas, my own research suggests that, in fact, Sikkim was, at least from the time of the confiscation of Darjeeling, indirectly colonised by the British. The British occupied a role as supreme overseer of the Sikkimese government which, in the early 20th century, was tentatively attempting to modernise by introducing organs of state, including political officers who had power over the kings (White 1986 [1909]:25). This supervision of local Sikkimese administration continued until India became independent in 1947, when Indians assumed supervision in accordance with the previous Raj policies. In the 1960s, following the Chinese annexation of Tibet, there was a series of disputes between India and China about the precise location and ownership of several areas of border territory in the Himalayas. Because of Sikkim's historical relationship with Tibet, China claimed that Sikkim was among the Himalayan areas that should legally be part of China. The diplomatic incidents between India and China made Sikkim a particularly sensitive area that was believed to be in danger of Chinese attack. In 1975 therefore, to counter this threat, Sikkim officially became the 22nd state of India, and was granted special privileges to ensure the maintenance of Sikkimese culture. The most prominent action of the Indian government was the amendment of the Constitution of India to include a clause that guaranteed Sikkim the right to retain its customs and made provision for the application of customary law in modern Sikkim.[1]

However, events in the past few decades show clearly that the implementation of customary law in Sikkim has been extremely problematic. This chapter presents a case study of some of the challenges to the full implementation of customary law by focusing on Pemayangtse Monastery, a Buddhist institution in west Sikkim that has remained essentially traditional despite facing significant changes and challenges since 1975. In this chapter, I outline the pre-1975 historical laws that the monastery was subject to in order to provide an understanding of the traditional Sikkimese relationship between Pemayangtse Monastery and the State. This may be considered as representational of the relationships between the State and other monastic bodies in Sikkim. The interaction between the State and central Indian governments and the monastery are often depicted as part of a wider relationship of tension between ethnicities, or as simply the clash between tradition and modernity (Arora 2006:31–2). However, this chapter will regard the issue differently. I believe that some of the fundamental problems concerning land rights in modern Sikkim are unresolved because of confusion about the role of traditional authority in a modern secular India on the part of both monastic and State representatives. The misunderstandings are perpetuated by the British colonial legacy in Sikkim, and are exacerbated by gaps in the historical archive of Sikkim. In this chapter, I outline the history of the monastery's estates, explore implications of gaps in the historical archive and conclude with suggestions for forms of reconciliation between the different stakeholders—monastic institutions and the State.

The gift: Chador Namgyal and Pemayangtse as patron and priest

As noted above, the monastery of Pemayangtse was considered the royal monastery of Sikkim until 1975 and remains an important institution in modern Sikkim, although with modified authority. The territory that forms modern Sikkim on the contemporary map was unified in 1642 by Lhatsün Namkha Jigmé when he and his colleagues enthroned the first king of Sikkim, Phüntsog Namgyal. The coronation of Phüntsog Namgyal marked the beginning of the Namgyal dynasty, which ruled Sikkim until the 19th century. This early link between religion and politics was potent, as the role of the *lama* as an adviser and legitimater of royalty remained powerful throughout following generations. After Lhatsün Namka Jigmé enthroned the first king, he returned to Tibet, but his spiritual descendants did not. People in Sikkim promulgated Lhatsün's lineage and developed a unique series of teachings known as Denjong (Sikkimese) Dzogchen. During his lifetime, Lhatsün Namka Jigmé was believed to have initiated institutions to promulgate his teachings in the form of monasteries.[2] The first monastery of Sikkim was founded at Dubdi in 1642 near the site of Phüntsog Namgyal's coronation; later in that decade Pemayangtse Monastery was founded a few hills away (BJGR:55). Lhatsün Namka Jigmé was said to have chosen the site because of its tactical superiority, as the political situation in Sikkim and surrounding areas of Bhutan, Nepal and the province of Tsang in Tibet was largely unsettled. In such a political climate, monasteries had to defend themselves and their Buddhist teachings. Pemayangtse's location close to the palace supports the idea that Sikkim was a part of the wider development of military and state-building activity in the Himalayas during the late 17th century. Given the links between the monastery and the royal family, its location, which would give the lamas an advantage in the event of conflict, suggests its strategic importance to the kingdom (BJGR:55).

In 1712, the third king of Sikkim, Chador Namgyal, donated large tracts of land to the monastery (BJGR:74). The size of the donation suggests that, by this time, the monastery was already supporting a large number of clergy. The original document that included Chador Namgyal's declaration, known as *Katen dang Sergi chagje* ('The Document with the Golden Handprint') (BJGR:74), has now disappeared, as many documents relating to Sikkimese history disappeared during the turbulence of the 20th century that saw the withdrawal of the British government and then the political turmoil that preceded Sikkim's joining of the Union in 1975. However, a copy of the original proclamation was made and stored in the monastery, and this serves as the declaration of the original boundaries of the monastery's estates. This document identifies the boundaries of the monastery's estates from the Ratung river to the hot-springs area of the

Rangit in west Sikkim and up the hill above the monastery. The area included 11 traditional constituencies, which suggests that, by the 18th century, west Sikkim was already widely populated.

The most interesting feature of this document is not the detail but the statement that ends it, in which Chador Namgyal declares that, 'until the sun and the moon fall, and until the mountain Kangchejunga, or the "Five Snowy Treasure Stores" crumbles, no force on this earth can take away the estates of this monastery' (PDDEC). [3]

Obviously, in making such a generous gift and reinforcing it with such strong words, Chador Namgyal had his own motivations. The most obvious was that, by giving the monastery the means to support its clergy, he could ensure the continued crucial support of the lamas of Pemayangtse, who acted as the legitimators of the kings of Sikkim. They were responsible for enthroning the crown princes and carrying out yearly ceremonies to clear obstacles for the kings. The lamas also had important advisory roles to the kings. By providing these estates, Chador Namgyal was recognising the legitimacy of the monastery as a holder of spiritual power. The reciprocal recognition that occurred between these two parties acted as an important covenant and impetus for the two groups to continue to serve the best interests of both parties and to perpetuate the country's status quo as a Buddhist monarchy.

British imperialism in Sikkim

Despite the words of Chador Namgyal in making his gift, the estates of Pemayangtse no longer remain intact. What has happened between the time of Chador Namgyal's declaration and the present to lead to the apparent transgression of traditional laws? This section of the chapter outlines instances of the ambiguities of traditional law and its implications for the monastery at present and in the future.

In order to understand the complexities of the implementation of customary law in modern Sikkim today, it is necessary to assess the legacy and impact of indirect British colonialism on Sikkim. Although Sikkim is often considered an uncolonised area, the presence of a British political officer in its capital, Gangtok, from the 1880s onwards meant that the Sikkimese government, including the monarchy, was effectively under British supervision (Risley 1894:v, passim; White 1986 [1909]:19ff). This supervision could not be dispensed with, as Sikkim had to its south the vast plains of colonised India, to the west Nepal (which often invaded), to the north isolated Tibet (with an ineffective army), and to the east an independent Bhutan, with which it had frequently fought (Aris

1979:248–9). In such a situation, Sikkim had no other powers to approach for help in seeking its independence from the British.

The British used many techniques to ingratiate themselves into local society. The 'divide and rule' policy, by which the British would select particular aristocratic families for favourable treatment, often practised on the plains of India, was also applied in Sikkim. This treatment was formalised in the *kazi* system, which appeared in British writings about Sikkim from the 1850s.[4] *Kazi*s, or landlords, are often considered an indigenous Sikkimese creation, but my research suggests that, prior to the British appointment of *kazi*s, holders of large tracts of lands in Sikkim did not have the level of power that they had following the intervention of the British. Although Sikkim had a long history of particular families being granted aristocratic status, they did not, historically, have the full rights that landlord *kazi*s were given by the British over land and the workers occupying it. Traditionally, aristocrats worked in a symbiotic relationship with local people, in which both groups had their share of production from the land and both were compensated for fulfilling their responsibilities. The *kazi* system created a privileged upper class for whom collaboration with the British was an attractive and lucrative prospect, and acted as a disincentive for privileged Sikkimese families to resist British influence.

As well as introducing a new class system in Sikkim, the British also pushed concepts of racial divisions (Risley 1894:ix–x). Although ethnic groups that were technically what we would today call Nepalese had lived in Sikkim for centuries, in the 1880s the British brought very large numbers of Nepalese Gurkha migrants into Sikkim to clear the forests of the south. They remained in Sikkim, and tensions that emerged later between social groups were not acknowledged as having their origins in the British practice of divide and rule, but were simply attributed to ethnic tension (Risley 1894: x). The British also re-categorised ethnicities in the hills, so that groups that had been in Sikkim from ancient times, such as the Tshong or Limbu, were relabelled *subba*s (tribes) of Nepalese. Families who had lived in Sikkim for centuries, Lhomontsongsum, who had followed the Lhopo kings of Sikkim were suddenly called immigrants. This creation of ethnic separation and lack of understanding led to the emergence of new tensions that had no precedent in Sikkim.

The making of modern Sikkim

Following independence, India continued to have control in Sikkim in much the same way that the British had. Sikkim remained of strong interest to the central Indian government because of its rich mineral resources and its strategic position on the Chinese border. After the Chinese takeover of Tibet in the 1950s, the threat of incursions into border areas in the northeast by Communist China became ominous, causing India to pay closer attention to its northeastern borders.

The British *kazi* system was considered to be an oppressive feudal system by those who supported the Indian Government. These supporters regarded members of the communities around the monasteries, including those within the boundaries of the Pemayangtse Monastery estates, as slaves who needed to be freed from landlords. The *kazi* system was officially abolished in 1949 (Boot 1996:45). The original manuscript of Chador Namgyal's declaration still existed at this time, and the lamas of Pemayangtse had the document accurately translated into English by people sympathetic to the monastery's cause so that it could be used as evidence of their claim to the monastery's original estates (PDDEC).

Following the Sino–Indian conflicts of the following decades, in the 1970s the Indian Central Government renewed its efforts to strengthen Sikkim's administration because of legitimate concerns about the vulnerable position of the border (Datta-Ray 1984:80–1). Political tension led to protests among different groups and to the destruction, sometimes violent, of property that included many important historical documents. Homes of people on both sides of the conflict were attacked and sometimes torched, and the ancient documents within the homes of the aristocracy and officers of the previous government were destroyed. The documents included original treaties and State legislation, as well as official and personal correspondence that pre-dated the creation of the Sikkimese State. Many documents that were not destroyed went missing in this period of unrest, as they were either hidden in places that were considered safe, and then forgotten, or taken out of Sikkim by associates of their owners. The political circumstances and turmoil of the 1970s have left a chasm in the historical archive of Sikkim, and impaired the monasteries' claims to the right to manage their own estates. In April 1975, Sikkim formally became the 22nd state of the Indian Union. A detailed account of the complete political events that led to this are outside of the scope of this chapter, but they had grave consequences for the Pemayangtse Monastery and other traditional authorities.[5]

Following the upheaval of 1975, special amendments to the Constitution of India guaranteed Sikkim's right to exercise customary law and to take measures to preserve its culture (Bakshi 2006:315). Most significantly, Sikkim became the only state in India to be allowed elected *sangha* representatives in the State legislative assembly. The new administrative status of Sikkim has, however, put monasteries and other traditional organs of authority in a difficult position. In recent decades, the situation has become more complex, as the lamas are now required to provide documentation for their estates and there is some disagreement within the Government about the legitimacy of land ownership by monasteries. Cases such as that of Pemayangtse Monastery remain unresolved, although lamas and the local government are taking tentative steps toward resolving some of the conflict about the rightful ownership of the land claimed by monasteries. Recent studies of Sikkim have seen conflict between the monasteries and the State as being based largely on grounds of ethnicity and identity (Arora 2006:31–52), or as stemming from the tension between tradition and modernity. I do not believe, however, that this situation has arisen from such straightforward dichotomies.

I see Sikkim's current dilemmas in implementing customary law as being related largely to misunderstandings between religious and State representatives. On the one hand, the government of Sikkim sees the monastery as an ambivalent institution that has no defined role in modern secular India. On the other hand, monasteries do not understand how to continue as advisers and spiritual leaders in a secular society. The division goes beyond the split between the secular and spiritual, and is intimately linked to differing concepts of authority.

Directions for the future

The only effective way to approach this dilemma is through meaningful dialogue between the State, the Central Indian Government and the monasteries of Sikkim. All parties need to be able to accept the different modes by which they each communicate, and attempt to find a middle ground among their epistemologies.

Customary law cases from overseas, particularly law relating to land rights, can illuminate the potential for future relations between the Sikkim State Government and monasteries such as Pemayangtse. In New Zealand, for example, the government created the Waitangi Tribunal during the 1970s to allow compensation to be made for land confiscated in the past, which has led in many cases to the healing of rifts between the descendants of the tribes who lost their land and the descendants of those who took it (Orange 1987:246). In several significant land rights cases in Australia (McNeil 2001:416–63) and Canada (McNeil 2001:250–80) previous government decisions have been overturned in favour of the indigenous inhabitants of the land. Case studies such as these exemplify the potential for reciprocal recognition between traditional and governmental authorities to take place and to reinvigorate community relations in a way that benefits all parties. A significant factor in these case studies is the recognition of proof of land ownership that extends beyond physical documents and into realm of collective memory.

Conclusion

A significant barrier in the current situation is a lack of awareness of the legacy of the past. In order for the Sikkim State Government and the monastery of Pemayangtse to be able to work co-operatively as well as in conjunction with their community for the benefit of that community, the monastery's traditional function needs to be recognised and its recent history clarified. Until the legacy of colonialism in Sikkim is accepted, respect for alternative modalities of power in Sikkim cannot be achieved. Indeed, Sikkim's situation is not unique within the postcolonial world, as many other indigenous peoples have also had to fight for the recognition of their traditional rights in the modern world. The pre-modern role of Pemayangtse was intimately intertwined with politics in a traditional *chösi* (spiritual and temporal power) system. However, under this system the monastery did not assume the responsibilities of the king except in extreme circumstances. The monastery traditionally acted almost as an accountability agent for the government, by endowing the king with legitimacy to rule and acting as a spiritual adviser.

There is still great potential for this relationship between monastery and State to be viable in the future. If the statement made by Chador Namgyal when he gave the land to Pemayangtse monastery in 1712 is taken as a statement of customary law, Pemayangtse's ownership of the wider Pemayangtse estates should not be disputed. Because a century of trauma has created gaps in the Sikkimese historical archive, Sikkimese monasteries are often without verifiable proof to support their claims over land titles. Nevertheless, even though a physical document may have been lost or destroyed, the Sikkimese people still remember declarations relating to land entitlements. In discussions of customary law, can collective memory also be accepted as legitimate as a form of verification in its own right? Is there a way to move past dominant imperial discourses and concepts of what can be counted as proof of title and ownership? In Sikkim, there may be such a way. The current political leaders in Sikkim are generous benefactors of Pemayangtse Monastery and pay respect to the senior lamas of the monastery in exchange for spiritual and political advice. In turn, the monastic body also appreciates the Government's support. The role of lamas as wise, politically astute advisers could be of immense assistance to local authorities in healing some of the tensions of the past, as all the involved parties may learn to regard each other positively and attempt to work together for the benefit of Sikkim, with or without verified physical evidence of land titles. Modern statehood can conceivably be reconciled with Pemayangtse and other traditional organs of authority in Sikkim, but only through mutual understanding of the alternative forms of authority that Pemayangtse as a spiritual and social cohesive force, possesses, not only for Buddhists, but for the Sikkimese as a people.

Ultimately, the history of modern Sikkim is one of alternative authorities and alternative ways of remembering. The British Raj, the Indian Government after independence, the lamas of Pemayangtse, and the inhabitants of Sikkim all have ways of knowing and remembering the events of the last two centuries. In this chapter, I have attempted to return agency to the original lamas of Pemayangtse through depicting the collective memory of the monastery, which has included the loss of parts of the estate and damage to the heritage of Sikkim. Through remembering the past in a non-confrontational, non-judgmental way, the potential for dialogue that can heal old wounds emerges. In turn, this path offers the opportunity to enable customary law to be applied in modern day Sikkim in a way that is meaningful and significant for the community of Pemayangtse and for other stakeholders in Sikkim's unique culture.

Notes

1. Article 371F of the Constitution of India contains these provisions (Bakshi 2006:315).
2. BJGR:72
3. This quote has been taken from the English translation of the document dated from the early 1950s and discussed later in the chapter.
4. See Carrasco (1959:272, fn265) for a discussion of the term '*kazi*' and its probable non-Tibetan origins and for a consideration of how it appeared and was used in the writings of British visitors to Sikkim, including Hooker and Campbell in the mid-19th century. In *The history of Sikkim* (BJGR), the word *kazi* is never used and the traditional *rgyal blon* (*gyalon*) and *lha mi* (*lami*) appear instead. However, in the English translation by Kazi Dawa Samdup (HOS), the term *kazi* is used, which suggests that by the time the text was written in the early 20th century, the terms were interchangeable. For more on the appearance of the term and concept of *kazi*, see Datta-Ray (1984:34–6), which discusses the Indian alteration of the original ministerial system in Sikkim.
5. See Datta-Ray (1984) for a detailed, though biased, account.

chapter four

Multiculturalism on the Tibetan border: the temple of Triloknāth in Lahul

Diana Cousens

Lahul is a region in the Western Himalayas comprising three river valleys and bordering Ladakh and Tibet. The culture of Lahul is a mixture of Buddhism, Hinduism and indigenous beliefs and practices. Historically, it exists within the Tibetan imagination as a place of pilgrimage with a special association with Avalokiteśvara. The temple of Triloknāth accommodates Buddhist and Hindu worship and pilgrims; the Hindu community perceives the principal deity, in fact, a form of Avalokiteśvara, as Śiva.

During my fieldwork at Triloknāth in 2006 I encountered a spectrum of attitudes towards the mixed nature of the temple. Some plains Hindus and Tibetan refugees were unhappy that the temple was not clearly 'theirs', but the Lahuli population and the temple priest worked hard to achieve a rare inclusivity. I argue that this accommodation demonstrates a model of communal harmony and that the possessive attitudes of some outsiders demonstrate a lack of understanding of the multicultural nature of Lahul.

Before I went to Lahul, I had read Elizabeth Stutchbury's PhD thesis (Stutchbury 1991) and other works by her and had gained the impression that Lahul was a kind of small Tibet that had been protected from the Chinese occupation over the border and from the devastation of the Cultural Revolution. In fact, I found it to be well integrated into India and that Tibetan was spoken only amongst Tibetan refugee visitors to the region. The local people speak three indigenous dialects, Manchad, Bunnan and Tinnan, which have an historical relationship to archaic Tibetan but have no script. The prevalence of these languages roughly corresponds to the three separate river valleys that constitute Lahul.

The temple of Triloknāth is in the Pattan, or Chandrabhāga, valley where the local language is Manchad, which is sometimes further specified as Upper or Lower Manchad and has a number of other names, such as Reungpa and Swangbash. Lahul is contiguous with Spiti, where a form of Tibetan called

Bhoti is spoken. Spitian visitors to Lahul, by extension, speak Bhoti. Visitors to Lahul from neighbouring Ladakh speak Ladakhi, which is also closely related to Tibetan. The resident monk at the Triloknāth temple is from Ladakh and speaks several languages and most local dialects.

As Lahul has for several decades been a district within the northern Indian state of Himachal Pradesh, which borders Punjab, Jammu and Kashmir and Ladakh as well as China (Tibet), the language taught in schools is Hindi, so the children all learn Hindi, including the Devanāgarī script. In Lahul there are isolated valleys and mountain tops with villages scattered amongst them that no roads reach. There are some bridges but there are also long stretches of rivers without bridges. Sometimes simple rope bridges and flying foxes join two river banks. Isolation is also intensified by Lahul's climate. It is cut off by snow from the rest of India for eight months of the year, when only a few helicopters get into the region. This physical isolation has ensured Lahul's linguistic diversity and the survival of customs and beliefs of great antiquity.

The majority of the population of the Chandrabhāga valley are Hindu, whereas in the other two valleys of Lahul the majority are Buddhist. Lahuli monastic Buddhism depends on Tibetan language texts, as does Ladakhi monastic Buddhism. There are Buddhist monasteries in the Lahul-Spiti capital Keylong and in nearby Mayanarla, where the monastic residents are not monks but householder *yogi*s. The Buddhist image of six armed Avalokiteśvara at the Triloknāth temple is the only Buddhist image that I observed in active use in the area around Triloknāth. There is a *devī* temple at Udaipur, about ten kilometres from Triloknāth, called the Markula Māta temple, which is said to have originally been a Vajrayoginī temple but has now been fully converted to a Kālī temple where animal sacrifice is regularly practised.

The Triloknāth temple is a complex entity with many layers of history and current devotional practice. The core of the temple, which is inside a modern outer building that forms a reception area and a covered walkway, is a classic stone *śikhara* of the type used as a Śiva temple in Jagat Sukh, near Manali and Bajaura in Kulu. Slightly more elaborated forms of the *śikhara* can be found in places like Baijnath and Mandi, where the *śikhara* core has an added *maṇḍapam*, or reception area. All of these stone *śikhara* temples are Śiva temples. Triloknāth is historically located within the Chamba administrative region. The town of Chamba can be reached on foot over some mountain passes and lies to the east of Triloknāth. Chamba also has *śikhara*-style temples similar to Bajaura and Jagat Sukh, and like those temples, their Hindu identity is not in doubt.

So the likelihood is that the Triloknāth temple was originally a Śiva temple that was converted to Buddhist use at some time in the past, just as the

Buddhist Markula Mātā temple was converted to Hindu use. I have noticed that modern scholars sometimes contest terms like Buddhist and Hindu, but at present these terms denote meaningful identities for current Buddhist and Hindu populations.

The central image in the temple is a form of Avalokiteśvara called Sugatiśandārśana Lokeśvara. The local Hindu population, who have no concept of Avalokiteśvara, identify the image as either Śiva or the goddess Bihara, whose name is also the name of the village of Triloknāth. The fact that the image is actually a Buddhist image is, however, acknowledged by the Government of Himachal Pradesh in a painted street sign outside Manali at the entrance to the road up to the Rohtang Pass. The sign lists 'Places of Tourist Interest' and mentions numerous places in Lahul and Spiti. For Triloknāth it says, 'Trilokinath [sic] temple is situated at left bank of river Chandrabhaga. A lifesize marble statue Bodhisattva Ablokiteshwara [sic] is installed in the hall of Trilokinath. Trilokinath temple is also symbol of communal harmony between Hindus and Bodhs'.

The white marble statue is wrapped in cloths and garlanded with necklaces of pearls, leaving only the face visible. It is unwrapped once a year in February during the festival of Yor for its ritual washing (*abhiṣekā*). This is at the time of the year - between October and May - that the roads in and out of Lahul are cut off by snow, so the attendance at this festival is largely confined to local people.

There is a widespread ban on the sale of photographs of the statue in the village of Triloknāth, although they can be secretly obtained from shops at the town of Keylong. The ban stems from the Temple Management Committee's insistence that all proceeds from the sale of photographs of the statue should go to the temple. There is a black market in photos of the image in Triloknāth but one has to know whom to ask in order to obtain one. A picture is available for sale at the temple to sell, but it is overpriced and unclear.

So the Triloknāth image has an ambiguous identity, is hidden in cloths and is known by different names, and it is quite difficult to see even a photograph of it. It can be viewed unwrapped in February, a time when there are no visitors from outside the valley. What is definitely known by all who come to the temple is that it is powerful, self-arising and possibly the most sacred image in the Western Himalayan region.

As mentioned at the start of this chapter, the Triloknāth temple attracts Buddhist and Hindu pilgrims and there is also a strong indigenous element to local Hindu practice. As a mixed temple, rare in India though not in Nepal, both

Buddhists and Hindus are able to come to the temple and interpret it according to their preconceptions. I suggest that the image is perceived in different ways according to the belief systems of the different viewers. The first thing the Hindu sees on entering the courtyard is a small covered shrine with a Śiva *liṅgam* and white marble Nandi. Hindu visitors ring the bell above the Nandi, touch the shrine and then, with palms together, touch their face. They may pour some water into the pot above the *liṅgam*. After going into the temple and lighting Indian incense, they are likely to come out and put the incense into the incense pot beside the *liṅgam* and to add flowers to it. The shrine is a scene of active worship. Incense is segregated—Indian incense, common to Hindu temples, is put outside in the *liṅgam* shrine, while Tibetan incense is burned inside the temple.

The sign over the entrance to the temple proper reads 'Om Namah Śivaya'. Inside is the walkway leading to the entrance to the anteroom/reception area. Hindu visitors prostrate themselves in a variety of ways and their perception of the Hindu identity of the temple is reinforced by the presence of a picture of Śiva and the *sādhu*'s sandal on the right of the entrance to the inner sanctum. However, the frame is surmounted by a white scarf, a *khatag* (in Tibetan, *kha btags*) — an article typically found in Tibetan temples. Hindu visitors frequently touch the doorstep at the entrance of the inner sanctum as they enter. In front of the inner sanctum are two pillars through which Buddhist and Hindu visitors squeeze in the hope of obtaining purification and gaining merit.

Both Buddhists and Hindus offer money and possibly other things, such as biscuits, *ghee* for the large butter lamps or white scarves at the altar and are given a sip of saffron water from a Tibetan jug called a *bumpa* (in Tibetan, *bum pa*) and some white sweets that look like rice but are pure sugar. Hindu visitors are given a wristband and Buddhists a neckband, although this distinction is not rigidly observed as nearly everybody gets a wristband made from the white scarves which are simply cut up into two- to three-inch lengths and kept in large quantities in a box in the inner sanctum. Hindu visitors will help themselves to the red vermilion powder, *kumkum*, kept in the small pot on top of the donation box just outside the inner sanctum.

Buddhist visitors walk past the Śiva *liṅgam* in the courtyard and go directly into the temple. Their perception of the temple as a Buddhist place is reinforced by the presence of images of Buddhist deities in the anteroom in front of the inner sanctum, a throne with a picture of the Dalai Lama, a Tibetan cabinet with further Buddhist images, offerings of butter lamps and water bowls in front of the images in the anteroom and in the inner sanctum, the presence of a Ladakhi *lama* officiating as the *pujārī*, and the image, which is recognisable as Avalokiteśvara particularly through the presence of the Buddha Amitābha seated in the crown. The gold-plated canopy above the image reinforces the Buddhist character of the shrine, with its images of Amitābha and the inscription of the *mantra* 'Oṃ Maṇi Padme Hūm'. The Buddhist identity is also reinforced by the existence of a circumambulation path around the inside of the temple lined by brass prayer wheels, a portable image of Padmapāṇi in a stone niche and the smell of Tibetan incense inside the temple. Outside, at the back of the courtyard, the Buddhist visitor will go to the Maṇi Lakhang, the room that houses a two-metre-high prayer wheel filled with paper copies of the *mantra* 'Oṃ Maṇi Padme Hūm', which is turned by the devout. In another corner of the courtyard is a room dedicated to the lighting of butter lamps, again a typically Buddhist ritual act. Surprisingly, Hindu visitors also turn the prayer wheels on the circumambulation path and the big prayer wheel in the Maṇi Lakhang. They also pay for butter lamps—large ones inside the shrine room and smaller, cheaper ones in the lamp offering room at the back.

Buddhist and Hindu sacred songs are played on the loudspeaker, so a musical setting of 'Oṃ Maṇi Padme Hūm' will be followed by a *bhajan* with the words 'Oṃ Nāmāh Śivaya'. Male Hindu visitors cover their heads with a handkerchief and conscientiously remove leather garments, such as belts, before they enter. The blessed food, or *prasād*, the white wrist-bands and the giving of blessed water are also customs common to Hindu temples. However, in Hindu temples the wrist-bands are not made from cut up *khatags*. The style of prostrations may vary between Hindu and Buddhist visitors, but some Hindus do prostrations that are in the Tibetan style.

In another part of the courtyard is a large fireplace for *pūjās*, called *havana kuṇḍa* in Sanskrit. This is used by both Buddhists and Hindus for their quite different ceremonies involving fire. The space is neutral, a plain, square, sand-filled box. It has no characteristics to predetermine its use.

An old *śikhara* spire sits at the back of the walkway. It is a remnant of ancient built structures and was damaged in an avalanche. It includes small bas-relief images of the tantric Buddhist god Vajrapāṇi, who is clearly visible, and what looks like Buddha and others, but these are obscured by layers of whitewash. If the whitewash was professionally removed much history would be revealed. The front area of the inner sanctum facing the *maṇḍapam* includes several meditating Buddhas carved in black granite that appear to be an integral part of the structure. The channel for the free flow of *abhiśekha* water—used for the ritual washing of images—is a part of the basic structure of the inner sanctum. The ritual washing of images is not a part of contemporary Buddhist practice amongst Tibetan Buddhists, but the seventh century Chinese pilgrim I-Tsing (1998 [1896]) attests that it occurred in Indian temples.

On special days, especially full-moon days and no-moon days, the *lama* performs a long chanting ceremony, or *pūjā*, in Tibetan in the morning and uses a range of Tibetan musical instruments, particularly the trumpet and drum. He prepares a large metal tray of offering cakes called *tsog* (in Tibetan, *tshogs*) made from barley flour, butter, sugar and fermented dried cheese. These are formed into pointed domes and are cut up and distributed with other standard foods, including large quantities of biscuits, white and boiled sweets, apples, bananas, bread and fried bread, and occasionally dried fruits and nuts, given out on ceremonial occasions. Large crowds come to the temple on these occasions, often many hundreds in the morning.

The pilgrims who come to Triloknāth belong to many distinct groups. There are local Lahulis, Spitians and Ladakhis, and plains Indians, including Hindu *sādhus* who identify Rishikesh in the neighbouring state of Uttarakhand as their home; there are mountain people from Kulu, just ten hours' drive away over the Rohtang Pass, and Tibetan refugees, most of whom were born in India, and many of whose parents were also born in India.

While I was there only about a dozen foreigners visited the temple, although a couple of busloads of Germans walked in and out of the temple, none spending more than half an hour there. The Dalai Lama has visited on three occasions.

The temple is served by two or three full-time policemen who are appointed to keep the peace and assist in the running of the temple. As the temple has been subject to sectarian conflict in the past, the presence of these police is a reminder that peace is fragile. However, there is usually communal harmony in the temple and, although some visitors may mutter privately that the temple is really 'theirs'—that is, really Hindu or really Buddhist—and that the others have corrupted it, at the time of my visit in 2006, the last incidence of conflict had been in 2004. In the absence of conflict, the police play an important role in the distribution of food on ceremonial days, and stand in for the *lama pujārī* in handing out blessed water and wrist-bands in the inner sanctum. The *lama pujārī*'s day begins at about five o'clock in the morning and the temple closes at eight o'clock in the evening. Between those hours he has almost no time to himself and is either constantly in the temple or preparing materials for the temple. He actually needs an assistant—a junior *lama*. In 2004, conflict arose when the then Sub-Divisional Magistrate of Udaipur appointed a Brahmin *pujārī* to share *pūjā* duties. It appears he had a sectarian attitude and was dismissed.

While I did not enquire deeply into the past conflict, I was made aware that both communities were happy with the Ladakhi *lama* and did not want the return of a Brahmin *pujārī*. Moreover, the presence of the Buddhist *lama* was seen to be in accordance with the ancient tradition of the temple. It was also said that sectarianism had been brought in by people outside Lahul who did not understand the Lahuli tradition of living together without conflict. On occasion, I observed the children of Tibetan refugees expressing sectarian views at the temple, but Tibetan refugees are outsider groups. Brahmin priests are also outsider groups, as there are no Brahmin priests native to Lahul.

The Lahuli people and the Ladakhi resident *lama* seem to have made a conscious decision to include all comers and a diversity of religious belief and overcome the potential for conflict. The real history of the temple is not a clear one. Its form is Śaivite and its principal image is Buddhist. Concepts of single identity and sectarian ownership must always be out of place.

Triloknāth is a living temple that attracts 40,000 pilgrims per year, most of whom come in the summer months. The contemporary needs of visitors have brought about significant changes, such as the development of accommodation and other facilities. The original characteristics of the temple have been modified and it has become a composite of old and new features and Buddhist and Hindu elements. At present the temple is a rare model of communal harmony, whereby the different communities come together and somehow see what they want to see and also co-exist. Persons chanting loudly in Sanskrit are followed by Tibetan monks performing *pūjā* in Tibetan. Somehow the appreciation of the deity has cut across the normal boundaries of religious and ethnic identity. In this it is, perhaps, a model for others, a temple for everyone.

The festival of Pori

One of the main occasions that pilgrims come to the temple in the summer months is the festival of Pori, held in late August. It is a great occasion that brings about 3000 people to Triloknāth from all over Lahul and its immediate neighbouring regions such as Spiti, Ladakh and Pangi. The festival lasts for three days and during that time the temple of Triloknāth is constantly full of pilgrims, forming a long queue leading into the shrine as they wait to take the blessing of the god.

The local cricket ground becomes the centre of the festival and hosts a variety of activities. These include a recently introduced volleyball tournament, a cultural program of local musicians and dancers, and animal sacrifice. The quiet main road and side streets are lined with stalls selling clothes, imitation coral and turquoise necklaces and wooden beads, cut fabric ready to be made into women's Punjabi suits, and plastic toys. Entrepreneurs run miniature roulette wheels and games involving throwing bamboo discs over prizes. Many of these businesses are run by itinerant traders, such as Tibetan refugees, plains Indians and Sikhs. The head Thakur of the village, the Kardar, and his wife invited her family to come and they set up a sweet stall. One room fronting the street became a kitchen with huge vats of boiling oil in which sweet *jalebis* were fried, and other pots produced golden *barfi*, made with sugar and chickpea flour. The volleyball tournament is keenly contested and each village has one or more teams. In 2006, as in 2005, the Himachal Pradesh police team won yet again, triumphing over Hinsa Red Star.

Pori began with the Thakur riding a white horse to the seven springs of Saptadhara, meaning 'seven springs', the place from which the white marble Triloknāth deity came. It is a four-kilometre walk up the mountain and he was accompanied by traditional musicians: drummers, a flute player and two longhorn players. It takes about two hours to reach the springs, where animal sacrifice is performed and other ceremonies take place.

I asked the Thakur the purpose of the trip to Saptadhara at the start of the festival. He replied:

> It is linked with the Pori festival. All the Thakur families and religious people of Triloknāth go there on pilgrimage in order to invite all the gods and goddesses to this holy place [Triloknāth]. Because the statue came from there, so we are inviting all the deities, gods and goddesses (Sinha 2006b).

So, in some senses, the procession up the mountain to Saptadhara is a ritual of remembrance of the mythological origins of the Triloknāth deity. A white horse is chosen because the deity is white and the horse is offered in Triloknāth's name (Sinha 2006b). It is also assumed that other gods and goddesses can come down to the village from the same place. In other words, the Triloknāth deity is not unique, but one of a class of beings to be found in Saptadhara. It is assumed that the invocation of the gods at the site will bring them down, clearly not in a visible form, to participate in the festival. So the festival has a component of interaction with the invisible world.

On the second day, the procession of musicians that went to Saptadhara came to the temple and the horse was led, riderless, around the temple's walkway in a ritual circumambulation of the deity. It is said that the Triloknāth deity is riding the horse.

> It is said that Lord Triloknāth rides a horse which takes him round the temple but is not seen, as the horse perspires in cold. This very horse is taken to Rana's [Thakur's] house who in turn rides this horse and comes to the fair and sits at such a place wherefrom he can see the entire fair and all the participants in the fair can see him (Bajpai 2000:62).

The procession of horse and musicians then proceeded to the ground where the Thakur was already seated on the roof of a building. The musicians set up camp at one end of the field and played traditional, repetitive music. Soon they were joined by dancers, mostly older people and initially both men and women who slowly danced in a circle, their hands raised in the air. Two women emerged with large containers of *arak*, a distilled spirit made from grain and euphemistically known as 'local wine', and plied the dancers with free drinks in plastic cups.

The drinking and dancing that are such a visible part of the Pori festival have been commented on by earlier writers. Vogel mentioned that, while the festival is performed in honour of the *bodhisattva*, in practice, it includes drinking, dancing and animal sacrifice. He also noted that the principal actors were not *lama*s but spirit mediums (Vogel 1972 [1926]:254–5).

Drinking and dancing at Pori were also noted by Ibbetson (1980 [1919]:18): 'The Pori *mela* is observed only in Trilok Nûth, and is accompanied by dancing and drinking. Held in Bhûdon'.

To the outside observer, drinking and dancing could be interpreted as simply fun-seeking behaviour, similar to the volleyball, but it has another meaning. As the deities have been invited to come to the festival and the Triloknāth deity has been brought invisibly on the back of the horse, it is thought that the deities are present. The Thakur told me that on the first day of the Festival of Yor, in February, when the high caste people dance, the deities are also believed to be dancing with the people. I did not ask whether the same belief is held for Pori, but it is quite possible. The Thakur said this of Yor:

> The Chahan people [low castes] are not allowed to dance that day. People believe that the benevolent deities of the forest and so on will dance with the local people. The dancers have their hands up. If the Chahan hands are held up and touch the *deva*s' [deities'] heads, the *deva*s will become impure. Chahans can dance on other days (Sinha 2006a).[1]

The drummers and flute-players, who are low-caste Chahan, stood to one side and played their flutes and drums and did not dance at this time in Pori. The drinking and dancing continued for three hours or more, in spite of the hot sun. Thousands of people sat in the stadium, mostly interested in the volleyball matches between different teams. The drumming continued and dancers kept on circling but the women left at an early stage. As the dancing got more crowded and disorderly, the circle form dissolved and became largely just a general drunken crowd of men milling around.

While the low-caste musicians may not be allowed to dance they are indispensable to the festival. The Thakur explained that for four years there was no Yor festival as the lower-caste musicians had got government jobs which means they now have to be paid to perform. Another factor in its postponement was the death of the medium, or *gur*, of the deity of Triloknāth and a new medium is yet to come forward. During Yor someone takes the role of the *gur*, but does not go into a trance.

The festival of Pori functions on many levels. On one level it has a vibrant commercial role. Large sums of money are made by the stall-holders and this boosts the economy of Triloknāth and the earnings of itinerant traders. It also has the social function of bringing people together in celebration. Friends and relatives who live apart from each other can reconnect. The small village's population of 300 suddenly becomes ten times larger. The festival also promotes the fame and prestige of the temple, as every pilgrim visits the temple and the temple is the site of some of the festival's ceremonies, such as the commencement of the processions on the first and second days.

The introduction of an organised musical program every night on a stage with sound equipment and a formal volleyball tournament has updated the festival in many ways and provided interest for different social groups. The volleyball probably reaches a younger generation. But these components are in addition to older and deeply rooted practices and beliefs that pertain to indigenous beliefs that are known as 'the religion of the valley', in Tibetan, *Loong-pai-chos*, first described by Harcourt in 1871 (1972 [1871]:65). Within these indigenous traditions the deity of Triloknāth has a place as a benign and gentle presence.

The Pori festival is one occasion where the overt concerns of the religion of the valley are very much in evidence. These concerns are predominantly with invisible forces of nature, many of which are perceived as dangerous and harmful. Animal sacrifice is performed at the beginning and the end of the festival to appease the *rākṣasas* (angry female spirits). Local gods make themselves known and their voices heard through rites of spirit possession enacted by the *gurs*.

Lahul has long been known as a place of syncretic merging of different religious traditions. According to Ibbetson (1980 [1919]:18):

> Lahul is the meeting place of the Aryan and Mongolian races and the people exhibit the characteristics of both, though the Aryan element predominates. Their religion is an impure Buddhism grafted on the ancient and probably aboriginal Nag and Devi worship which is similar to that of Pangi and is found as far up as the junction of the Chandra and Bhagi rivers—Chortens, prayer flags, *mani* walls and other symbols of Buddhism are common. The Buddhist temple is at Trilok Nath and the chief Devi shrine is that of Mirkula Devi at Udaipur.

The Pori festival demonstrates how the religion of the valley provides a substructure upon which Buddhist and Hindu identities are placed. It is not an independent religion, but a point of view through which the world is perceived and which co-exists with differing levels of Sanskritic Hindu affiliation and

Buddhist practice based in Tibetan language, as described to a certain extent above.

Late in the afternoon of the second day, the *gur* arrived at the festival grounds. On his entry he was propitiated by two young men holding plates of burning juniper. He came into the crowd of dancing and drinking men shaking a chain of many links and proceeded to beat himself with it. Others also became entranced, grabbed the chain and tore off their jackets and shirts and whipped their backs. They were in a frenzy, whipping and circling, moving their hands about, clearly undergoing a catharsis. The principal *gur* grabbed the chain from one of the participants and wrapped it around the other man's neck. It looked as though he was trying to strangle the other man—at any rate, it looked dangerous. The other man recovered his senses and left the group. The *gur* then stripped off his own jacket and shirt and resumed whipping himself with the chain, appearing to go into a frenzy, but only for a short time. He quickly put his shirt and jacket back on and left.

At about nine o'clock in the evening the amplified music program—traditional Lahuli singing coming from the stage at the cricket ground—was overwhelmed by traditional drumming. It was time for the animal sacrifice. About ten people surrounded a sheep at the place of the drumming. The Thakur held a traditional hand-forged knife and others helped hold the sheep.

There was a small fire and a pot of water. The sheep was splashed with water and water was poured in its ears. The sheep didn't move and people waited. I did not see the sheep shiver but at some point it must have been observed to shake and the Thakur swung his iron blade at its neck. It took a number of blows to kill the sheep which was held by several people. Then its head was severed and thrown on the fire. The body was carried off and given to the Chahan who play the musical instruments. It was believed that this would appease all the devils and angry spirits that harm the crops, cause floods and other disasters, and bring about the untimely death of the Thakurs. In reply to my question about the benefit of sacrificing the sheep, the head Thakur said: 'It satisfies the devils and appeases those living around the gods and goddesses' (Sinha 2006b).

While the sacrifice was going on, the cultural program continued at the cricket ground where most people faced the stage and did not see the sacrifice. Perhaps the music was more interesting; perhaps this method of protection from harm is no longer so compelling for some people. Nevertheless, on the following day everybody came and watched the rite of spirit possession.

The role of the *gur* in Lahuli culture has been described by TK Ghosh (2002:180–1):

In Lahaul, there is a certain inter-action between the Buddhists and the Hindus. This is especially found in implementing the superstitions of the ancient animistic faith which sometimes requires magico-religious ceremonies for driving away the evil spirits or spirits in cases of sickness or any other adversity. In such cases, when prayers and havans of the Buddhist Lamas prove ineffective, drastic remedies are called for and sacrifices must be offered. But, since the Buddhist Lamas would not commit to such taking of lives, a Hindu Bhatt from the Pattan valley, or a *goor* [*gur*] from the Chandra valley has to be called to carry out or execute the requirements of such a necessity. Bhats [sic] are counterparts of the Lamas in the Pattan valley, which is predominantly Hindu…The *goor* is the *chela* (disciple) of a *devta*. The *devta* manifests himself through the *goor*. The *goor* goes into a trance, and the *devta* then answers the people's queries through him. The *goor* is generally a Lohar and keeps long hair…However, the priest of the *devta* is always another man. The Bhatt performs the required sacrifice of a sheep or a goat for which he is given one leg of mutton. The *devta* makes his wishes and desires known through the *goor*. He does not perform any puja but merely acts as a seer.

This quotation notes the possibility of either a Hindu *bhatt* or a Buddhist *lama* being called in to assist in the case of 'sickness or any other adversity', suggesting an interchangeability of religious specialists. The *lama*'s methods are gentle and do not require sacrifice. If the need is more extreme, 'drastic remedies are called for and sacrifices must be offered'. So the decision to undertake a sacrifice is made not on grounds of intrinsic affiliation of faith but on grounds of degree of need. The sacrifice takes place and the wishes of the god are made known through another religious specialist, the *gur*.

The role of the *gur* is well known in Lahul. From interviews with several *gur*s I noted that in some senses he is a classic shaman, with a period of chaos that indicates his vocation, a rite of initiation, leading to a special role as the intermediary with the deity.

On the last day of Pori a party of between 30 and 50 pilgrims, with an equal number of sheep, left on pilgrimage for the Śiva shrine of Mani Mahesh, near Brahmour in Chamba, which they reach on foot, climbing over high mountain passes. Mani Mahesh has a *swayambhū liṅgam* in a Śiva temple set on a mountainside. It also has a sacred lake.

Before they departed, the crowd assembled around the bus stand. Women, in rows six deep, filled the curved edge leading up to the fields. People were sitting on the roofs of all of the buses and cars parked in the stand to get a good view. Eventually the Thakur, holding a pot containing hot coals and smoking green juniper leaves, arrived and stood at one end. The sheep and pilgrims were assembled. A circle was formed which included other members of the village but no women, other than me, were visible in the front line. The crowd chanted 'Jai

Bhāgavati Ki Jai' in solid repetition, neither loud nor soft. There was shouting as a man in a red shirt ran into the centre whipping himself with chains. He was in a frenzy and circled the crowd with popping eyes. Others ran in, tore off their shirts and took the chains from the first *gur* and beat themselves. Mostly no-one said anything clear; the sounds were just guttural cries, occasionally addressed to the crowd. The first *gur* handed over the chains to others and came out of his trance, but remained in the circle. Up to four *gur*s at a time were circling in a trance. One *gur* with a particularly wild face pointed at people in the crowd and clearly berated them. Another *gur* with long red hair stuck out his tongue periodically—identification with Kālī was unmistakable—and uttered some prophecies for the pilgrims. At one point the *gur* who had been pointing at and berating the crowd ran right into the crowd and pulled a young man back with him. He then embraced him and beat him with the chains. He bit his neck—it looked like a lovebite— and kissed him, with a full open-mouthed passionate kiss involving tongues. The young man also went into trance. The *gur* with the long red hair also embraced him. The young man shouted in ecstasy. Set free of these embraces he also circled the crowd in a trance before coming to, putting his shirt back on and going back into the crowd.

There were several explanations as to why the young man was embraced, bitten and kissed. The Thakur said he was an incomplete *gur* and the other *gur*s were trying to make him complete. The *gur* with the long red hair said they were trying to free the *gur* from some devil-powers that had attacked him and that they were successful.

Each of the *gur*s only remained in trance for about five minutes at a time, then they came to and put their shirts and Kulu hats back on. Periodically, some would resume the trance. After about 20 minutes, the trances stopped, the circle was broken and the pilgrims moved forward with their sheep to begin the seven-day round trip to Śīva's shrine. Although there were no women going, I was asked if I was going and found that women were not excluded from the pilgrimage.

I asked the Thakur to explain the spirit possession at the start of the Mani Mahesh pilgrimage. He answered:

> On the last day of Pori 30–40–50 people go to Mani Mahesh. The *gur*s tell all about the future, some bad things happening around. If there is any person who is affected by some bad things then they cure them with a particular *mantra*. At the moment there is no particular *gur* of Triloknāth. All the *gur*s this morning were of Kālī Mātā and Kelling—Kārttikeya.

When he was asked why one *gur* kissed the other man, the Thakur replied:

The man was an incomplete *gur* and the *gur* was trying to make him a complete *gur*. There were only *gur*s of gods. All the *gur*s who went into trance are established *gur*s who have performed as *gur*s in the past.

He related the *gur*s' prophecy as 'that the Thakur had managed the whole *mela* [festival] well'.

How do we interpret the trance possession? As others have noted, it is a collective event. Uma Singh Mahajan (2002:342) gives this interpretation:

> Trance possession is not a single, individual or isolated statement or performance by an isolated or alienated member of the community. It is a cross-cultural part of religious practice and sensibility; a community event directed towards a common goal, for the well-being of the collective good as seen, for example, in the celebration of individual and community rites of passage. In this sense, the trance possession is not an individualized behavioural deviance of wish fulfilment, but the expression of the collective unconscious of the community.

Whether the community has a collective unconscious or not is, perhaps, open to debate, but it can definitely be said that the trance possession reflects a widely held belief in the immanence of the divine and its ability to interact with ordinary people.

I spoke to one of the *gur*s who enacted the possession at the bus stand and asked him to explain how he had become a spirit medium. Dolit Ram was 21 when he went on pilgrimage to Mani Mahesh and was subject to a 'spiritual attack'. He became unconscious and 'it was just like clouds came'. He was taken to the temple of Kārrtikeya, one of the sons of Śiva, who is called Kelling in this region. As the sun went down, he went consciously into the temple and the *pujarī* slaughtered a sheep and painted his whole body with blood and then he became unconscious. He was wearing only a loincloth. At some point he saw a light. There were other *gur*s in the temple who whipped him on his back with a 24 kilogram chain and he felt no pain. Still unconscious, he whipped himself with the same chain and still felt no pain. He had no memory of what had happened but said that if somebody had not been a genuine *gur* they would have been killed by the whipping. He is now the *gur* of the wrathful goddess Kālī Mātā and conspicuously stuck out his tongue during the trance possession in the morning. He made various prophecies but had no memory of what had taken place during his intervals of possession in the bus stand.

The role of blood and sacrifice locates the spirit mediums outside of Brahminic and Sanskritic culture. Mahesh Sharma (2001:43), in one of the most substantial works describing this region, made the following observation:

> The ritual of sacrifice also has a bearing on the social structure. Sacrifice has always been used against vegetarianism. Blood has been perceived as a norm of the ritually low, while vegetarianism with ritually high. Sacrifice involving

blood has been associated with indigenous, while vegetarianism is symbolic of brahmanic society. Thus, the goddess of sacrifice, Kali, is associated with crematoriums, funeral pyres, death and darkness. She destroys humanity, harms any one 'who crosses her'. If not appeased she unleashes disaster, illness, or death. Opposed to her are the 'mother goddesses' as Parvati (the mountain goddess), Lakshmi (who bestows wealth), Sita (of earth), or Savitri (the virtuous one), the benevolent aspect of the fierce one, who are never offered sacrifices.

Low-caste temples and functionaries provide services that are sometimes wanted by higher castes, and there is the potential for appropriation by higher castes over a long period of time.

> In the nineteenth century, the popular centres of belief had no brahmin pujari—priests but only low caste functionaries, and were popular among the low castes, the Muslim buffalo-herders, and 'tribals'. The upper castes visited these shrines concerning certain psychic maladies, a category of healing in which only the low caste functionaries specialised. Economically, these shrines neither had any state patronage, as did the Sanskritic shrines, nor a wide catchment area which would ensure a large inflow of liquidity. However, due to the changing political scenario and consequently the political landscape, a nexus developed between the state and some of these shrines. Consequently their catchment area started enlarging and with the extension of royal patronage, they became popular and economically affluent centres.:.The fallout of the process was that many local shrines got universalised and this was reflected in the growth of high caste pilgrims to these shrines. The brahmanised deities also became associated vertically and horizontally with the Sanskritic deities, though arbitrarily ranked and always in a subordinate capacity (Sharma 2001:182–3).

While this may be the large-scale trend in the Western Himalayan region, the absence of Brahmin *pujarīs* and the enthusiasm for animal sacrifice and trance possession suggest that, in the Chandrabhaga river valley, at least, the old practices are not in danger of dying out. The Triloknāth temple is insulated from direct engagement with identification as either a low-caste shrine or a high-caste shrine as it has always been in the care of a Buddhist *lama*, under the jurisdiction of the Thakur as *kardar*, who has hereditary control of the temple. The Buddhist *lama* is from Ladakh and is outside the Hindu caste system. No animal sacrifice is performed in the temple. The person who carries out sacrifice, the Thakur, may leave for the sacrifice from the temple but it takes place outside the temple. A delicate balance takes into account Buddhist prohibitions against animal sacrifice but still recognises the authority and power of the Thakur.

The day after the Pori festival I had another conversation with the Thakur who I noticed was writing something in Hindi. When asked what it was, he said it was a letter to the newspaper, complaining that the Temple Management Committee had not properly invited the medium from the Markula Mata temple. That medium was the most important in the valley and his absence meant that the rite of trance possession was incomplete. He said that the correct way to invite the medium was to visit him and offer him a goat, but this had not happened. In his letter he also mentioned that he was not happy about carrying a large financial obligation in relation to the festival for which he was not reimbursed. The organisation of the festival takes about two months which diverts him from his income-generating work. He gets no income from visitors to the temple, as was the case in earlier times. As will be shown further down, there is a conflict between the new conception of the Pori festival, with its stage-shows and volleyball tournament, and the older traditions relating to religious practices. In the past, the central events of the Pori festival were related to the pacification of the local gods so as to ensure the protection of the Thakur and the village people. In his letter he wrote:

> The reason for getting the *gur* of Mirkula Mata to perform the left-handed worship of Triloknāth is to make sure that the family of the Thakur and the villagers do not suffer the wrath of the God. The family of the Thakur has experienced the anger of the God many times in the past. If it happens again [because of this], who is going to bear the responsibility?[2]

There is clearly a conflict between old and new ideas of the festival. New institutions, such as the Temple Management Committee, have provided a new layer of authority, but older forms of authority embedded in Thakur's role persist and the village's expectations of the Thakur have not entirely changed. The equation of the festival with stage-shows is in conflict with its earlier role where it was the place for what the Thakur refers to as the 'left-handed worship of Triloknāth'. These types of conflicts were not expressed in any aggression or argument but in the quiet form of a letter to the newspaper.

The Pori festival has social, commercial, sporting, recreational and religious elements. Probably all of these are needed to make it meaningful in different ways to the different participants. The Triloknāth deity and temple have an important role in auspicing the festival by bringing down the deities from Saptadhara and by attending the festival, with the invisible deity being carried to the cricket ground on the back of the horse. But the Triloknāth deity is also just one benign and gentle deity amongst a pantheon of good and bad forces. The festival's sacrifices and rites of possession enable the local people to engage with and appease a myriad of beings who interact with their lives. They can dance with the deities and they can hear them speak through their *gur*s. The festival also acts as a preliminary event to the major annual pilgrimage to Mani Mahesh, the site of another self-arising object, a Śīva *liṅgam*. In this way the village of Triloknāth is linked with the religion of Chamba, the region which formerly acted as its suzerain.

The Pori festival brings together a spectrum of Buddhist and Hindu beliefs, underpinned by ancient indigenous ideas. It brings together the peoples of the region—Lahuli, Pangi, Ladakhi, Spitian, and others from Himachal, including Tibetan refugees and Sikhs. It is changing over time, with new ideas and new events taking an increasingly prominent role. How these old and new elements can co-exist is a matter of negotiation that is still under discussion.

At the start of the festival the horse and the procession commence their journey from the Triloknāth temple and go up the mountain to the place where the god first came. The associated rituals are a combination of Hinduism and the religion of the valley. The animal sacrifices and spirit possession are a part of an indigenous understanding of a world deeply linked to gods and demons with whom the Lahuli have a relationship. All visitors and participants respect the temple and its ambiguous deity, which arose out of the world around them. The capacity for the locals and the visitors to allow many different views and practices to co-exist and mingle is a model for communal harmony and a reflection of a tolerant, inclusive and syncretic spirit, which is characteristic of Lahul and of the temple of Triloknāth, where layers of identity and ideas of the deity co-exist and occasionally merge.

Notes

1   Ibbetson (1980 [1919]:18) describes the festival of Yor too: 'The Or *mela* is held on the full moon of Phagan, in Trilok Nath and Margraon, and like the other *melas* the chief accompaniment is drinking and dancing'.

2   'The historic Pori-Mela ceremony at the Triloknāth shrine performed without the Gur', letter to the paper by Veer Bahadur Sinha Thakur, translated by Dr Jayant Bapat, Honorary Research Fellow, Monash Asia Institute, Monash University. The Thakur kindly gave me a copy of his letter in Hindi, which I had translated in Melbourne.

The Triloknāth deity. (Black market photo; no photographer attributed. All other photographs by Diana Cousens.)

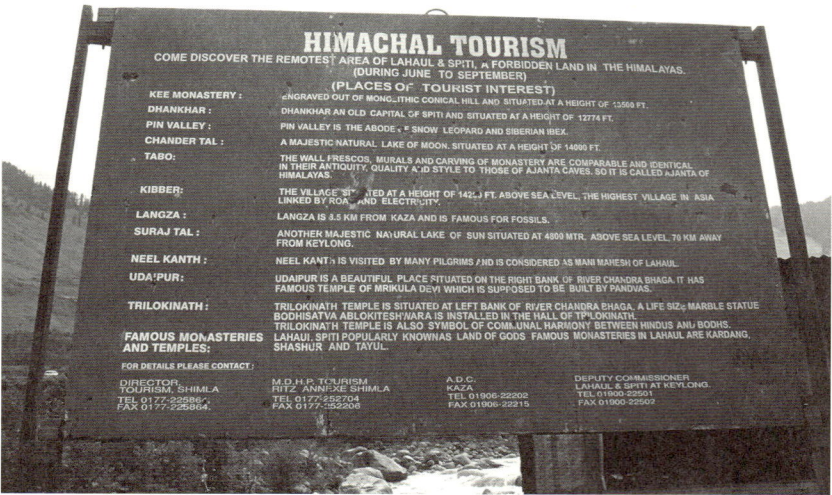

Sign at entrance of road to Rohtang Pass outside Manali. Identifies deity as Avalokiteśvara and the temple as a 'symbol of communal harmony between Hindus and Bodhs'.

The statue wrapped with offerings in front

The Markula Māta Devī temple of Udaipur

Bajaura temple, a śikhara Śiva temple in Kulu

Resident *lama* performs a pūjā with *tsog* offerings on table

The Jagat Sukh śikhara Śiva temple near Manali

Crowds come to the temple on full-moon day

View into the inner sanctum, with pujārī, Lama Rinchen Dorje

Śiva liṅgam in Triloknāth temple courtyard

Maṇi prayer wheel in Maṇi Lakhang

Old śikhara at back of walkway

Abhiśekha outlet and prayer wheels

Vajrapāṇi image on old śikhara

Triloknāth village, seen from Hinsa

chapter five

Ama Adhe, the voice that remembers

Isabella Ofner

Over the past decades, an increase in Tibetan diasporic life-writing has provided a growing and sympathetic English-reading audience with insights into Tibetan culture and religion.[1] These Tibetan autobiographies, testimonies and prison memoirs are part of the greater body of postcolonial literature and, as such, are an attempt to voice experiences that have been silenced by hegemonic discourses. By definition and intent, postcolonial literature is the attempt to resist master discourses through literary self-representation; in its struggle to re-interpret the coloniser's representations of place and native society, postcolonial literature engages with and challenges foundational hegemonic concepts and discourses. Postcolonial writing, especially ethnic autobiography, sets out to be sensitive to historical readings from the margins and serves as 'politicized activity [that]… resists the exploitation of knowledge by the interests of power to create a distorted historical record' (Harlow 1987:116).

As examples of postcolonial writing, Tibetan autobiographies likewise attempt an interspersion of knowledge about Sino–Tibetan historical relations produced by the colonial centre by presenting alternative narratives to Chinese versions of history and disseminating them in the global economy of culture. Characterised by distinctly subversive writing practices, these works of literature become part of a distribution mechanism centred around neo-colonial structures of strategically marketed 'exoticism' that collapses cultural differences in order to satisfy an increasingly global desire for predictable otherness as the latest Westernised product of the exotic East (Huggan 2001:4).

Targeting middle-class Western audiences, postcolonial writing mainly appears in English (often translated into English). This hints at a larger process of cultural appropriation, in which postcolonial literature is confined by what Graham Huggan terms 'a discourse of *translation*' (Huggan 2001:4, 15), through which the unfamiliar and the culturally different become understood, domesticated and subsequently neutralised for Western aesthetic consumption. In this global market, competition for symbolic value among exotic goods, including postcolonial literature, and their producers is bestowed through a system of hierarchisation that legitimises writers, for example, according to elaborate codes of difference in cultural production (Bourdieu in Huggan 2001:4). As Graham Huggan (2001) persuasively argues, 'exoticism' is as much an aesthetic as it is a political strategy within the hierarchy of cultural production and representation. Exoticism not only accompanies neo-colonial and neo-imperialist power, but also effectively disguises the underlying political motives by which colonised, marginalised people become dominated. I would add that the subsequent appropriation of exotic products through the practice of decontextualisation is the most effective strategy of disempowerment.

Given that our globalised world still'bears witness to the unequal and uneven forces of cultural representation involved in the contest for political and social authority within the modern world order' (Bhabha 1994:171), it becomes difficult to imagine how postcolonial writers may evade this domesticating process of strategic othering. In their aim to authorise the postcolonial self from objectification by the dominant discourse, Tibetan diasporic autobiographies are caught between the need to present their versions of history and the danger of becoming appropriated as just another instance of exotic otherness. In this article I propose a reading of Adhe Tapontsang and Joy Blakeslee's *Ama Adhe: the voice that remembers* in which I apply Graham Huggan's theory of the 'postcolonial exotic' to interrogate the various strategies by which this Tibetan woman's life-narrative negotiates the possibility of exotic commodification through a self-empowering vision of using the market for her own ends. In identifying Ama Adhe's autobiography as *testimonio*, I offer an alternative reading of postcolonial alliances with neo-colonial commodity fetishism as an instance of assigning new agency to the exotic other.

Conferring authenticity

In her work on Tibetan autobiographies, Laurie McMillin (2001) identifies a number of authenticity markers, including spiritual inclination, nationalist feelings and life in exile, that feature prominently in the body of diasporic life-writing. To become valuable contributions to the Tibetan struggle, these texts play into Western exoticisation by circulating popular images of an 'authentic' Tibetan—humble, pacifist, stateless and marginalised—in the hope for emotional, material and political support, because, as McMillin points out, 'to be worthy of support is another way of being authentic; to receive support is to have one's Tibetan-ness affirmed' (McMillin 2001:132ff). Alexandra Schultheis, in her analysis of subjectivity in Tibetan autobiography, argues that Tibetan life-writing is often read and judged according to its perceived capacity to offer readers 'spiritual relief from the dissatisfactions produced by modern materialism as well as a self-gratifying identification with an oppressed people' (Schultheis 2006:5). Feelings of spiritual alienation, dissatisfaction with technological process and desire for primitivist myths feed the need for Tibetan accounts of suffering and liberation; yet, paradoxically, it is precisely this want for exoticism that not only ensures the successful circulation in the global cultural arena, and is, therefore, potentially emancipating for Tibetans, but is also identified as the 'prison' from which essentialised enunciations of Tibetanness are made.[2]

Ama Adhe fits within these Western parameters of purity to identity and authenticity. Through tropes and figures of speech used frequently in public rhetoric about Tibet, *Ama Adhe* reiterates the core values of the authentic Tibetan. From Adhe Tapontsang's privileged and carefree childhood and adolescence in pre-colonial Kham, we follow her story in the Tibetan resistance, to subsequent imprisonment and, finally, escape to Nepal where she is able to fulfil her promise to recount the suffering of her people. Her childhood and adolescence are described with a near-mythic sense ('our land was known as *Metog Yul*, or Land of Flowers' (Tapontsang 1997:5)),in sharp contrast to the general social, religious and environmental demise since the Chinese invasion and colonisation of her native land ('the Tibetans began comparing the Chinese presence to a Tibetan proverb about leprosy—that it kills one slowly as the fingers fall away from the hand' (Tapontsang 1997:63)). Adhe's narrative thus follows tropes connected with Tibetan life-writing; combined with her strong faith in the teachings of Tibetan Buddhism and her continuous struggle for Tibetan independence, Adhe Tapontsang's compliance with the expectations of a Tibetan autobiography verifies her narrative within the parameters of neo-colonialist discourses of 'truth' and 'authenticity' (Kaplan 1992:123). I argue, however, that *Ama Adhe* produces slippages through which our assumptions and expectations of an autobiography of an authentic—and, therefore, exoticised—Tibetan life story can be challenged. Before I examine how *Ama Adhe* establishes ways to resist exotic commodification, it is important to outline the vested interests of both the Tibetan community in exile and a sympathetic Western audience in creating a normative value system of Tibetan authenticity.

The experience of displacement has been salient in the construction of Tibetan diasporic identity. While regional affiliations have played a greater role in the formation of cultural identity prior to 1959, the common loss caused by the trauma of exile has led Tibetans to 'become increasingly aware of how much they share culturally, linguistically, and religiously' (Powers 2004:144). Even so, the Tibetan diasporic community has been careful to promote the idea of a pan-Tibetanness among disparate groups of people from various parts of greater Tibet since the beginning of exile. The remarkable success of maintaining their heritage in diaspora is often attributed to a 'process of enclavement', the role of the 14th Dalai Lama as spiritual and political leader, and the continuous emotional and financial support from individual donors and international aid agencies (Klieger 1989:55). As well as cultivating a strong sense of solidarity, the Tibetan diasporic community has focused on cultivating shared traditional social practices in order to preserve the cultural heritage of Tibet. The urge to re-establish and preserve traditional cultural and religious institutions in an effort to counter assimilation informs not only the official policies of the Central Tibetan Administration in Dharamsala, India, but also individual choices in language use, dress code and cultural ceremonies (Diehl 1997:125). Stuart Hall explains that the idea of a shared, essentialised cultural identity, which reflects a common history and provides the community with a certain sense of oneness, is paramount in all postcolonial struggles (Hall 1990:222ff).

In the continuous struggle against social disintegration and the threat of assimilation into the new social and natural environment, diasporic communities often seek to strengthen a collective identity derived from the shared history of displacement and the identification with a specific origin. In an attempt to counteract assimilation, diasporas often rekindle feelings of nostalgia and reinforce the desire to return to the homeland. It is not surprising then that traditional values and tradition have become the core identification factor for the Tibetan community in exile; yet, in their attempt to resist the making and remaking of identities, the Tibetan diasporic community practises a strategy of essentialism through which '[s]tasis and purity are asserted—creatively and violently—*against* historical forces of movement and contamination' (Clifford 1997:7). The focus on the past and tradition complicates choices of acceptable representations of Tibet and this process of selection is inextricably intertwined with the question of authenticity and the need to preserve a distinct Tibetanness in diaspora. Several scholars note that the public discourse in the Tibetan diasporic community is clearly defined by this 'strategic essentialism' (to use a term coined by Gayatri Spivak {1988b:205}) in which hybridity and syncretism are devalued as potentially undermining the idea of nationhood in diaspora.

The need to preserve the memory of Tibet with all its attributes of culture, religion and language must, therefore, be seen in the context of the challenges posed by both colonisation and life in exile. However, some scholars have emphasised that the creation of a narrowly circumscribed Tibetan history and identity has been produced partly through an interaction with the West. While the century-old Western idealisation of Tibet as a place of mysticism removed from the trials and tribulations of modernity has resulted in material and emotional benefits for Tibetan diasporics, the exchange between Western financial and Tibetan 'symbolic capital'[3] has strong repercussions for the representations of Tibet and Tibetans in the production of diasporic literature. The exchange referred to here is that between Tibetan refugees and their Western donors; for financial and political support from the West, Tibetans offer non-material goods, such as Buddhist teachings, traditional values and customs, which 'validate their status as "Tibetan refugees", and make them worthy recipients for financial sponsorship in the eyes of foreign donors' (Prost 2006:234). It can thus be argued that the present-day formulation of an essentialised Tibetanness in diaspora is a convergence of the diasporic commitment to preserve their traditional culture with the consciously constructed self-presentation to a potentially supportive Western market. Audrey Prost notes that diasporic Tibetan and Western representations of an idealised Tibetanness 'happily coincide in awarding high symbolic currency to the preservation of "authentic" (largely Buddhist) Tibetan lifestyles' (Prost 2006:241).

This convergence of ideologies places growing pressure on the community as it becomes difficult to remain pure in diaspora. Essentialised notions of Tibetanness further negate the hybridising effects of life in diaspora. Though the Tibetan community in diaspora attempts to rigidly enforce an essentialised cultural identity, diasporas can never, in practice, maintain an ideology of purity or sustain their 'illusion of spatial isolation' (Featherstone 1996:48). John Powers suggests that the 'unanimity of the Tibetan sources we are considering is partly a reflection of pressure for people to conform their beliefs to the norms of the group' (Powers 2004: 128); indeed, the freedom of thought and expression, as laid down in the constitution of the Tibetan diasporic community, can be heavily circumscribed. Although Powers claims that the majority of diasporic Tibetans subscribe to the essentialist representations put forth by the Central Tibetan Administration and a small number of Western-educated Tibetan diasporic intellectuals, he notes that 'there are also powerful mechanisms to bring doubters into line' (Powers 2004:129). As a result, literary output in the Tibetan diasporic community becomes 'both the site of identity formation and the site of the *struggle* over identity formation' (Ashcroft 2001:4 [italics as in the original]).

Although this exoticisation and its subsequent commodification as Tibet chic have been under attack within academia for some time, popular Western discourse still adheres to the concept of Tibet as violated Shangri-La In her article on popular images of Tibet, Calla Jacobson notes that contemporary idealisations are not only connected with present-day Tibet and its people but are simultaneously extended to include Tibetan society in the past to create a narrative of a 'traditional society that was, until the Chinese occupation, frozen in a kind of unchanging stasis, isolated outside of the flow of history' (Jacobson 2004:54). In what Edward Said recognised as the 'flexible positional superiority of Orientalism' (Said 2000:7), Tibet, its society and religion are to this day still categorised and represented in an assumed difference and separateness from the West. This ties in with Gayatri Spivak's repeated appeal to vigilance against the belief that our current period of decolonisation has simply interrupted Western representation of the non-West as a stable object of Western knowledge. It becomes clear that this idealisation of Tibet and its people works through a hierarchisation of certain popular aspects—Buddhist, non-violent, nationalist, colonised—of Tibetan culture over others and that adherence to these markers confers authenticity to the Tibetan subject. In this idealisation, popular rhetoric is simply another instance of oppositional thinking and, as such, 'dehumanizing, perhaps no less so than obviously racist characterizations' (Jacobson 2004:54). The exoticising tendency is not restricted to popular discourse but is also discernible among Western intellectuals and political activists. In their attempts to aid and give voice to the marginalised they run the risk of mainstreaming Tibetan enunciations into a common narrative of the peaceful, spiritual and oppressed —and, therefore, without agency—victim.

Not just an authentic autobiography?

In the light of these tensions of expectation within which postcolonial, or ethnic autobiography is created, marketed and consumed, I agree with Caren Kaplan that 'the burden of ethnic autobiographical writing is to participate in at least two different registers at all times, even two separate temporalities' (Kaplan 1988:148). Yet, while acknowledging the burden that these converging constraints place on ethnic autobiography, I argue that this double vision provides a perspective through which postcolonial life-writing can challenge the dominant model of genre *from within* and, therefore, allow for alternative readings for the colonised subject. I agree with Alexandra Schultheis that this could also contribute 'to the wider project of speaking with the subaltern by expanding what counts as academic theory to encompass other epistemologies, technologies, and enunciations of selfhood' (Schultheis 2006:4).

Ama Adhe is a series of transcribed interviews, written in collaboration with Joy Blakeslee, an American writer specialising in historical research and human rights. It begins by challenging generic assumptions of the autonomous and self-conscious I dominating the narrative style in autobiography through the author's insistence on speaking not just for herself but for her community:

> I have traveled a long distance from the land of my youth, from the dreams and innocence of childhood, and have come to see a world that many fellow Tibetans could never have dreamed of...Those I once knew are gone, and I have given them my solemn promise that somehow their lives will not be wiped out, forgotten, and confused within a web of history that has been rewritten by

those who find it useful to destroy the memory of many I have known and loved (Tapontsang 1997:3).

Adhe Tapontsang's choice to use the Western genre of autobiography, with its focus on the subject's individualism in a metropolitan context, in order to publicise her experience as a representative voice of the Tibetan community, leads me to identify her work as an instance of *testimonio*. John Beverley has defined *testimonio*, which is used mainly in conjunction with Latin American indigenous autobiographies, as an example of confessional writing told, 'in the first person by a narrator who is also the real protagonist or witness of the events he or she recounts' (Beverley 2004:31). While this definition is essentially that of autobiography and memoir, *testimonio* is further defined as a representative genre of the marginalised—the woman, the child, the slave, the subaltern—and as an attempt to interpolate hegemonic discourse to assume agency as a *subject* of history. It is, therefore, an instance of what Barbara Harlow terms 'resistance literature' that aims at presenting a people's freedom struggle to attract sympathy and support from outside their cultural group. Written in a situation of urgency, oppression, poverty or marginalisation, *testimonial* literature is not centred on the individual fate of the subject of autobiography but rather on the representation of collective destiny. In contrast to Western autobiographical writing, *testimonia* 'renegotiate the relationship between personal identity and the world, between personal and social history...[they] are tied to a struggle for cultural survival rather than purely aesthetic experimentation or individual expression' (Kaplan 1992:130). Because they refuse to be limited to simply mirroring the individual 'I' of the *Bildungsroman*, *testimonia* are often read as 'identical, and coterminous, with the nation itself' (Fraser 2000:77). Thus they approximate 'the symbolic function of the epic hero, without at the same time assuming the epic hero's hierarchical and patriarchal status' (Beverley 2004:33). Adhe Tapontsang tellingly remarks in the prologue of her testimony: 'Somehow I have survived, a witness to the voices of my dying compatriots, my family and friends...I do not understand the reason that this has come to be my part to play; but I understand very well the purpose of what must be said' (Tapontsang 1997:3). Adhe Tapontsang's narrative cannot, therefore, be read only as a personal account; by virtue of her survival of 27 years in labour camps in Chinese-occupied Tibet, her life story has representational value for her people. It 'evokes an absent polyphony of other voices, other possible lives and experiences' (Beverley 2004:34) which are connected and enunciated through her testimony. Because it is an instance of what Caren Kaplan terms 'out-law genre', I argue that Adhe Tapontsang's *testimonio* can be seen as a subversion of 'the individual bourgeois author (the sacred subject of autobiographical narrative)' in order to construct *a collective self*—'a kind of collective consciousness that "authorizes" and validates the identity of the individual writer' (Kaplan 1992:121). However, by producing a life-narrative that undermines the 'auto' in autobiography (the insistence on the 'I' to the exclusion of community), *Ama Adhe* complicates the issue of 'authenticity'. What we have here is not simply the individual account of a colonised Third-World woman, but a multi-layered text that dispels the myth of authenticity through identification with the exotic other.

In speaking for the collective through an individual life story, *testimonio* does not privilege the individual of traditional autobiography and her experience but acts as an appropriation of this Western literary form through which the subaltern acquires agency. In this appropriation *testimonio* defies what Marxism sees as the inability of the subaltern to voice its history through any means other than being 're-presented' by the dominant group. The strong evocation of 'truth' by the narrating 'I' must be regarded as 'the mark of a desire not to be silenced or defeated, a desire to impose oneself on an institution of power, such as literature, from the position of the excluded or the marginal' (Beverley 2004:34). After her release from labour camps in 1985, Adhe sees the radical changes that have been implemented during her imprisonment, both in the natural environment and within the social structure of her people. Having survived the harsh 27-year sentence, she recounts:

> A thought began to grow in me: 'I must go to India to inform His Holiness and everyone in the world, whomever I meet, about how my people perished from the Chinese atrocities.' It seemed that unless I could find people to tell the story to, I could never be satisfied. In me, there was no feeling of 'living' in Tibet. (Tapontsang 1997:206)

It becomes clear that the sole intention of this life-narrative is to act as political testimony of collective suffering in order to elicit international support for Tibetans within and outside of Tibet. In this intention I see Adhe Tapontsang's active role in using the exotic fetishism prevalent in the West to champion the cause of her people. To achieve this, the myth of authenticity is played out using clichéd stereotypes and representations both textually and paratextually. As I have outlined above, the narration of Adhe's life story follows closely the limits by which readers can identify *Ama Adhe* as authentically Tibetan. Yet more importantly, authenticity can be detected much earlier in Adhe's narration through what Wendy Waring classifies as 'paratextual traces...that render the process of cultural production visible' (Waring 1995:455). As Graham Huggan (2001) points out, the writer herself is only part of the authentication process; book covers, reviews, publishers, book prizes and readership all contend in confirming and conferring authenticity to authors and their works. The book cover of *Ama Adhe* reinforces certain expectations of Tibetan life stories: Adhe's portrait in traditional Tibetan dress and with the Buddhist *mala* (rosary) at the centre of the dust jacket immediately establish the link to Tibetan Buddhism. This is emphasised by the 14th Dalai Lama's Foreword and a photograph showing Adhe and her second husband in front of the Potala in Lhasa. The quotes at the back of the book reiterate the individuality of this autobiography as a tribute to the 'powers of the human will' in the face of 'immense degradation and suffering'. However, in the background of the front cover the mass movement of Tibetans is depicted, which, together with the Dalai Lama's description of the book as 'a moving testimony of both the suffering and the heroism of the Tibetan people' (Tapontsang 1997:vii), revokes the individuality of the account by stressing her experience as an evocation of representative authenticity.

Indeed, *Ama Adhe* frustrates assumptions about knowing her situation because she resists not only singular interpretation but also intimacy between herself and the reader. In what Jacques Derrida terms 'an inquisitorial insistence' on the part of the reader, we often expect autobiographical writing to reveal the innermost depths of its narrative (Derrida 1979:87). While Adhe Tapontsang's story is told purposely for us, it nevertheless evades the perception of solidarity through an insistence of difference. Adhe Tapontsang describes, for example, scenes of intense suffering through what I term the 'withholding of intimacy' for us readers. Adhe recounts the experiences of several women, including herself, of repeated rape by a Chinese guard during her first years of imprisonment in the Dartsedo labour camp. The tone of her narration approximates factual observation through her use of the third person to establish distance between herself and her experiences, as well as between the reader and the women suffering sexual violence: '[The warden] took an interest in young and attractive women prisoners. They were often called by him to clean his rooms and do his laundry. During this work, he also repeatedly raped them' (Tapontsang 1997:112). Although her narration then shifts back to first person, Adhe Tapontsang's account remains distanced, disclosing no emotional reaction to the aggressive behaviour she encounters:

> I was one of these women. Three others were also selected for this duty: Nangtso Wangmo, from Lingkarshe, a region bordering Lithang region, and Dolkar and Yangchen from Chatring. We were called in rotation and raped. As a precaution against pregnancy, he forced us to drink musk water immediately after intercourse (Tapontsang 1997:112-13).

The documentary style in reporting the names and regional affiliations of the women raped establishes Adhe's truth claim and works to unearth the forgotten (hi)stories of her people. Crucially, Adhe Tapontsang brings to light the suffering of Tibetan women, key subalterns in the already marginalised Tibetan issue. In their article on memory, gender and transmission, Marianne Hirsch and Leo Spitzer (2007) interrogate the use of gender as a category of analysis for testimonies of survivors of genocide. Gender, according to Hirsch and Spitzer, may shift the focus away from the extreme trauma suffered by female and male survivors. To support this claim, they quote Claire Kahane, who acknowledges that '[i]f hysteria put gender at the very center of subjectivity, trauma, in its attention to the assault on the ego and the disintegration of the subject, seems to cast gender aside as irrelevant' (Hirsch & Spitzer 2007:140). In narrating the Tibetan occupation and subsequent religious and political persecution, Western coverage and Tibetan *testimonia* have mainly focused on the collective plight of Tibetans, omitting almost completely the gender-related violence that occurred during and since the initial colonisation, such as the incidents recounted in the passage above. If, however, as Kahane argues, colonisers and perpetrators ignore the gender of their victims, it is very important to bring the category of gender back into to our discussion of trauma and violence. While I want to avoid simplifying the traumatic events by attributing them to gender difference and to exaggerate and celebrate the efforts of Tibetan women and the pain they endured over those of Tibetan men, I argue that the quotation from Tapontsang's writing above can sensitise us to the gendered experience of trauma. Although *Ama Adhe* presents a collective narration, her focus on the gendered violence, which is often absent from Tibetan *testimonia*, also provides an important but neglected means of understanding the complexity and breadth of gendered suffering and ensuing resistance in the Tibetan struggle.

By offering her narrative for consumption in an urban context, Adhe Tapontsang can give voice to those erased by Chinese versions of history. Her testimony is, therefore, a powerful tool—'a weapon, a way of fighting back' (Beverley 2004:xvi)—against silencing by the coloniser. Her recounting of her own sexual abuse in the same documentary fashion may be indicative of post-traumatic suffering in which narrative distance helps to deflect the emotional and physical pain endured; yet I propose an alternative reading focusing on what Doris Sommer calls an 'ethical reminder of difference' (Sommer 1999:137). While Adhe Tapontsang's *testimonio* addresses us directly and specifically in order to make the story of her people known, we must bear in mind that she speaks to us from a position of cultural and political otherness. The safeguarding of her own trauma in the quote above keeps not only her experiences but also us, the readers, at a distance. It therefore withholds the 'complicity between narrator and reader' of traditional autobiography in which we expect to find 'a tighter bond of intimacy than is possible in manipulative and evasive narrative fiction' (Sommer 1999:132). By denying us insight into her 'individual' suffering, she not only frustrates our expectation of the immediacy of knowledge through autobiography but also signals her story as being *representative* in its *exemplary* way. Through this narrative device Adhe Tapontsang reminds us of her role as spokeswoman for the collective suffering of Tibetans since the Chinese occupation.

I agree with Alexandra Schultheis that postcolonial discourse should 'recognize the religious, colonized woman as well as her collaborative text as active participants in discourses of modernity rather than its victims' (Schultheis 2006:4). At the same time, we must acknowledge the necessity for Tibetan *testimonia* to collaborate in a collective movement based on international modernist ideas of sovereignty and human rights. While the purpose of Tibetan life-writing is to assume agency, and thus to enter history, the publishing and marketing networks they enter into inevitably follow their own agendas. In the case of Tibet, the feeling of urgency to preserve its religion for the common (read Western) good of humanity is especially evident in the rhetoric of Western popular discourse. It comes as no surprise then that this motivation also influences the publishing world interested in Tibetan literature. While it addresses the politically and culturally destructive situation for her community in Tibet, Adhe Tapontsang's narration from the margin runs the risk of being 'exoticised' in the desire to read (or publish) another story of 'cultural otherness' (Huggan 2001:14). This raises the question of the problematic appropriation of ethnic autobiographies into evocations of what Robert Carr has called 'Otherized communities and their worlds' (quoted in Kaplan 1992:123) that serve as pretexts for the 'accumulation of knowledge and power' of the Western reader. Translating the self and narrating the other are, however, part of a *dual* process 'shot through with relations of power and desire' (Duncan & Gregory 1999:5). This desire can be seen as the risk of silencing the Other by filtering her experiences through the grid of dominant systems of representation. In other words, what we have come to expect of Tibetan autobiographies can complicate our potential to read and hear heterogeneous enunciations of Tibetanness. Joy Blakeslee interprets Adhe Tapontsang's distanced tone in narrating her personal suffering as 'a reflection of the Tibetan language and culture itself' (Tapontsang 1997:x). Since Blakeslee does not speak Tibetan, this interpretation is indicative of the popular assumption about Tibetans' innate capacity to exhibit great strength and compassion, even when faced with great suffering and adversity. I argue that this reading affirms and interprets silence on the part of the subaltern woman; however, it does 'not necessarily address the voices of the dispossessed' (Emberley 1993:74). I suggest an alternative: perhaps we have to concede that Adhe's silence may be strategic, a resistance to the co-operative act of sharing the 'innermost' aspects of her story. After all, *Ama Adhe* sets out to be more than just the individual life story; even more so, her strategic silences evade our control over the shaping of her collective self. Although she is willing to participate in her own objectification for political purposes for both the means and ends of social action (McLagan 1996:5), Adhe Tapontsang simultaneously resists a recasting of herself as victim without agency.

Given the role literature plays in the production of cultural commodification and its interdependence with patriarchal and hegemonic structures, ethnic autobiographies are intentionally written for and read within Western discourse of exotic fetishism. Tibetan life-writing also engages with the global marketplace by 'detail[ing] the Tibetan subject's engagement with militaristic, economic, and cultural colonialism' (Schultheis 2006: 5) with the aim of eliciting Western support for the Tibetans' political cause. However, reading and interpretating in a metropolitan context allows for the appropriation of Tibetan life stories within the often-benevolent discourse of Western academia, popular media and transnational political activism. This situation brings with it the danger of what Spivak calls a 'domesticated Other' in which Tibetan life-narratives are read in an expectation of their subalternity by which the reader's 'own position of relative authority and privilege [is] left uncontested in the process' (Beverley 2004:xvi). John Beverley (2004:38) reminds us that the control of representation 'does not only flow in one direction'. As I have argued above, ethnic autobiographies have the power to avail themselves of existing literary forms and the global marketplace in order to make their stories heard. Though their reading within the dominant discourse by academics, activists, editors and the general public can lead to these stories being represented as subaltern or as exotic, thereby, re-marginalising (or re-subalternising) them, Tibetan life-narratives can use literary forms and the marketplace for their own agenda. I argue that Adhe Tapontsang's refusal to share with us the emotional and physical implications of her sexual abuse and the insistence on her collective self is an instance of the appropriation of an existing structure for her own ends. In resisting our desire for the innermost aspects of her narrative, she refuses not only to allow her readers to identify with her but also to be commodified as another example of authentic Tibet chic. *Ama Adhe* invites us to reconsider 'the increasingly facile adoption of the notion of a homogenized Other, for a celebratory, oppositional politics of the margins or minorities' (Bhabha 1994:75). I argue that what Adhe Tapontsang forces us to come to terms with

> is not someone who is being represented for us *as subaltern,* but rather an active agent of a transformative cultural and political project that aspires to become hegemonic in its own right: someone, in other words, who assumes the right to tell the story in the way she feels will be most effective in molding both national and international public opinion in support of the ideas and values she favors, which include a new kind of autonomy and authority for indigenous peoples (Beverley 2004:92-93).

As consumers and critics of Tibetan *testimonia*, we have to acknowledge that, while no actual power can be assumed in writing history, they are evidence of subaltern historiography and, as such, of an attempt to demystify whatever material interests and ideological methods are being negotiated and preserved against other parties. One way to resist turning Tibetans and their life stories into examples of exoticised otherness is, therefore, to undertake a careful reading that appropriates them 'as neither an idealized victor in the face of irrevocable oppression nor as a passive victim of some inevitable force of exploitation... but as a contradictory subject involved in alternative strategies of resistance' (Emberley1993:20-21). In collapsing differences in Tibetan autobiographies to fit the profile of the 'authentic Tibetan' lies the danger that the multiple experiences of Tibetan diasporics become appropriated, benevolently interpreted and finally silenced. Any attempt to essentialise this heterogeneity in order to 'constitute the colonial subject as Other' must, therefore, be seen as an instance of 'epistemic violence' (Spivak 1988a:280) which a critical reading needs to account for.

Notes

1   Tibetan self-representations appeared in the form of English autobiographies as early as 1957; McMillin (2001), however, only identifies a marked increase of various literary forms in Tibetan diasporic secular literature since 1990.
2   For an overview of Western romanticisation of Tibet, see Bishop (1989), Lopez (1999), Huber (2001) and Jacobson (2004), amongst others.
3   A term used by Audrey Prost (2006) to refer to the non-material 'goods' Tibetans deliver in their exchange with Western beneficiaries.

chapter six

He who shall not be named: the Shugden taboo and Tibetan national identity in exile

Wokar Tso Rigumi

In June 1996 the Tibetan government-in-exile passed a parliamentary mandate prohibiting the worship of a relatively obscure deity called Dorje Shugden, following the Dalai Lama's earlier strictures against the practice. Although the ban had no legal jurisdiction, and may even be considered illegal under the 'right to freedom of worship' enshrined in Article 25 of the Indian Constitution, the mandate found its place as a social norm amongst Tibetan refugees in India. An understanding of Dorje Shugden worship as a degenerate cult has percolated into public discourse, leading to social ostracisation of Shugden devotees. Along with a general public aversion to the practice, systematic campaigns have also been organised to abolish the practice in some monasteries, encourage voluntary withdrawal at public ceremonies and expel Shugden worshippers from government-run institutions.[1] Given this volatile situation, most remaining Shugden worshippers do not admit openly to their faith; and if some do employ a collective presence to assert their identity, other Tibetans often circumvent such gatherings.

Though the controversy has now abated in exile, a few prolific Shugden groups based in Europe have attracted global attention by staging vocal protests against the Dalai Lama for persecuting Shugden worshippers. In the wake of the recent Chinese valorisation of the Shugden cause,[2] Tibetans in exile accuse Shugden supporters of colluding with the enemy. One severe accusation of such collusion involved the brutal murder of three monks heading an anti-Shugden campaign. Many claimed that Shugden devotees from Tibet had committed the murder with Chinese backing. Although the perpetrators were never caught, the Indian police corroborated the accusation (Phull 1998).

Given this controversy, a tone of cautious scepticism has also crept into publications in the mainstream media that generally write about Tibetans in adulatory tones (Woodward 1998). There has been no shortage of strident attacks indicting the Dalai Lama for being a tyrant perpetrating religious persecution (Al-Jazeera 2008; Backman 2008; Hitchens 1998).[3] But beyond these somewhat vapid meditations by newspaper columnists, there is a more entrenched significance to the Shugden conflict in its connection with Tibetan politics in exile. The question is not a matter of ascertaining whether it is a case of religious persecution or whether the Dalai Lama is a scheming autocrat beneath a charming persona. Instead, the controversy calls for an analysis of the conflict of interests between the Shugden supporters and the Dalai administration. Shugden supporters proclaim the deity as a vanguard of Gelug purity that is under threat from Gelug hierarchs like the Dalai Lama, who disregard this need for preserving its doctrinal purity. The Dalai administration denounces Shugden worship as a cult that promotes divisive sectarianism.

I will argue that Tibetan nationalism in exile has as its legacy a theocratic society led by the Dalai Lama, who has to strive against his own sectarian affiliations to dispense his role as its ecumenical head, and that the Shugden controversy can be seen as a conflict with this structure. Drawing almost entirely from the meticulous historical analyses compiled in the authoritative and lucid account by Georges Dreyfus (1999), I have attempted to look at this aspect of the current Shugden controversy in the context of exile politics as a crisis of national unity.[4] An interpretation of the Shugden's theological underpinnings, which overlap into a number of tendentious arguments, is beyond both the scope of this chapter and my knowledge. But in my opinion the conflict is not purely a case of religious misunderstanding detached from larger political motives. What I have attempted to do is trace the emergence of Shugden as a symbol of Gelug exclusivism, the conflict engendered therein, and how that has played out in exile politics. I also address a contemporary social taboo against pronouncing the name of the banned deity amongst Tibetans in exile, an issue that has not been analysed before.

A brief history of the Shugden deity

In the periods of power vacuum that followed the downfall of the monarchy in the 9th century, Tibet underwent bouts of intense political intrigue. There were many conflicts among the great monastic strongholds that had emerged as centres of socio-religious power after the ascendancy of Buddhism. In the mid 17th century, after a protracted struggle with some other competing religious hierarchs, the fifth Dalai Lama (1617–82), a prominent hierarch of the Gelug sect, took over the administrative reins in Lhasa with the help of his Mongol patron Gushri Khan. The Dorje Shugden controversy is a tangential event linked to this momentous historical event of the Dalai Lama's ascendancy as the head of a theocratic state in Tibet.

Perhaps from a self-conscious consideration of his acquired position as the temporal leader of the realm, as well as his own family background and personal spiritual calling, the Dalai Lama was attracted to the Nyingmapa sect. The fifth Dalai Lama's inclination towards this older sect of Tibetan Buddhism was disliked and regarded as dubious by some factions within the Gelug school (Dreyfus 1999:6). The third Panchen Lama, Drakpa Gyaltsen (1618–55), a contemporaneous Gelug hierarch of the fifth Dalai Lama, also censured him, subtly but derisively, for his Nyingmapa leanings.

This third Panchen Lama, who also had a history of close rivalry with the fifth Dalai Lama, is the historical person with whom the Dorje Shugden deity is equated.[5] Acknowledged for his superior intellectual and academic prowess, the young Drakpa Gyaltsen had been a candidate for the coveted position of the Dalai Lama, but having lost to the fifth Dalai he was appointed as the third Panchen Lama. After a successful visit to the Chinese imperial court and a victory over the Dalai Lama in a scholarly debate, the third Panchen Lama was found dead in suspicious circumstances with a ceremonial white silk scarf stuffed down his throat (Dreyfus 1999:3). It is from this historical incident that Shugden devotees draw the legend of the origin of the Dorje Shugden deity. According to this legend, the dead Panchen was reborn into a wrathful spirit protector to ensure the purity of Gelug standards—a cause that he had championed in his lifetime through his opposition to the fifth Dalai Lama's laxity in adhering to those principles.

Birth of a legend from fragments

While Shugden devotees cite this legend as the aetiological myth of the deity, there are many grounds to challenge a direct correlation between Shugden and the slain Panchen.

Firstly, there are divergent interpretations of the historical event at the time that belie this claim of the re-incarnation of the Panchen into a spirit. Such an ominous event as the untimely death, or perhaps murder, of a hierarch of Panchen's stature caused a huge stir in monastic circles. In the turmoil, riven by the animosity between the Dalai administration and the Panchen supporters, speculation about his death abounded.[6] At the time, it was the Dalai Lama who announced that the Panchen had been reborn into a spirit, in order to denigrate his rival's memory. The insinuation that a spiritual master of such high standing had been reborn into a spirit would have been rightly taken as an insult by Panchen supporters at the time. A prominent Gelug historian refuted this claim as sacrilegious to the memory of the Panchen, claiming that the spirit was actually that of the Dalai's prime minister Sonam Gyaltsen. As a retort to this defamatory allegation made by the Dalai administration some Panchen sympathisers at the time claimed that the Panchen had been reborn as the Chinese emperor. Some others subverted this allegation to claim that the Panchen had indeed been reborn as a spirit, but only after committing wilful suicide to be gloriously reborn as an indomitable wrathful spirit-protector of the sect.

Secondly, the polymorphous nature of the deity linked with the Shugden narrative also makes the narrative of the slain Panchen as the Dorje Shugden deity quite murky. The practice of propitiation of the Shugden deity, in many local forms but with the same aetiology and symbolism, is extensive across Tibetan regions and predated this incident. Shugden draws from the aetiological myth of the *gyelpo* spirit, a treasure-protecting, wrathful red spirit of a person, often a religious one, seeking to extract revenge against those involved in his death. One of countless spirits in Tibetan mythology, this entity is not aligned with any sectarian denomination.[7] From his anthropological studies in Nepal in the late 1970s, Stan Mumford (1995:132) writes, 'In Gyasumdo the lamas are Nyingmapa, yet most of them honor Shugs-ldan as a lineage guardian picked up in Tibet in the past by their patriline'.

The legend of the Panchen as Shugden deity protector of Gelug purity is not a continuous narrative passed on through the ages. Panchen supporters attracted to his latent Gelug supremacist attitude and derision of the Dalai's Nyingmapa sympathies may have developed a counter-allegiance towards the slain rival, regarding him as a sort of martyr for Gelug purity. But the legend seems to be a tangential narrative prompted by the resentment Panchen supporters held against the fifth Dalai Lama in his own time. It dissipates into relative anonymity thereafter. Noting the localised nature of the legend, Stephen Batchelor (1998:para 10) says, 'After the death of the Fifth Dalai Lama in 1682, the controversy between these factions of the Ge-luk school slips into the shadows and we hear only occasional references to Dorje Shugden for the next two hundred years'.

Rekindling a legend, beginning a controversy

In the light of these discrepancies, we must examine how the slain Panchen/ Shugden as spirit protector of Gelug purity has emerged as such a strident narrative in recent years. According to Dreyfus, the Panchen/ Dorje Shugden narrative explicitly became the vanguard of Gelug exclusivism with a charismatic Gelug monk called Pabongkha Rinpoche (1878–1941), who is predominantly responsible for the present persona of the deity (Dreyfus 1999:15–19). Pabongkha had imbibed the practice from his mother. After a period of ill health, which he considered to be chastisement by the deity for straying from strict Gelug dictum, he established an unwavering commitment to the Dorje Shugden deity. Greatly disturbed by poor discipline and the decline of standards in Gelug monasteries he visited across Tibet, he spearheaded a revivalist Gelug movement from the 1930s. In this endeavour to restore the lost glory of Gelug practice, Pabongkha elevated the Dorje Shugden, a minor deity at the time, to supreme protector of the Gelug sect (Dreyfus 1999:15–19). By invoking the emotional narrative of the slain martyr and the wrathful symbolism of the deity, he had founded the perfect foil to stand as a protector of Gelug purity.

The contemporary controversy among Tibetans in exile began in the 1970s when a pro-Shugden leader, Dzemay Rinpoche (1927–96), published a text known as *The yellow book*, which listed Gelug lamas who were supposed to have suffered bodily harm or a shortened life as a result of Shugden's anger for not adhering to pure Gelug practice (Dreyfus 1999:23). Dreyfus notes that this was the first text to create a narrative promulgating Shugden's anger as a deterrent to peripatetic Gelug practitioners.

The Dalai Lama was apparently disturbed by the potentially divisive nature of the text. Within a year or two of *The yellow book*'s publication, he stopped worshipping the deity; two decades later, he articulated his concern by publicly disavowing the practice. Following the Dalai Lama's proscription of the deity, the government-in-exile issued an official edict to ban the practice. It claimed that Shugden was detrimental to three key aspects of Tibetan identity in exile: the person of the Dalai Lama, the unity of Tibetan people, and the integrity of an enlightened Buddhist practice.[8]

Shugden as a taboo

Curiously, in spite of vocal debate and sporadic violence, the majority of lay Tibetans in exile have devised a defence mechanism to deal with the whole controversy, which puts a most ironic twist to this war of rhetoric. The rejection of the deity by edict promotes a discourse about national unity and enlightened Buddhist practice; however, old superstitious legends have resurfaced in retellings of the story of the Dorje Shugden amongst common people.[9]

A deep rejection has transformed into a naming taboo in which people desist from uttering Shugden's name. Tai Situ Rinpoche, a prominent hierarch from a non-Gelug school says, on a CD released by the government-in-exile, 'As Kargyüdpas we do not take his name because of fear'.[10] I have often heard advice against taking his name or looking at his picture, lest he appear in one's dreams. Such a myth strengthens the taboo, inflating his insidiousness so that he is seen as capable of luring people even in their dreams. Before this practice emerged among Tibetans in exile, there was no historical precedent for a naming taboo relating to Shugden. This may be attributed to the fact that earlier, the conflict was a part of the elite power struggles within monastic circles, and, consequently, held no resonance for religious practices of the masses.

Instead, Tibetans now refer to him by the euphemistic title Gabbar Singh, the name of the foremost villain in Indian cinema, famous for his sadistic malevolence and booming laugh.[11] But Gabbar Singh's repeated appropriation into the repertoire of Indian popular culture has subverted his original quality as a fearsome villain to a much-bandied joke in the Bollywood-coloured imaginative psyche of the subcontinent. The use of this pseudonym for the Shugden deity serves as an 'anti-legend'. According to Bill Ellis (2005:124, 126), anti-legends, 'unlike official denials, arise from the folk process [and]...mimic credible stories that provoke tension among listeners only to dispel this tension with a punch line or some other well-known humorous device'. Unnaming the Dorje Shugden adheres to the official ban of the deity, not just by opposing the practice but denying him any effective agency by erasing his identity. Renaming him after the caricatured figure of Gabbar Singh serves as an anti-legend, deflating his ominous image.

There are other fragments connected with these lay rumours about Shugden that can be conceptualised as 'anti-legends'. In lay interpretations, Shugden is perceived as a primordial, wrathful spirit to be feared rather than as a deity with theological ramifications and a historical past. Shugden is a hungry and grasping spirit who seeks to satiate his eternal emptiness by luring as many souls as he can. He is an immensely pliable deity who responds immediately to fulfil the material wishes of devotees, but unless constantly propitiated, promptly punishes them with catastrophes. Virtually everyone has a cautionary tale about a family they know that has had catastrophic experiences. These myths reflect an anti-legend's mechanism of the distortion of legends to 'serve as ways of distancing listeners' (Ellis 2005:124). They instil the need for absolute rejection and a vigilant attitude. You may talk about the deity to warn others, but these allusions are safe only if you call him 'Gabbar Singh'.

Shugden in a schema of cultural memory

Given the plethora of myths that have attached to the Shugden controversy, I have sought to explore how they have succeeded in finding meaning in the schema of cultural memory of Tibetans. Jan Assmann (1995) has described cultural memory as collective understanding or constructions of the distant past, through which a social group makes sense of its history and conceives its identity. Assmann notes that there are two modes through which cultural memory transmits a moral order, 'one being normative—that which is expressed and enforced by some law, the other being narrative—which is articulated and dispersed through a culture's countless discursive registers' (Brockmeier 2002:27).

The theoretical narrative/normative binary has helped me to plot what I see as the significant phases in the dissemination of the Shugden in the cultural memory of Tibetans.

ACTUAL HISTORICAL EVENT
↓
CONFLICTING LEGENDS ABOUT PANCHEN'S DEATH
↓
PABONGKHA'S NORMATIVE COMMITMENT
↓
DALAI'S NORMATIVE OPPOSITION
↓
FOLK LEGENDS OF SHUGDEN

This somewhat simplistic plotting of an arcane controversy is, of course, incapable of providing a complete interpretation of such a complex issue. But it serves my aim of clarifying one aspect of the Shugden issue as an artefact of cultural memory. While the historical event of the Panchen's demise led to diverse conflicting myths, Pabongkha's installation of Shugden as a supreme protector of the Gelug sect instituted a normative commitment to the deity. In the same vein, the Dalai Lama's edict against Shugden worship as a degenerate practice constitutes an opposition that is normative in nature. This in turn has led to folk narratives amongst lay people that underline their understanding of Shugden.

Denying Shugden: affirming national identity

While literal interpretations of its history lead to exasperated confusion, this approach has led me to a greater appreciation of the cultural meaning of the Shugden problem amongst the Tibetan people in exile. Dorje Shugden has an entrenched relationship to the emergence of Tibet as a theocratic state and the Dalai Lama's rise to power—riven by the conflict between his sectarian affiliations as a Gelug hierarch and his duties as the head of a society. Another attempt by the present Dalai Lama to invoke the ecumenical discourse of Buddhism and Tibetan nationalism has provoked the alter ego of Gelug puritanism to rise again after 350 years.

While this controversy has been recognised by some scholars as a crisis of national unity for Tibetans in exile, the situation has also been rejected as an anomalous product of a misguided Tibetan political consciousness. Ursula Bernis takes such a view:

> Thus, I am treating the Dorje Shugden conflict as the most obvious symptom of a larger identity crisis. I believe it will not begin to be solved until the currently instituted political practice of merging religion and politics has been adequately scrutinized (Bernis 1998:part 3,1).

I argue that interpreting this identity crisis as an anomalous situation that can be rectified by transforming Tibetan polity to some universal norm is in itself misguided. On the contrary, the self-conception of national identity amongst Tibetans, no matter what form it takes, must be analysed as a legitimate response shaped by their own history. As Benedict Anderson (1991:12) has clarified, 'nationalism has to be understood by aligning it, not with self-consciously held political ideologies, but with the large cultural systems that preceded it, out of which—as well as against which—it came into being'. The Dalai hegemony forms the overriding historical context within which contemporary exilic Tibetan nationalism is always defining itself. Faced with outside scrutiny, even the Dalai Lama's position as the head of a unified Tibetan state has often been a part of strategic positioning, while political arrangements in Tibet before 1959 clearly reflect a fragmented polity with no unified state.

One may also argue that this controversy also reflects Homi Bhabha's argument of nation as a narrative strategy that seeks to perpetuate itself as a timeless, eternal presence in the psyche of a people (Bhabha 1994:212). According to Bhabha this strategy plays itself out in a performative/ pedagogical dynamic. The pedagogical refers to the totality of institutions and practices that teach a people to adhere to a unifying discourse of an exclusive national identity. The performative refers to the mundane daily activities through which people undertake to assert themselves as acting subjects within that discourse (Bhabha 1994:211). In this case, while the official edict issued by the government-in-exile forms the pedagogical discourse of national unity for Tibetan people, the anti-legends adopted by the people re-interpret the edict on their own terms to perform that expectation as subjects of the nation. The lay anti-legends merge with the official dictum in such a performative/pedagogic equation to transform the coercive dictum of the state into a cultural norm, resulting in the successful grassroots enforcement of the ban.

In its performative aspect, the nation also presents itself as an accessible space that will allow its subjects to articulate internally antagonistic and minority voices (Bhabha 1994:212). The pro-Shugdenites' condemnation of the ban as religious repression and a denial of human rights can be seen as part of this performative, albeit minority, subject voice within the nation-narrative. The violent opposition to Dorje Shugden is also symptomatic of the Andersonian 'reassurance of fratricide', whereby antagonism is realigned and inscribed as 'family history', but always within the prerogative of the supreme nation (Anderson 1991:199).

In conclusion, it could perhaps be asserted that a cultural studies perspective has extended the materialist accounts and historical analyses to tease out the nuances of the Shugden controversy as a nub of contestation for Tibetan nationalism in exile. From such a perspective, the Shugden controversy has led to a crisis in the creation of a protean national identity in the form of a multi-sectarian theocracy, with a Gelug hierarch at the helm. With this crisis, Bhabha's conceptualisation of the 'nation as narration' with a performative and pedagogical dynamic has explicitly come to the fore in the struggle to maintain the integrity of a Tibetan nation in the psyche if its people.

Notes

1. For example, in a campaign run in some monasteries in southern India, where there was a systematic program for voting and swearing against the worship of the deity. For documents and pledge-sheet from these events, see Shugden Society (2008).
2. The issue has been used by the Chinese media to malign the Dalai administration (for example, Focus 2008). According to the website dorjeshugden.com, the current Chinese-anointed Panchen has been seen to endorse the deity.
3. In one of the earliest mainstream articles about the Shugden issue, Christopher Hitchens (1998) paints a particularly negative picture of the Dalai Lama as being merely the progeny of modern public relations who is as human and embroiled in domestic power struggles as any other politician. Michael Backman (2008) asserts, 'To enhance his authority, he has sought to merge the four traditions into one and place himself at its head'.
4. I have limited the details of the historical and theological context to what is necessary for my arguments; my primary focus was to extend Dreyfus's historical findings as narratives and phenomena of cultural memory and dissemination.
5. Dreyfus (1999:3) says: 'Very little is known about the events that took place in the next ten years but it seems quite clear that there was a contentious [relationship] between the two lamas' estates'.
6. Many conflicting claims were made at the time about the cause of the Panchen's death, including natural causes, murder as result of political machinations, suicide committed in despair, and voluntary strangulation as a martyr. For a detailed account of these claims, see Dreyfus (1999:7–9).
7. Dreyfus also excavates a contemporaneous legend of a *gyelpo* that caused trouble to the Sakya theocratic estate. At the time it was notorious around Lhasa and may have seeped into the Shugden story as well.
8. Perhaps it is not too rash to propose that, by opposing Dorje Shugden in terms of the specific denominations that the Gelug exclusivists gave it, the Dalai Lama unwittingly legitimated their version.
9. I cite these legends from personal experience.
10. I have not been able to trace the title of the recording. It is one among many media releases relating to Shugden put out by the Tibetan government.
11. Gabbar Singh, a character from a 1970s Hindi blockbuster 'Sholay', is arguably the most memorable villain in Indian cinematic history.

chapter seven

Tibetan clerical attitudes to armed conflict: the cases of Tāranātha and the 14th Dalai Lama

David Templeman

Buddhists have consistently raised important points concerning the topic of war and armed struggle. Sometimes they have sought and produced what they believe to be convincing textual justification for their views. Among the major issues they have sought to clarify are:

- the possibility of Buddhists engaging in killing, with reduced or somehow ameliorated consequences;
- the moral dimensions of Buddhists permitting war to continue and doing nothing to end it;
- the range of moral questions raised by Buddhists attempting to justify their active engagement in war.

These issues are frequently easily (perhaps, glibly) answered by reference to *sūtras* and their commentaries which claim to give authoritative response to such dilemmas. However, there is surprisingly relatively little in those early texts that can be seriously considered as being authoritative.[1]

From the time that Buddhism first came under state protection and patronage within the Buddha's own lifetime—something that the Buddha himself was keen to see happen—it has been caught up inextricably with the roles, functions and obsessions of rulers. The ruler supplied patronage for an order of monks and in return gained reciprocal blessings from that meritorious deed. In later times such rulers might well have even been portrayed as being 'true' Buddhist rulers for their meritorious actions, whether or not they were regarded as such during their lifetimes.

However, all rulers, without exception, also needed to defend their borders, subdue unruly neighbours or expand their kingdoms whenever possible. Whether these actions were performed out of a purely imperial motivation or, more charitably speaking, to ensure the safety and prosperity of the populace, is a moot point. These are core roles of rulers. If they do not take these roles they may be said to have tacitly abandoned their right to rule. These sorts of activities might appear to have set such rulers in a position diametrically opposed to what we believe might or should have been the accepted norms of Buddhism, whether such norms actually were generally accepted by that particular ruler or not.

Throughout history, the ruler's need to protect, expand or subdue has never prevented Buddhist monks from offering prayers and rituals to assure the ruler (*their* ruler, in contrast to the ruler of the *others*) of success on the battlefield, with an apparent lack of concern for the moral problems involved in such actions. Neither, it appears, has such religious sensibility prevented various Buddhist rulers from sometimes using the armed forces at their disposal.[2]

Perhaps the most frequent and certainly the most difficult moral possibility facing one who would in some way take up arms allows us to decide whether or not the enemy poses a danger to Buddhism's very existence. From that viewpoint one may either defend the doctrine or abandon the struggle entirely. *Prima facie* this might appear to be a reasonable criterion but, ultimately, it faces the same moral problem as all other choices inasmuch as at some stage armed struggle becomes a likely possibility.

In examining a narrow selection of cases in which Tibetan prelates handled these problems in quite different manners, the point that emerges most clearly is that of the sometimes fraught relationship that exists between the monastic upholders of Buddhist tenets, their lay patrons, those who defend Buddhism with acts of violence and the act of armed struggle itself.

As we shall see in the next section, there emerges an awkward sense that Tāranātha for example, became drawn into a kind of devil's pact with his masters, being called on to perform a variety of actions that could be considered to have formed a crucial and intimate part of the war which raged between the neighbouring provinces of Tsang and Ü. Tāranātha's ambivalent stance towards war and his Buddhist attitude to certain aspects of it, is illuminating in this respect.

Tāranātha and Tibet's Civil War

This section of the chapter takes as its subject, the person of Tāranātha (1575–1634), a renowned Tibetan prelate. It specifically examines his position in the prosecution of Tibet's so-called Civil War which raged sporadically between 1603 and1621, a stance which I describe as being 'uninvolvedly involved'. Tāranātha became drawn into the Civil War largely because of his role as the major ritual priest to the rulers of Tsang in southwestern Tibet. These rulers, known as the Depa or Desi, became ineluctably engaged in a protracted struggle with the forces of Ü, or Central Tibet, which was nominally under the religious control fourth and fifth Dalai Lamas, hierarchs of the Gelugpa tradition of Tibetan Buddhism. The Gelugpa were supported by their willing allies, the Khalkha and Oirat Mongols, in their struggle for a more secure patron base and an enhanced religious influence.

The key elements which mark the overall mood of the 16th and 17th centuries and must inform our understanding of its events were the gradual deterioration of secular aristocratic power and the growing conflict between the ascendant Gelugpa and the various 'non-reformed' sects, such as the Kargyüdpa. The links between the Gelugpa and the Mongols were initially revitalised by Sonam Gyatso, later known by the title Third Dalai Lama (1543–88). He reminded the Mongol Khan that theirs was not a new relationship in which the Tibetan prelate was simply proselytising in a new 'convert field'. Instead it was in fact an old one that was being revitalised in their current lifetime. This served to link the Mongols irrevocably with the Gelugpa and this calculatingly expedient move thereby set the scene for future trouble with the powerful and ambitious Tsang rulers. The recently ascendant Tsang 'Kings', as they became known in 1611, felt under direct and immediate threat. This sense became especially strong when they saw potentially fortifiable sites becoming forcibly converted into Gelugpa monasteries, backed up by hostile Mongol forces and funded by families with whom they had chequered pasts and uncertain futures. In short, they saw their future existence as rulers coming under palpable threat.

How did Tāranātha, an eminent Buddhist prelate and renowned meditator, certainly among the most important religious figures in Tsang at the time, manage to work so intimately with his patrons, the various Depa of Tsang? This question becomes more pointed when we realise that these rulers were not some sort of unilaterally meek patrons, but were clearly bent upon pursuing a 'war of liberation' from what they regarded to have been malign foreign influence. Moreover, in the larger picture, the Tsang rulers sought to actively reshape Tibet's value systems to allow them to become more appropriately aligned with more ancient values. This almost *revanchist* position was combined with a palpable sense of being the sole defenders of their own non-Gelugpa religious traditions. The Tsang rulers considered their somewhat aggressive stance towards the Gelugpa as a 'defensive war' maintaining the prestige of the Kargyüd and Jonang traditions of Buddhism, for which they were the major patrons and which had come under direct threat from the Gelugpa.

Clearly any outright refusal to participate in any manner in the defence of the realm would have cost Tāranātha dearly. The Tsang rulers had been extremely munificent sponsors of the building, decoration and maintenance of Phüntsokling monastery, an undertaking extremely close to Tāranātha's heart. To have actively opposed them would have cost Tāranātha not only control of the temple but also possibly any further role in the ritual life of the rulers.

We note from Tāranātha's own writings that he appears to have been unable to devise a strategy that sat comfortably both with the demands of his conscience and with the overtly expressed and tacitly hinted wishes of his masters. Perhaps rather mechanically (we are not informed directly about his state of mind at the time), Tāranātha performed a wide range of ritual activities, some of them directly connected with the various military campaigns. Nevertheless, even those rituals not intimately connected with the rampant militarism of the times were intentionally focused on sustaining the rulers of Tsang through activities such as life-lengthening ceremonies and healing rituals. With hindsight, these might be considered to be quite as compromising as, for example, Albert Speer's avowedly 'innocuous' activities which substantially supported the Third Reich in our own times. The range of activities we discover from Tāranātha's autobiography (Tāranātha 2000 [1633]) which he performed for the Tsang rulers include:

- blessing the troops before battle;
- offering Buddhist homilies to the soldiery to mollify any reservations they or the rulers might have harboured about their involvement in the war;
- performing various acts of augury and sortilege for the Tsang rulers;
- transferral of Tāranātha's own tutelary deities to various ailing rulers;
- enacting both life-enhancement and death-proximate ceremonies for the Tsang rulers and their families;
- giving religious and other advice to relatives and close bondsmen of the Tsang rulers;
- offering benedictions for the crown princes belonging the royal house.

It may be noted throughout Tāranātha's autobiography [3] that he preferred to employ fine-sounding Buddhist homilies concerning the moral duties of a good ruler rather than giving sound advice to his secular masters, even in situations where the latter might have been of more use. It appears to be the case that Tāranātha preferred to see the good, or at least the potential for good, on all contending sides.

I believe that it was this trait that prevented Tāranātha from being a completely honest adviser who could be relied upon to proffer unbiased (and potentially unwelcome) advice, as indeed a Buddhist monk should have been able to do in such situations. Whatever the case, both Tāranātha's presence and his multifarious ministrations were largely ineffective in reducing either the ferocity or the prosecution of the Civil War itself. I suggest that this failure to deal with situations directly, as they merited, resulted in part from Tāranātha's injudicious reliance on his Buddhist beliefs as his sole guide. This largely Buddhist focus simply did not allow him to address the issues as they presented themselves in real life. The day-to-day events stand in some contrast to the largely contemplative, visionary life that Tāranātha lived for much of the time. In short, I believe that he failed to see that his clients were not simply pious patrons defending Buddhism but were also rulers who were enjoined by the obligations of their ascendant position to act decisively and sometimes distastefully in a combination which encompassed both military adventurism and defence of the faith.

We note that, in bestowing his advice on the ruler Phüntsog Namgyal (1550–1620) towards the end of the Depa's life, Tāranātha avoided the polarities, such as the duality of Kargyüd (good) versus Gelugpa (enemy), which his master had employed himself out of necessity. Instead Tāranātha used a safely noncommittal point of view to avoid the issue. For example, in avoiding the pitfalls of the Depa's unambivalent view of the 'enemy', which were for him clearly the Gelugpa forces of Central Tibet and their Mongol allies, Tāranātha somehow sat awkwardly (and safely) in the middle.[4] He said,

> Although the enemy are the Yellow Hats (Gelugpa), I myself have the deepest and most surpassing faith in the mighty Tsongkhapa. Concerning the (Gelugpa) monks of Drepung, who have deeply held tendencies and whose minds are reactionary, I pray for their evil tendencies. I also pray that the Buddha's teachings might spread amongst them. I also pray that this dispute might become entirely tranquil and peaceful and that the monks do not fall completely under its influence (Zongtse 1994:72–3, my translation).[5]

It is in examples of general statements such as this that we note Tāranātha sitting comfortably between contending sides, expressing his great respect for Tsongkhapa, his concern for the monks of Drepung and his reliance on the words of the Buddha as his mainstays, but in fact adroitly avoiding the vexed issue of the war itself.

It is evident that Tāranātha's manner of resolving almost every tension by means of an overarching Buddhist sentiment derives partly from his belief that the apparent world of direct experience (the Civil War itself) was only a guise for deeper and ultimately far more 'real' experiences. An example of such a sentiment might be the Buddhist idea of the 'ultimate unity of opposites'. In practice, this meant that, for Tāranātha, there was neither a 'side' nor an 'enemy', nor, ultimately, even 'death' itself. This philosophical belief might go some way to explain his detached manner of recording deaths he heard of or witnessed *in re*. One might even suggest here that in his eyes the tragedy of the Civil War became minimised because in Buddhist belief 'nobody' was actually killed, there was no 'killer' and no such thing as an act of killing. In his advice to Phüntsog Namgyal, Tāranātha gave further encouragement to the Depa in words that were based squarely upon the Buddha's tenets. This teaching encouraged Tāranātha's lord to focus on distinguishing between the opposites of attachment and rejection, and to find a middle way between those apparent opposites. Tāranātha's intention in this was to bring all manner of contradictory phenomena into concordant agreement by liberating the Depa from the same tensions that plagued Arjuna when he was about to do battle with his kin in the Indian epic, the Mahābhārata, a text with which Tāranātha had been extremely familiar since 1603 (Tāranātha 2000 [1633]:126–7).[6] It must be remembered that this advice was proffered at a time when the Civil War was at its height and when the Tsang forces, although frequently defeated previously, still possessed a reasonable chance of success.

It is true to say that, for the most part, Tāranātha seems to remain aloof from any overtly expressed desire to end the Civil War. In fact, in most cases Tāranātha simply alludes to it rather than referring to it directly. We almost never find reference to it at all in his general writings, as if it never impinged upon his life. The exceptions to this are where he directly advises or counsels the rulers of Tsang. It is almost as if he regarded it as being entirely the business of those rulers, and that his involvement was merely to act for them, solely at their request. I am unable to locate any expression in his large autobiography, or even in his tripartite secret autobiographies (Tāranātha 2000 [1633]) in which Tāranātha unambiguously requests the Tsang rulers to scale down or cease their war preparations or to reassess their various aggressive stances. On the rare occasion that he expresses concern, he does so in a veiled and allusive manner.

Perhaps this sense of preferring to remain somehow self-protectively distant from the tragic events was an intimate aspect of Tāranātha's psychological make-up. What we do note in Tāranātha's writings is that he expresses only mild and vague Buddhist sentiments of regret at war *in general* rather than at the *actual* war raging all around him. For example, in the middle of a very lengthy section dealing with various tantric empowerments and practices he was involved with, Tāranātha refers to the plight of the area of Lhorong which had become surrounded by Mongols in the upper and lower regions of its northern flank in just two lines. He mentions in passing (actually in only 12 words) the protracted holding action of the ruler, Dekyi of Tingkyé and the eventual liberation of the area from the Mongol grip. In the very same line as that extremely brief reference, Tāranātha immediately reverts to the religious sphere, almost downplaying and negating the importance of the armed defiance of the Mongols. He says '... having freed [Lhorong] from that encirclement, I performed certain acts of the *Dharma*...' (Tāranātha 2000 [1633]:408).

It appears that Tāranātha mollified his Buddhist monastic vows somewhat by expatiating in the most general terms on the folly of war, worldly alliances and similar topics. However, one might argue that he actually felt quite comfortable bolstering the Tsang rulers and backing their armies with his Buddhist rituals. It is precisely in what Tāranātha does *not* say that we may detect an almost steely edge of commitment to the stance of his secular masters.[7] A closer reading of the autobiography (Tāranātha 2000 [1633]) than I have so far been able to undertake might reveal that Tāranātha could well have felt that his masters were, in fact, entirely correct in their bellicose response to the armies of Central Tibet and their Mongol allies that his ministrations to both the court and the army were entirely appropriate in those circumstances. In the final analysis, despite Tāranātha's avowed commitment to a sense of non-sectarianism, (Tāranātha 2000 [1633]:231, 482), he was also acutely aware of the fact that a Gelugpa victory would mean an end to the Kargyüd/Jonang coalition of the two most important sects in Tsang, which strongly influenced the Depa, and he was concerned to employ all means to avoid such an eventuality.

Although rare, we do occasionally find the suggestion in some of Tāranātha's words that he was capable of being quite critical of certain Tsang strategies, if only in broadbrush ways. These criticisms were so broad that accusations of treachery or fifth-column activity could not possibly be levied against him. For example, in 1608 he said to Karma Tensrung, who had led the army into the heart of Central Tibet to counter the Mongol army there,

> Whatever wild and unruly thoughts might arise in your mind, it seems to me that the blessings of the Karmapa will protect you. Others will be unable to protect those whose *karma* reaches its fruition today. Right now, this is how I evaluate your life! (Zongtse 1977:348–9, my translation).

The immediate point to note, apart from the play on the word '*karma*' is, why is it to be the Karmapa and not Tāranātha himself who was able to offer effective protection to Karma Tensrung? Perhaps this was a relatively safe way for Tāranātha, distancing himself from potential displeasure, to say that he disagreed with the venture overall and that the fruition of the ruler's *karma* would ultimately be the responsibility of other lamas and certainly not his. Whatever the interpretation Karma Tensrung placed upon it, Tāranātha could not be accused either of failing to do his duty or of being directly opposed to his ruler's ambitions—a fine balancing act indeed!

Expecting to discover more examples that would have been appropriate from a Buddhist master, I was surprised that I could find only one occasion in which Tāranātha gives absolutely direct and unambiguous advice to his patrons. In 1623, when the defeated Tsang ruler still wanted to make a last-ditch stand against the Mongols, he simply advised him in these words: 'It would be an appropriate strategy if the ruler were to decide not to lead his armed forces out' (Zongtse 1977:354, my translation).

Although this is not the place to examine each and every function that Tāranātha fulfilled for his masters, in one of his abovementioned roles, that of predicting the future, Tāranātha at times did manage to display an impressive accuracy. Towards the end of his life, in about 1632, he made the telling prediction for the King: 'The Tsang ruler's life having been prolonged somewhat, he will not remain long at Samduptse.[8] As for the Mongols, they will pervade throughout the land of Tibet. As for this monastery [Phüntsokling], it will only flourish poorly' (Zongtse 1994:69–70, my translation).

In his specific reference to the ruler's life and to his beloved monastery of Phüntsokling, Tāranātha turned out to be entirely correct. Karma Tenkyong was murdered in 1642 and Phüntsokling was converted from a Jonang to a Gelugpa monastery shortly after Tāranātha's own death in 1634. This might not be regarded so much as an example of Tāranātha's prescience but rather as one in which Tāranātha demonstrated his ability to shrewdly observe the *realpolitik* of the times, something which the myopia of the various Tsang Depa prevented them from accomplishing by themselves.

On another occasion, his predictions again seemed to be interestingly prescient. In 1611, when Tāranātha was 37 years old, the Tsang ruler, Phüntsog Namgyal invited him to Samduptse, where Tāranātha bestowed the following advice on his patron: 'If someone offers no harm whatsoever to the Buddha's teachings, then it seems to me that…such a person will be able to offer the ruler an appropriate stratagem to prevent the army of Central Tibet from coming here' (Zongtse 1977:350, my translation). Distancing himself from the issue at heart, he went on to say: 'As for myself, I say that both the large and small monasteries will be unharmed and that the enemy army will bring about no great destruction at all' (Zongtse 1977:350, my translation).

This proved to be accurate in several of its aspects. Although the Tsang forces were repelled in their attempt to invade Central Tibet by powerful Mongol forces and considerable harm was wreaked on many monasteries, the armies of

Central Tibet did not in fact invade Tsang at that time. More importantly, 1611 was the year in which the rulers gained complete mastery over the region and became known as 'Kings' of Tsang.

Sometimes Tāranātha's prognostications about the war went horribly wrong, even though their ostensibly noble intention might have been to alleviate debilitating fear among the populace. For example, in 1603–04 Tāranātha had a vivid dream in which the goddess Tārā appeared before him. Even though war was looming ever closer to Tsang at that very time, Tāranātha said that the portents that he had seen in his dream of the goddess Tārā should have been sufficient to alleviate the whole area from any fears or concerns residents might have felt. He proclaimed that Tārā would in fact protect the whole of Tsang from the Mongols. He was unutterably wrong in this prediction and the area was invaded shortly thereafter with much bloodshed, among both the military and the local people (Tāranātha 2000 [1633]:231–2).

Tāranātha believed that his strong faith in Tārā would protect him from all physical harm on his various wanderings around Tibet. However, despite being a Buddhist monk and, therefore, disinterested in his own physical welfare, he allowed himself, on the ruler's insistence, to be accompanied by a corps of archers acting as his bodyguard, as if he felt that perhaps Tārā's guarantee of safety would be insufficient (Tāranātha 2000 [1633]:231–2). Of interest here is that Tāranātha barely made a protest about being accompanied by the military, almost as if he recognised their role as being somehow mandatory for the success of his ongoing travels. Tāranātha seems to make no further mention of the apparent inconsistency in which the life of a Buddhist, sworn not to cause harm to others, is protected by those who are expected to kill and to lay down their own lives protecting him.[9]

The pursuit of war seems always to bring in its wake a measure of looting and pillaging. One might assume that a Buddhist prelate of Tāranātha's stature would not allow himself to become involved in even the smallest aspect of this process. However, this turns out not to have been the case at all. In 1617 certain important sacred objects from Narthang monastery were bestowed upon Tāranātha. The rulers of Narthang had been defeated by Tāranātha's own protectors, the Tsang Kings in a brief but vicious campaign. The texts, images and a small *stūpa* from Narthang were ceremonially accepted by Tāranātha and placed within his Phüntsokling monastery without a single question being raised as to the propriety of such an offering (Zongtse 1977:351). This was no ordinary loot gleaned from distant strangers either. Tāranātha had been in a long relationship with the rulers of Narthang and its various monasteries, performing ceremonies and rituals, engaging in public teachings and employing their artisans

(Tāranātha 2000 [1633]:182; 399–400). One might have expected at the very least that Tāranātha would have declined such treasure out of respect for his erstwhile friends, but that was not to be the case at all. The treasures all ended up at Phüntsokling as items known as 'supports', that is, as well-displayed, precious objects intended to encourage both faith and respect from the faithful.[10]

In the last few years of Tāranātha's life the Depa Karma Tenkyong commenced a policy that should have elicited a clear and strong reaction from Tāranātha, but somehow he utterly failed to condemn it in any of his later writings. Karma Tenkyong feared that his enemies, the Mongols, might seek to make citadels or defensive sites within his own region of Tsang, clearly running counter to his own strategic imperatives of expansion. To prevent these incursions Karma Tenkyong developed a policy of dismantling each and every fortress and isolated location which might have offered the Central Tibetan forces and their Mongol allies any shelter whatsoever. Included in this process was the razing of not only potential military structures but also, more importantly for our purposes, hermitages and meditation retreat sites belonging to several different sects. There is little doubt that even hearing of such a proposal would have been a heartbreaking experience for someone like Tāranātha, who was profoundly aware of the importance of hermitages and longed to spend more of his own time in such locations. It would have been impossible for him not to have heard about the Depa's plan and, considering his wide-ranging travels, it also would have been unlikely, even in those later years of his life, that he not actually seen a variety of hermitages being destroyed. Yet we find not a word against this policy either in his autobiography or in his secret autobiography. Can we assume that his silence on this matter and his apparent unwillingness to make any criticisms of his patron's policies represented Tāranātha's complete acquiesence to whatever his patron wished and his total subservience to his policies? A reasonable reading might be that Tāranātha concurred with whatever plans his masters might have hatched, as long as his own personal prebend remained untouched.

This historical example of Tāranātha offers a complex vignette of a fraught and sometimes awkward relationship between a major monastic prelate and patrons who saw war as a solution to what they perceived as incursions into their territory. The next example I cite discusses the equally difficult relationship between the present 14th Dalai Lama and the so-called Tibetan guerrilla movement, the Chuzhi Gangdrug. In this section I am primarily concerned with examining the awkwardness of the Tibetan Government-in-Exile in fully acknowledging the Tibetan guerrilla resistance movement as embodying a legitimate and worthy means of defending Buddhism and the long-term ramifications of that reluctance.

The 'real world' of the Chuzhi Gangdrug

Speaking in the 1980s on the topic of possible justification for armed struggle, the 14th Dalai Lama said that defence of Buddhism by violent means was only permissible when and if the last Buddhist practitioner was threatened with extinction, and not before then. This statement lies somewhere on the borderline between the ingenuous and the disingenuous and does not appear to be really helpful at all. The Dalai Lama's statement suggests that the entire edifice of Buddhism must be reduced to a single person before physically violent (and possibly effective) measures may be legitimately taken. However, as we know from the corpus of Vinaya texts, a community of practitioners cannot survive if only one person is saved. The requirements for ordination necessitate that there be at least six other *saṅgha* members present for the ordination to be effective. This ostensibly reductionist and idealist view offers an interesting comparison with the Dalai Lama's stance towards the activities of the Tibetan resistance movement between the late 1950s and the mid 1970s, which is examined below.

Part of the reason for His Holiness's reluctance to fully and incontrovertibly enunciate the huge debt the Tibetan people owe to the Chuzhi Gangdrug lies in the almost imperceptible transition in Tibetan attitudes towards what may be considered 'justifiable' violence. This has changed from overtly expressed approval and great respect for the activities of the Chuzhi Gangdrug in the 1970s to a present-day sense of public embarrassment coupled with a privately held view of respect. I suggest that this transition has been largely brought about through the influence of Western supporters of the Tibet issue, either as 'concerned citizens,' as *dharma* students or as well-wishers for the Tibetan cause. Both groups have exerted a major influence on the way Tibetans have perceived themselves and upon how Tibetans present themselves to the world. The desire of Westerners for Tibetans to be peaceful, contemplative and forgiving has coloured much of what has been written about Tibet by non-Tibetans since the early 1970s. As a result of this shift, Tibetans have created, in effect, a calque of themselves to the West in several important areas.

The case of the Chuzhi Gangdrug, the 'Four Rivers and Six Ranges' (otherwise loosely referred to as the Tibetan guerrilla movement), allows us to note something of the problems that arise when a rather idealistic Buddhist stance is confronted with a perceived need for armed struggle.

To what extent can a Buddhist become involved in violent activities, even in defence of the *dharma*? The ramifications of this question become clear in the attitude of the present Dalai Lama in relation to the Tibetan Chuzhi Gangdrug guerrilla fighters who fought what they perceived to be a fully justified struggle against the invading Communist Chinese between 1956 and 1974. For a variety of reasons, the nobility and personal sacrifice of their cause was never fully recognised and acknowledged by the Tibetan Government-in-Exile at the time who appeared unable to take a lead for fear of causing offence either to the Dalai Lama or to various overseas supporters. As a result, this lack of forthrightness caused much pain to the fighters themselves and latterly to their descendants.

The process of downplaying the Tibetan armed struggle, especially after the early 1980's a struggle that has been reduced in effect these days to the level of a museum-display set-piece, is connected at its core with the difference between the particular views Tibetans have of themselves and how they want the world to perceive them on the international stage. To enable such an expediency, the Chuzhi Gangdrug's cause was never accorded the fullest recognition in the post-1980 period by the Tibetan Government-in-Exile. To accord full recognition would have run diametrically counter to the image the Government-in-Exile wished to present to the wider world. McGranahan notes that what should have become a major aspect of Tibet's heroic history has in fact been deliberately downplayed as a result.

> Although one might expect that the story of the popular armed struggle would be at the centre of national narratives of modern Tibet, it is not. Histories of the Tibetan resistance have not yet secured a place within state-sanctioned national history in exile' (McGranahan 2006:127).

McGranahan's approach, especially her 'arrested histories' analysis, takes a slightly different approach to mine. She suggests that the aim of presenting a palpable sense of Tibetan unity to the world is deemed to be of far greater value than the official recognition of the facts of the resistance which would risk fracturing that apparent unity (McGranahan 2005:574–6). In broadening her analysis, I suggest that in the process of making themselves more 'acceptable' to their Western supporters, those Tibetans in exile who have nurtured this attitude of presenting 'unity above all else' have disenfranchised certain other aspects of their culture almost entirely, including that of the doomed, yet inspiring, armed resistance to the Communist Chinese. This disinclination to officially recognise the Chuzhi Gangdrug because it resorted to violence in defence of both the person of the Dalai Lama and the nation is but one area in which Tibetans have attempted to alter the way the West perceives them. In other cultural aspects, such as the sanitising of its attitudes towards women, Tibetans have also attempted to 'defer the past' through the process of 'arrested history' suggested by McGranahan. Even more actively, they have attempted, consciously or unconsciously, to change Western perceptions of the past in line with their own predelictions and inclinations.[11]

Formed in eastern Tibet as early as 1958, the very name of the resistance, Tensrung Dragmag, contains the Tibetan word '*tensrung*' which may be translated as 'defending the teachings' (of the Buddha). (*Dragmag* may be translated as 'army'.) It was largely under this aegis (and sentiment) that the Chuzhi Gangdrug acted. In their eyes, a considerable rationale for their activities was directly connected with the defence of religion.

A graphic representation of the values that motivated Tibetan fighters may be noted in aspects of the flag of the Chuzhi Gangdrug which reflect something of the idea of the defence of Buddhism and of the Tibetan attitude towards the idea of what might constitute a just war. In its simplest form, the flag simply depicts two crossed swords on a golden ground. However, rather than being simply the swords representing 'two deities' (McGranahan 2006:109), we must note here a more nuanced interpretation. The bottom sword is in fact a Tibetan fighting sword, angle-tipped with a decorated hilt—a true war sword intended for no other purpose than killing.[12] As if to temper the war sword's usage and limit it to appropriate situations only, a sword of an entirely different type is superimposed above it. This is the 'flaming sword of Mañjuśrī', the Buddhist deity of wisdom, and it is shown with a *vajra* hilt, a lotus pommel and tip wreathed in divine flames. The golden yellow colour of the flag's ground tells us that what is being defended is the Buddhist *dharma*. The uppermost sword represents Mañjuśrī's innate wisdom. It severs the bonds that conjoin the opposites of wisdom and ignorance. Its representation on the flag reminds the fighter that he must understand precisely when to use and when not to use violence. The sword's *vajra* hilt shows the wielder's unswerving indomitability, while its pommel shows that the killing must be done from a basis of purity and compassion, represented here by the lotus. The flaming sword tip symbolises the historic links between the wielder and the mythologised, ancient Tibetan dynastic era, in which a flaming sword was said to have been one of the symbols of the Supreme Ruler, the Tsenpo, Trisrong Detsen.

Clearly the symbolic sword takes precedence over the war sword by virtue of its placement over and above it, suggesting that war must only be undertaken with some sort of religious sanction or, at the very least, with understanding. The topmost sword also serves to remind the flag's viewer that the foundations for such struggle and resistance must be tempered by certain Buddhist tenets. In this respect, the flag demonstrates an awareness that resistance of all types, including violence, may become permissible where Buddhism is perceived as being under threat. It was this understanding that was a basic motivation for Chuzhi Gangdrug resistance.

In 1958, realising that the Communist Chinese were becoming far more demanding in their relations with Tibetans, the Dalai Lama said that, 'the people of Tibet will stoutly resist any victimisation, sacrilege, and plunder' (McCarthy 1997:138). This relatively clear statement was taken by the Chuzhi Gangdrug to mean that an active and, where necessary, violent resistance had the imprimatur of His Holiness. Although reluctant to give his fullest blessing to the activities of the Tibetan resistance fighters, a flavour of this sanction was bestowed upon its leaders by the Dalai Lama in 1959 when he wrote to the Chuzhi Gangdrug leader, Gonpo Tashi Angdrugtsang, acknowledging his previous years of struggle against apparently insuperable forces,

> [Because of your] unshaken devotion towards the cause of Tibet's Buddhist Faith and political stability [*chabsee*]...in commanding the Chuzhi Gangdrug victoriously against the spiritual foe, Communist Chinese force, [you] will be honoured with your promotion to the rank of General...you will report here soon to receive the honour...and will display similar gallantry and intrepidity [of] action, to sub-side the enemy henceforth. Any other devoted heroes who laid conspicuous heroic deeds will be honoured with due heroic rewards (Angdrugtsang 1973:101, 106–7).[13]

McCarthy notes that, some years after this expression of support, certain of the Tibetan infiltration teams, trained by the United States Central Intelligence Agency (CIA) and air-dropped back into Tibet, carried with them a letter of encouragement from the Dalai Lama. Unfortunately no example of this letter appears to have survived and we do not know the letter's actual phrasing. Because much of McCarthy's book is based upon a lengthy 1959 interview with Gonpo Tashi Angdrugtsang himself, we might be persuaded to accept that such a document of encouragement did indeed exist, but must remain open to reviewing its import if an example of this document eventually emerges (McCarthy 1997:241).

The Dalai Lama's tacit support in 1959 appears to be countered in 1970 in what I believe is a previously unknown source. On 14 April 1970, four Tibetans closely associated with the Chuzhi Gangdrug in Mustang sent a letter to the then Indian Prime Minister, Śrīmati Indira Gandhi. The letter contains a paragraph expressing their profound concern over the disruptive work of a person they considered to be a Chinese agent who had been planted among them. More importantly for our topic, there is a strong sense of betrayal apparent in the broader text of the letter at the lack of government recognition of their work. This is evident in the words, 'We too appealed to H.H. the Dalai Lama and discussed with his Ministers and Private Secretary who...also denied any connection whatsoever with this Guerilla Army'.[14]

By 1975, some months after the Chuzhi Gangdrug had finally ended its campaigns in the Lo area of northern Nepal,[15] His Holiness the Dalai Lama was still apparently unwilling to openly recognise their efforts in forthright and clear language. He said merely that he had 'sympathy' for the Chuzhi Gangdrug whose efforts and sacrifice he said had '...helped Tibetan morale.' In the final analysis, he said that it was not really a matter of whether he approved or not of their actions (McGranahan 2005:577). Implicit in this obfuscatory understatement is His Holiness's apparent unwillingness to sanction the actions of the resistance, running counter to his profoundly felt Buddhist principles as they did. This is perfectly understandable, but placed him in a rather invidious position at the time, especially in light of the fact that he had specifically requested the Chuzhi Gangdrug in northern Nepal to cease their activities so as not allow further embarrassment to His Majesty's Government of Nepal by operating against China from Nepalese territory.

In reviewing his 1975 statement, the Dalai Lama was to clarify further his stance towards the Chuzhi Gangdrug. More recently, adopting a substantially different position, the Dalai Lama has said that there was indeed a role for armed resistance if the cause being fought for was a rightful one. He goes on to note that those participating in such actions must be willing to accept the karmic consequences of such actions, even if they were performed in defence of Buddhism (McCarthy 1997:132).

Part of the problem with the rather ambivalent attitudes of the Dalai Lama towards the actions of the Chuzhi Gangdrug is linked to both his own personal viewpoint and his vows as a monk. A monk is expressly forbidden from all acts of violence and may not encourage them in others. However, as an expedient (and it may be noted, an unsatisfactory) solution to this quandary we can find many examples of the adroit avoidance by Buddhist clergy of the moral problems attached to violence. These may be as creative as invoking the textually unfounded concept of 'killing with compassion' employed so effectively in the Chinese monastic resistance to Japanese aggression in the 1930s (Xue Yu 2005) and extend to the simple ritual absolution from the karmic results of killing. This latter expedient means was employed in 1958, for example, at the monastery of Dzogchen in Kham. In view of the demands brought upon them by turbulent events in eastern Tibet which necessitated their direct physical involvement, the monks disrobed temporarily before a senior monk as witness and thereby absolved themselves from their vow of harmlessness (McCarthy 1997:162). Even the tutor to His Holiness the Dalai Lama, the Venerable Trijang Rinpoche, said in 1959 that it was permissible for Tibetans to take up arms against the Chinese if there was no other option to defend the Buddha's teachings.

Conclusion

The shifting positions adopted by the Tibetan Government-in-Exile, and the varying views offered by His Holiness the Dalai Lama have not only caused some confusion in the minds of veteran fighters. Those of them still alive feel utterly disenfranchised and have seen their role as being whittled away from active and committed 'freedom fighters' to that of being simply the 'guardians of the life of His Holiness' in recognition of their role in escorting him to safety in India, which is how they are most frequently portrayed in Tibetan history and recent memory. Their willingness to sacrifice themselves for the ideal of the defence of Buddhism, the person of His Holiness and the land of Tibet no longer suits the dynamics of the Tibetan Government-in-Exile who prefer to encourage the vision of Tibet as a pacifist and morally blameless society. In a model such as this there is little scope for the faith-filled, dynamic and heroic fighter against insuperable odds.

Notes

1   The world of text and that of reality are strange bedfellows, as Schopen (1997) has demonstrated. The contrast between what texts say one *should do* and what is *actually done* is remarkable and Schopen's approach to a 'realistic' understanding of how Buddhists acted in the world has been most informative.

2   In facing the problem of appropriate response in times of war, a ruler may easily become confronted with a series of difficult choices. He might choose to: retain an ultimate reliance on non-violence and utterly separate himself from all aspects of the struggle, consequently ceding the state to the enemy; critically examine the nature of the struggle and decide either to engage in it or to abandon all connection with it, perhaps adopting the mendicant way of life; or, defend what he regarded as being of value, using whatever he believed to be appropriate means.

3   Both Tāranātha's 'Autobiography' and his tripartite 'Secret Autobiography' are to be found in Tāranātha (2000 [1633]).

4   In this non-commital positioning of his views, I suggest that Tāranātha was faced with a problem similar to that experienced by the Dalai Lama from the late 1950s to the mid 1970s, which is discussed later in the chapter.

5   The terms 'Yellow Hat' and 'Tsongkhapa' refer here to the Gelugpa sect and its 14th century founder. We find Tāranātha referring to his faith in Tsongkhapa in his autobiography (Tāranātha 2000 [1633]:410).

6   Arjuna's dilemma and its solution are to be found in the Bhagavad Gītā, the sixth book of the Mahābhārata. Arjuna, faced with impending battle involving his close kin at Kurukṣetra, is advised by his charioteer (Lord Kṛṣṇa in disguise) that there ultimately exists neither killing, nor relatives to be killed, no grief and no karma rising from such internecine warfare, as long as one's mind is constantly fixed upon the Lord and one remains detached from the apparent world.

7   This 'steely edge' seems to be evident in Tāranātha's reactions to many of the events he saw unfolding around him. We almost never find any expressions of heartfelt grief at various tragedies that Tāranātha certainly saw with his own eyes. He was not necessarily an unfeeling person, but as has been noted above, his approach to conflicts and tragedies seems, by present-day standards, to be marked by a prevailing sense of distance from the events themselves. For example, when in 1594 he heard of the collapse of the iron suspension bridge at Chubori in Central Tibet, with great loss of life, we find not a word of regret or any expression of compassion that we might otherwise expect. Instead Tāranātha simply notes that, as the pilgrims on the bridge had just come from a Tārā temple and some had recently taken certain initiations from him, they would no doubt be well served in their rebirths. It is not as if Tāranātha were located in Tsang at the time of the collapse, far away from the tragedy, hearing about it at a remove. In fact he was ministering to those very same pilgrims just before their deaths and he travelled to Lhasa just a few days after the tragedy, in effect completing the pilgrimage they had embarked upon (Tāranātha 2000 [1633]:149, lines 1–150, line 2).

This sense of removal from real-life suffering is evident in some of Tāranātha's poetic writings. He records fulsome expressions of great regret and sadness at Buddhist suffering in the abstract in his c1610 'A tsa ma' poem, in which he regrets and bemoans suffering, evil rebirth, greedy tendencies and the wilfully blind actions of sentient beings (Tāranātha 2000 [1633]:250, lines 2–251, line 3). It is instructive to compare this poem with the similarly titled '10 fold A tsa ma' work written by the first Paṇ Chen Lama, possibly in 1612 (Panchen 1969 [c1612]:14 lines 6–106, line 2). One of the only occasions that Tāranātha seems to have been genuinely affected by sufferings he observed was in 1606–07, when he was travelling to meet the Tsang army to give it certain religious advice. Having seen at first hand the situation of the already oppressed villagers *en route* and the burden which his party placed upon the local populace, he requested that the requirement for village corvée labour be removed while he was on his travels. Here, of course, the tantalising question remains, what sort of advice would/could Tāranātha have given to the soldiers? Would it have been the usual lama's stock-in-trade comprising life-enhancement ceremonies, teachings on *karma*, homiletics on the 'just war' of defending the Buddhist Dharma or was it possibly something more overtly connected with the pursuit of war, such as exhortations to bravery and self-sacrifice within the teachings of Buddhist 'selflessness'? Regrettably we are not informed further on this.

8   This is the name of the fortress/palace complex in the town more commonly known as Shigatse.

9   Of course such an inconsistency has been noted concerning the heavily armed guards who surround the present Dalai Lama. Despite his frequent touching of the weapons of his guards and his beneficent smiles towards the protecting soldiers (as in, for example, the 2009 film *The Dalai Lama: 50 years after the fall of Tibet* by Ritu Sarin and Tenzing Sonam), the larger ramifications of the military as protectors must not be overlooked. Comparisons have been made between such a high level of protection and the relatively minimal level of military presence employed on most occasions to protect Mahātma Gandhi, for example.

10 On the use of captured religious items as talismanic emblems of victory, enhanced by their having been captured in war, see Davis (1997), especially chapters 2 & 3.

11 Certain recent research has demonstrated that what we refer to as Tibet was an infinitely more complex entity than has been imagined. AlthoughTibetans, especially those in exile, would have liked the Nyemo 'Incident' of 1969 to have been a revolt against the Chinese presence and scholars claim that it possessed '… undeniably nationalistic characteristics…almost an independence movement…' (Smith 2008:128), recent documentation and interviews show that it was likely to have been something else entirely (Goldstein, Jiao & Lhundrup 2009).

12 Such ostensibly utilitarian swords are also frequently depicted in the hands of wrathful deities, many of whom also act as Defenders of the Teachings.

13 McCarthy (1997:172) provides an alternate translation of the same citation. The choice of words is informative, suggesting a somewhat different attitude towards the Chuzhi Gangdrug activities. These guerrillas are noted as being part of a national cause without direct reference to the Chinese as being 'spiritual enemies'. His translation of the same sections reads, 'You have led the Chushi Gangdrug with unshakable determination, resisting the Chinese occupation army in the national cause of defending the freedom of Tibet'.

14 The letter expressed concern at what were perceived as the anti-Chuzhi Gangdrug machinations of Bey Shen-Si, secretary to Gyalo Thondup, the brother of the Dalai Lama who was the main conduit for CIA funds to them. Bey Shen-Si was accused of diverting into his own pockets, funds intended for the Mustang guerilla fighters and he is accused of killing ten guerilla fighters and their horses in Mustang on 21 February 1970 in what the letter refers to as a 'Red Guard' type action. The letter was signed by Namgyal Dorji, Lo Nyendra, Rinchen Tsering and Chadzo Tashi. In March 1970 I made handwritten copy of a draft of the original, which is in my possession.

15 Generally referred to in Western writings as 'Mustang' (*lo smon thang* / *lo yul*).

chapter eight

A modern portrait of a Tibetan incarnate *lama*

Gillian Tan

Changes in Tibet over the past 50 years have significantly altered many aspects of contemporary Tibetan culture, society and religion. This chapter will detail the changes brought by, and affecting, one contemporary incarnate *lama* in the eastern Tibetan region of Kham. In what follows, I introduce the *lama* and his works, framing his actions within the larger context of other incarnate *lama*s. Fundamental to my general argument is the proposition that changes in this area of Kham are filtered primarily through the *lama*'s actions. But more than that, changes are wrought at the level of structure because of the unique combination of divine, social and political authority vested within the figure of the incarnate *lama*, whom locals believe to be a human incarnation of the divine. Through a detailed ethnographic account of the *lama*'s monastery and the way he works, I argue that his actions maintain the structure of Tibetan culture and society, even while he performs[1] his divinity to create transformative results within the structure itself. Ortner (1989) has written about a similar process of simultaneous adherence to tradition and creativity in her history of Sherpa Buddhism in Nepal. What are the implications of these transformative structures to the people and place of this area of Kham?

Background

Khenpo Dorje Tashi is a Tibetan *trulku*[2] born in Minyag Dora Karmo. As a child, he was recognised as the seventh incarnation of Jalse Rinpoche[3] and sent to the local monastery, called Samgyé, which is of the Nyingma sect. Later, he went to Derge Dzogchen, the famous teaching college of Dzogchen in Kham, Eastern Tibet. After ten years of study in Dzogchen, he returned to the Lhagang area where he studied with Khenpo Zhara Chudrak, as well as with Tsopa Dorlo Rinpoché.

In addition to being locally revered[4], he has become the most politically influential *rinpoché* in Ganzi Tibetan Autonomous Prefecture. He holds the Vice-Chair of the Provincial Religious Affairs Commission, is a representative of the Sichuan Province People's Consultative Congress and a member of Sichuan University's Buddhist Research Centre. He is the highest-ranking Tibetan religious official in Ganzi Prefecture, the second-highest ranked in Sichuan Province, and is closely connected to the national government in Beijing, mainly through his network of wealthy supporters and his charitable, development-oriented work in Lhagang township. During the 1990s he founded a welfare school in Lhagang town which has grown to be a success story that is well publicised in the Chinese media and well regarded locally. He also has global support through his relationships with international development organisations and foreign universities and his teachings to disciples in Hong Kong, Singapore, Malaysia and elsewhere.

Dorje Tashi's religious, bureaucratic and political positions, combined with his domestic and global appeal, are, in many ways, not unusual of incarnate *lama*s on the Tibetan plateau. The most prominent example is the figure of the Dalai Lama, who, as the incarnation of Avalokiteśvara, the Buddha of Compassion, is the highest emanation in Tibetan Buddhism. However, as the temporal leader of the Tibetan people, he also performs secular functions of governance, rule and diplomacy. The office of the Dalai Lama emerged from the union of these roles, when Sonam Gyatso petitioned Altan Khan to provide patronage over the land of Tibet in exchange for priestly ministrations in 1578.

Other notable examples from the past include the 16–17th century incarnate *lama* of the Jonang school of Tibetan Buddhism, Tāranātha. Templeman (2008) writes of the tension that emerged from Tāranātha's deep involvement with his wealthy patrons, the ruling elite of the Tsang hierarchy that were leading Tibet to civil war. This involvement was fundamentally at odds with the *lama*'s private desires for the leisure time to perform his solitary meditations, which stemmed from Buddhist teachings. Yet, as Templeman (2008:61–2) notes,

> In Tibet the process of forming alliances with ascendant patrons is not unique to Tāranātha. Indeed, even the briefest perusal of other Autobiographical and Biographical literature from the period makes it evident that linking oneself to a focal centre of power was an accepted, and acceptable, strategy for any ambitious Lama (*bla ma*).

More recently, the renowned *tertön*, or treasure-revealer, Khenpo Jigme Phuntsog, has been credited with the revival of Tibetan Buddhism in the eastern area of Kham, through his discoveries of old and buried religious texts—known as '*ter*', or treasure—and has established a famous teaching college in the nomadic area of Sertha, about 90 kilometres north of Minyag Dora Karmo. To do this, he nonetheless needed the support and patronage of local Sertha officials to proceed with his work. Furthermore, Germano (1998:84–7) has reminded us that Khenpo Jigme Phuntsog also spent a considerable amount of time at Wutai mountain where he cultivated a strong following of Chinese disciples who continued to provide important networks for his work. As the ethnography unfolds, we will see that this last point finds an important parallel with Dorje Tashi's work in Minyag Dora Karmo.

In his own behaviour, then, Dorje Tashi follows in a long line of incarnates. These historical antecedents adopted a hands-on approach to their affairs, as distinct from the *lama*s and saints who chose to meditate alone in caves and hermitages. Through their involvement in life, they inevitably aligned themselves with politics, either through ruling patrons or wealthy benefactors. The breadth of their connections was never merely limited to the immediate area, but extended beyond borders and kingdoms.

Yet the political and historical events of the past 50 years have also created contingent occurrences that do not have historical precedents. The figure of an incarnate *lama* has always been intrinsically connected to the monastery of which he was part and through which he exerted his authority. Tucci tell us that: 'the prestige of a monastery derives in all cases from the 'incarnate', which it shelters within its walls' (Tucci 2000 [1978]:134). The incarnate was crucially dependent on his monastery, leading to an important interdependence between the person and his monastery. Following the Chinese takeover of Tibet in 1959 and the subsequent departure of many high-ranking monastic officials and incarnates from Tibet, a significant separation occurred between incarnates and their monasteries. This separation created a space in which manifold changes and ramifications have occurred: monasteries have created new leadership roles and structures; incarnates outside of Tibet have built substitute monasteries; and incarnates within Tibet have seen new opportunities that have allowed them to creatively remodel their roles.

Incarnates within Tibet, such as Dorje Tashi, have taken up these opportunities, which include the potential to advance and/or reconfigure their positions, in terms of both traditional status and more recent bureaucratic posts. That is, they are able not only to rise within the structure of existing monasteries but also to create new spaces outside the system of monastic institutions. I now turn to an ethnographic account of a new monastery, Dorje Tashi's *stūpa* complex, known as 'The Golden Stūpa' (Sergichöten), to describe the unique combination of divine, social and political authority configured by the interstices of sociopolitical changes in Kham and the divine creativity of Khenpo Dorje Tashi.

A new 'monastery': the Golden Stūpa complex

One day while sitting with Dorje Tashi, I asked him, 'Aku Dordra, which is your monastery?[5] Samgye monastery? Dzongsar?' He smiled and replied, 'The Golden Stūpa is my monastery'.

Figure 1: Khenpo Dorje Tashi's Golden Stūpa complex and Zhara mountain. Photo: Kunchok Palzang

Dorje Tashi built his Golden Stūpa complex in 2002 on grasslands he had purchased from the nomads of Lhagang village for an undisclosed sum of money. It is a work-in-progress and, in its ever-growing construction and refurbishment, is the revelation and culmination of Dorje Tashi's work—a mighty icon for his various donors and supporters to point to, a symbol of his goals and aesthetics, and a testament to his work and willpower.

To place into perspective the radical shifts that Dorje Tashi has introduced through his Golden Stūpa complex, we should remember the particular significance of a *stūpa* in Tibetan culture and religion. *Stūpa*s are 'sacred structures containing relics of all kinds and constructed according to a design of which the various elements are symbolic;[6] '[it is] a psychocosmogram like the *maṇḍala*' (Tucci 2000 [1978]:259).[7] However, *stūpa*s are also associated with the tomb of Śākyamuni, 'erected over his remains [to be] the primary symbol of his passage into a supramundane state, thus coming to be accepted as the supreme symbol of otherworldly aspiration' (Snellgrove 1987:29). In time, as the building of *stūpa*s spread across India and Tibet, they would be the vessels for incarnates and their relics. A *stūpa*, then, is pre-eminently sacred—a fact that is both highlighted and ignored in the Golden Stūpa complex of Lhagang.

The Golden Stūpa complex is positioned at the confluence of the three holy mountains surrounding Lhagang: Jambayang, the deity of wisdom; Chenrezig, the deity of compassion; and Chana Dorje, the deity of protection/power.[8] To the northeast is Zhara mountain. The Golden Stūpa complex thus occupies a prime geomantic position in Lhagang. People live in close proximity to the *stūpa*. They wash and defecate a short distance from it—practices that are considered disrespectful in Tibetan custom. According to custom, one must be clean and spiritually pure in the presence of sacred persons and objects. One monk, for example, when arriving at Kokonor Lake in Qinghai Province, stopped a few hundred metres from the lake because he had not washed his face. He was not deterred by the fact that other people were going to the toilet beside the lake. Though residents of the Golden Stūpa complex are extremely reverent towards Dorje Tashi, they remain unperturbed by the numerous breaches conducted towards the sacred symbol of the *stūpa*.

In its design, the *stūpa* (see figure 1) is suspended above the ground, atop a two-storey building and completely covered in gold leaf. The first storey of the building is the prayer hall for the monks, similar to the main hall in a monastery. The second storey contains a vast collection of religious books. The two levels of the building are rarely used on a daily basis. The *stūpa* and building are surrounded by a pathway, which residents use to circumambulate clockwise around it. Immediately beyond the pathway are the buildings and rooms in which Dorje Tashi, the monks, the resident Chinese disciples and guests live.

The Golden Stūpa complex is surrounded by three perimeters of buildings and walls. The last perimeter, a three-metre high wall, was still being constructed in 2006. In its numerous enclosures, the Golden Stūpa complex of Dorje Tashi occupies a separate and isolated world in the Lhagang grasslands, emphasised by its perfect symmetry of construction, its high walls, and its red, closed doors.

The Golden Stūpa compound has become a prominent landmark in the high grasslands of Lhagang township. Tourists to Lhagang inevitably visit the compound because it is the major tourist attraction of the area. Busloads of chartered tours from the Chinese cities of Chengdu and Chongqing head to Lhagang, particularly for long weekends during the eastern lowlands' hot and humid months of July, August and September. The standard route of these tour groups is to head directly to the shiny lure of the golden spire. Even though the Golden Stūpa complex is hidden from the initial approach into Lhagang town by the hill called Drölma, tour operators know to go round the bend in the road to arrive at the complex. Word of mouth is apparently still the most effective form of advertising. On reaching the complex, many Chinese tourists pay an entry fee of ten *yuan* (US$1.50) to indulge in a cursory walk around the main building. More pay 25 *yuan* (US$3) for a 15-minute ride on brightly-decorated ponies, walked by residents of Lhagang village. Local residents have become dependent on the tourist dollar and set up white tents behind the compound in the summer months to sell snacks, play recorded Tibetan music and shout to any passer-by that horse rides are available.

More importantly, the Golden Stūpa complex is Dorje Tashi's teaching and meditative base. It is not, however, a conventional monastery, even though about 11 monks reside there. The monks come from nearby farming villages and nomadic areas. While some, already ordained as monks, followed Dorje Tashi from another monastery, a handful are robed but not fully ordained. Tucci (2000 [1978]:136) refers to these persons as *répa* and writes that they are usually robed in white. The existence of these persons, particularly among people of the Nyingma sect, which emphasises *ngag*, or the practice of *mantra*s and *tantra*s[9], goes some way in explaining the presence of two Tibetan women at the *stūpa*, introduced to me as 'friends' (but implying wives) of two of the monks.

Dorje Tashi conducted teachings at the Golden Stūpa a few times a year, corresponding to important festivals and ritual times. These teachings were mainly delivered in Chinese to a Chinese audience. Local people of Lhagang chose to perform their daily circumambulations around the original Lhagang monastery and attended ritual festivals at that monastery. They rarely entered the grounds of the *stūpa* complex and often did not hear Dorje Tashi teach.

Life in the compound was a matter of routine.[10] Every morning, disciples and guests woke to the sound of recorded music coming through the surrounding audio system. The music was a mix of traditional chants and modern Tibetan songs. The sound signalled the time—seven o'clock, half an hour before the morning meal. But a few people—the Chinese cook and his helpers—had been up since six o'clock in the morning to begin breakfast preparations. Breakfast was always a selection of rice porridge, hard-boiled eggs, steamed buns, peanuts and the occasional pickle. Sometimes, yoghurt was served and butter tea, but never *tsampa*,[11] the staple meal of all Tibetans. Tibetans living in the *stūpa* had their own supply of *tsampa*, which they ate in their own rooms.

Lunch and dinner occurred at noon and six o'clock in the evening respectively. The dishes provided were vegetarian, reflecting Dorje Tashi's own dietary tendencies, although he occasionally ate meat on doctor's orders, 'to regain strength'. The Tibetans living in the *stūpa* ate huge portions of rice, green vegetables and tofu, in contrast to the *tsampa*, yoghurt, butter and meat diet of their nomadic relatives. The seating arrangement at meal times never varied. Tibetans sat in a wider circle around the table where the food was laid out, next to the kitchen. Everyone had an individual large enamel bowl, which they heaped with rice and other dishes before taking their seats around the table. The Chinese disciples would place their food into their own bowls before sitting in another room where tables and chairs were arranged in proper dining style. At meal times, Tibetans and Chinese never mixed. By default, I wandered towards the Tibetan side, joining the monks, women and one other foreigner, who had come to oversee a project involving input of traditional Tibetan texts into

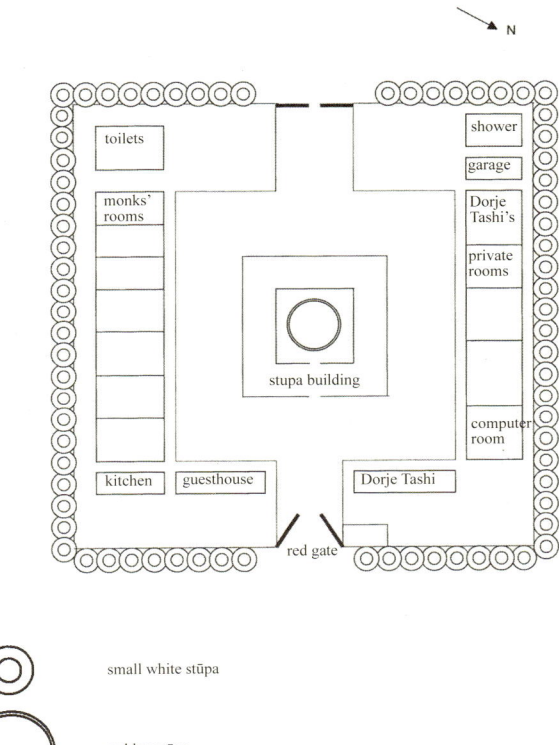

Figure 2: Diagram of Dorje Tashi's golden stūpa complex

electronic format. The project is jointly supported by an American development organisation and an American university and is another indication of the depth and breadth of Dorje Tashi's connections and vision.

In between meals, everyone did their own work and, in the Golden Stūpa, all tasks were either in direct service to Dorje Tashi or done to fulfill his wishes. After breakfast, most of the younger monks headed towards the computer room to continue entering Tibetan texts into a software program as part of the American-funded project. Older monks sat in their rooms and meditated or read, while one or two others carried out Dorje Tashi's daily commands, which included travelling back and forth between the *stūpa* complex and Dora Karmo in order to oversee the work at the boarding school.

Chinese disciples, in turn, were assigned their respective tasks, some of which were specific to the complex and others concerned with Dorje Tashi's other projects. The cook had tasks in the complex, as did his wife, who was the gate-guard. During their time in the *stūpa* complex, this couple slept apart, even though Dorje Tashi had told me that he generally left it up to individual couples to decide their own sleeping arrangements. Dorje Tashi's driver, a Chinese woman named Wosar who had left a good job and her family in Beijing to serve him in Lhagang, performed tasks relating to projects beyond the complex. She assisted with the logistics and operations not only of the complex but also of the welfare school in Lhagang and with the construction of the boarding school in Dora Karmo. In addition to driving the maroon Isuzu pick-up truck, her job included buying food and other provisions. Another disciple, Xiao Sun, lived sometimes in the complex and at other times in Dorje Tashi's Chengdu office, about a 10-hour drive away. She managed his correspondence and financial accounts relating not only to donations from other disciples but also to grants from international development organisations. Yet another secretary, Zeng Mei, came to Lhagang only during special times when more logistic support was required. Otherwise, she took care of operations and finances from the Kangding office, about three hours away by car. Wosar and Xiao Sun had short-cropped hair in the style of nuns and were generally regarded as such.

Divinity and charisma

Wosar and Xiao Sun represent an important group of people who are integral to Dorje Tashi's work because of their dedication to his teachings and personal sacrifice to serve him. Another equally important group to Dorje Tashi's work, mainly because of their substantial financial contributions to his projects, is the range of Chinese disciples and supporters, primarily from the eastern seaboard of China but also from as far away as Singapore and Malaysia. In this section, I outline how Dorje Tashi performs his divinity and activates his charisma in order to re-create traditional structures while advancing the structures themselves.

Here I must note that I am borrowing from and using Weber's definition of charisma in a particular way. Weber framed charismatic authority as one of three modes of political domination (the other two being bureaucratic and legal authority) and stated that as a 'pure' type, '[charisma] is the very opposite of the institutionally permanent' (Weber 1991 [1948]:248).

Charisma also refers to:

> an extraordinary quality of a person, regardless of whether this quality is actual, alleged or presumed...the magical sorcerer, the prophet, the leader of hunting and booty expeditions, the warrior chieftain are such types of rulers for their

disciples, followings, etc. The legitimacy of charismatic rule thus rests upon the belief in magical powers, revelations and hero worship. The source of these beliefs is the 'proving' of the charismatic quality through miracles, through victories, and other successes, that is, through the welfare of the governed (Weber 1991 [1948]:296).

In this sense, charismatic authority displays its etymological roots in 'the gift of the divine'. It is in this sense of charisma that successful incarnates in Tibet are presently able to forge new positions within existing monastic institutions or create new monasteries from which they exercise charismatic authority but through bureaucratic and legal frameworks.

As Lindholm (2003:3) noted, however, 'this primary form of charisma cannot last. If it is to survive, it must be rationalised and rigidified into a new tradition...the visionary must be replaced by the bureaucrat; the priest must take the place of the prophet'. This echoes Weber's conclusion that when the organisation of charisma becomes permanent (or institutionalised), the followers surrounding the charismatic leader become routinised. In Tibetan history, this crystallisation of charisma occurred around the system of incarnation, which eventually came to have foundations in both bureaucratic and legalistic authority. The charisma of incarnate *lama*s, therefore, is manifest in a different way from Weber's articulation of the ideal type of charisma because it is inextricably tied up with bureaucratic and legal functions. Yet, even though all incarnate *lama*s occupy positions of political authority that are both bureaucratic and legal, not all are able to activate charisma. Or more accurately, they are charismatic to varying degrees.

Under Weber's definition of the term, Khenpo Dorje Tashi is perhaps not the most charismatic incarnate *lama* in the Lhagang area. That distinction possibly lies with another incarnate, Trulku Druga, who is able to inspire fits of frenzy and exaltation in his audience, much like Christian charismatic speakers who are able to move their believers to speak in tongues and shake their hands in uncontrolled ecstasy. Nor is Dorje Tashi a renowned treasure-revealer and master in the way that another incarnate *lama*, Khenpo Jigme Phuntsog, was. Yet Dorje Tashi is at present the most successful of the incarnate *lama*s in this area of southeast Kham. The measure of his success and charisma lies in his unique ability to persuade a varied network of disciples to join in and serve his purposes and projects. With these disciples, his divinity is performed and charisma is evidenced in different ways.

The Golden Stūpa receives a steady stream of visiting disciples from eastern China and overseas. Dorje Tashi usually receives these disciples in his second-floor breakfast room, a large room filled with an array of colours, designs and objects. Butter lamps and bowls offering water lined one side of the wall, above vases filled with pastel-coloured plastic flowers. On another wall, cabinets housed an entire floor-to-ceiling collection of religious books. Plush wall-to-wall carpets of an incessant and colourful design covered the ground. In the middle of the room was the personal space of Dorje Tashi, where he sat cross-legged, surrounded by boxes of Ferrero Rocher chocolate, sachets of instant coffee and tea from Singapore and chocolates from Belgium.

It was in this breakfast room that he received a family of four from Fujian—husband, wife, son and daughter. They prostrated themselves before him three times. The atmosphere was silent and he looked on as they unpacked the bags of gifts they had brought—ornately carved crystal vases, huge plastic lotus flowers with plastic dew drops ingeniously stuck to random petals, boxes of expensive-looking tea and chocolate, a special tea-mug, and more plastic flowers. As they unwrapped each gift, they placed some at the altar, and gave others to him deferentially, with their heads bowed, before retreating backwards. The mother and daughter did not approach; the son, a boy of perhaps 12 years old, approached once, in awkward shyness, and handed Dorje Tashi some special plastic flowers. He smiled in thanks and the boy immediately retreated backwards, facing him but with his eyes down. In general, they were far more reverent towards him than the monks and local Tibetans were. When they had finished, they all prostrated again and took their leave, walking backwards in a bowed posture until they left the room. Dorje Tashi turned to look at me with a big smile and chuckle, characteristic of the manner in which he would often transition between situations and people, restoring attention to the present.

Performing divinity rests in the audience's continued reception and seeking of the divine, as well as in the diviner's ability to elicit a response. In the vignette above, Dorje Tashi was able to perform his divinity in multiple ways. His seated silence was one manifestation and his somber demeanour in the family's presence was another. With other, more familiar, disciples, both his outward manner and method of interpersonal engagement were markedly different.

One warm summer day, I went to see Dorje Tashi in the white tent that was erected at the back of the *stūpa* grounds in those summer months. He was seated in his usual position at the centre of the tent. To his right sat three Chinese women in their mid-40s, who looked to be quite relaxed with him. He himself was smiling and joking. 'Ah, Nyima Yangtso![12] Come and join us', he said when he saw me approach. The low Tibetan-style tables were filled with plastic-wrapped candies, biscuits and nuts. Each guest had a paper cup filled with milk tea and held in a plastic container. As I sat to his left, facing the other guests, he looked at them and said, 'She is a research student from Australia, but she was born in Malaysia, isn't it?' He looked at me to verify this information. 'Yes,' I replied.

'And now I'm from Dora Karmo', I added jokingly. 'Ha ha!' he said, 'yes, now she lives with Tibetan nomads. We are from one hometown'.

'Do you speak Tibetan?' one of them asked me. 'Yes, I do', I said. 'But I'm still learning'. The same one added, 'Wah, that's very clever. Is it very hard? We'd like to learn'. I had heard this sentiment expressed before. Wosar, one of Dorje Tashi's resident disciples, had taken to learning '*ka kha ga nga*', the euphemism for the Tibetan alphabet. 'Yes, quite hard to learn well', I replied truthfully, aware of how much I still had to learn. 'Where are you from?' I enquired. The one who had spoken before—she was the most loquacious—replied, 'I'm from Shenzhen. And she is, too', she gestured to her left. 'But she's from Guangzhou', indicating to her right. Dorje Tashi added, 'They are my close friends'. I smiled and drank the milk tea that had been placed in front of me.

I had interrupted their conversation, which they continued after these formalities had finished. The woman from Shenzhen told Dorje Tashi that she thought it was a wonderful idea to give the students from the Xikang Welfare School the responsibility of caring for the new students of the boarding school in Dora Karmo. This is what they had been talking about: Dorje Tashi was toying with the idea of dividing the new students into groups of five, each group with an older student from the welfare school assigned as a mentor and carer. It was a good way to manage the new students and introduce them to the general rules of the boarding school as well as to the standard rules of hygiene that they probably did not learn from their parents in the black tent. The woman from Shenzhen added that the best way to learn about management was to do it. She obviously had a longstanding interest in the wellbeing of the students from the welfare school. The other women were more reticent, although they also added their comments and suggestions about Dorje Tashi's ideas for the boarding school in Dora Karmo, particularly for the living conditions and guidelines for the new students. He listened to their comments carefully, presumably remembering their advice for fuller consideration later.

This was a strategy he employed frequently with many different people. I recall when he asked me, during a return visit to my field site, as we sat on a hill in Dora Karmo looking down at the boarding school he had built, what I thought of a fence around the school and its grounds. His question caught me by surprise. Even though I had known that he planned to build a fence around the land he had purchased for the school, I was not expecting him to seek my opinion. He looked ahead and drew an imaginary circle with this right hand, 'What about a fence made out of white rocks?' he asked. I looked at him and smiled, 'Well, there really will be a circle of white rocks in Dora Karmo,[13] then!' He laughed, 'Yes, yes, that's my idea'. I felt, then, quite special that he had thought to ask my advice on something. It made me feel included in his thoughts and plans. Perhaps the three women felt the same way when he talked about his plans with them. It was one of the ways in which his charisma was manifest.

After another round of milk tea was served, he suggested that we take a walk around the Golden Stūpa complex. We walked outside to where another construction project was unfolding. He was planning to build an outer wall that would be three metres high. The small *stūpa*s that served as the present wall and surrounded the perimeter of the grounds were in the process of being painted white. We followed him around as he talked to the construction workers about their progress. One of the women asked him about this new wall and he said that he planned to plant grass in the space between the current perimeter and the new wall. She added that it would be nice to have some tables and chairs so that people could sit and read on the grass.

It was always an experience walking around with Dorje Tashi because it was such a show-stopping event. Everyone immediately stopped what they were doing, walking or talking for example, and adopted a bowed stance, waiting until he passed before they resumed their activities. If men were wearing hats, they would immediately take them off. These moments were a reminder that, for those who believed, we were in the presence of a divine being. And when we returned to the tent, Dorje Tashi as the divine being re-emerged. He must have been inspired because, as soon as he sat down, he started to talk about three ways of knowing—through the mind or heart, through speech and through the senses. He gave examples of each of these ways of knowing, but said that the highest form of knowing is through your mind or heart.

He also said that it was wonderful, even necessary, to know about other things, other languages, other ways of knowing, seeing and experiencing the world, but most important of all, it was crucial that one knows one's own mind and follows that path. In life, one must follow one's path. And this path is not necessarily obtained through education, because there are those who are educated but who do not know their own path. Rather, the path is acquired through reflection and through searching; only by knowing one's mind or spirit will the path become clear. We had been treated, unexpectedly, to a teaching.

Conclusion

The divine plays an integral part in the lives of nomads. This divinity is not just channelled from above, as a *deus ex machina*, but needs to be enacted in practice, through negotiations, manoeuvre, and performance. This chapter has detailed how Khenpo Dorje Tashi, a divine incarnate from Dora Karmo, guides his fellow nomads in transitions towards an unknown future, how he negotiates and performs his divinity, while drawing on a wide network of support for his own perception of how his people should interact with the changes they encounter. In his actions, he follows in the pattern of divine incarnates of the past, merging divine and political functions into one institution while creating events that serve to alter conventional structures.

But more importantly, Dorje Tashi knows and follows his own mind or spirit, thereby moving through his own path in the world. In this manner, he navigates his own movements through policies of the Chinese bureaucracy, requirements of international development organisations, requests and expectations of Tibetan nomads and his Chinese disciples, and interactions with foreigners. And because of his divine authority and charisma, he inevitably shapes the movements of Tibetan nomads and all others who look to him for direction and guidance. Dorje Tashi both influences, and *is*, the change that has come to Dora Karmo and this area of Kham.

Notes

1. Performance, in this chapter, is used in the broadest anthropological sense described by Goffman (1959) and Turner (1967) as any public display or communication that influences other people.
2. *Trulku* is the term used to describe a *rinpoché* within a specific lineage, that is, one with a distinct and traceable previous incarnation.
3. His previous incarnation was Pelma Tsewang *rinpoché*.
4. This comment refers specifically to my field site. In the larger area, opinions of Dorje Tashi are far from homogeneous. Throughout my fieldwork, I was privy to various contrary opinions of him and his work.
5. I used the Tibetan word, *gomba* (*sgom pa*) which means 'monastery'. The word '*Aku*' means a 'paternal uncle' and is used as a title of respect.
6. The symbolism, as Snellgrove has elaborated, is that of the *dharma-kāya*, or absolute Buddha-nature (Snellgrove 1987:37).
7. Refer to the diagram of the Golden Stūpa complex.
8. Together, these three deities are known as the Rigsum Gonpo, or 'Protectors of the three families' and are regarded as the protectors of Tibet.
9. Sometimes the Nyingma are referred to as 'Ngag Nyingma' because of their strong reliance on *mantras* in their practice. The Nyingma also permit marriage of *lamas* under certain circumstances.
10. This manner of routine is also observed by Tucci (2000 [1978]:125–6) in traditional monastery life.
11. *Tsampa* is a paste made from mixing roasted barley flour with butter and hot tea.
12. The author's Tibetan name.
13. Dora Karmo means 'circle of white rocks'.

chapter nine

Laughing Vajra: the outcast clown, satirical guru and smiling Buddha in Milarepa's songs

Ruth Gamble

According to one telling of his tale, the Tibetan poet and saint Milarepa (1042 to 1123 CE) left instructions for his disciples to dig underneath his hearth for relics after his death. They were expecting to dig up buried treasure, but instead uncovered a magic sugar cube wrapped in a piece of cloth and a last testament, which they proceeded to read out solemnly, hanging on its every word. It explained how the relics worked and gave advice on meditation practice. Then it ended with the line: 'And if anyone says, 'Mila was rich', stuff their mouths with shit!' (gTsang 1999:866). His students, we are told, despite their grief, cracked up laughing.[1] Their teacher was still playing jokes on them. Even after his death he was still living up to the name his teacher Marpa had given him as a young man—Zhaypa Dorje, the Laughing Vajra.

It might seem incongruous that Milarepa, an ascetic among ascetics, the most revered *yogi* of the Himalayas, chose to make his last testament a joke, but anyone who has read Milarepa's story in Tibetan or heard his tale told, either by professional bards or enthusiastic, amateur storytellers, will recognise humour as one of its major elements. In particular, a close reading of the tapestry of songs and stories that recount Milarepa's life reveals he is portrayed by three main humorous types: an outcast clown; a satirical *guru*; and a smiling Buddha.[2] An analysis of these types is where this chapter is headed, but, in order to get the most out of this analysis, it seems prudent to begin by contextualising Milarepa's story and then by assessing some of the obstacles to enjoying this humour, in particular the ambivalence of Western and Indian traditions towards religious humour. It is also helpful to look briefly at the humour of his antecedents and inspiration, the Indian *siddha*s, to establish lineal precedents for his humour, before dedicating the remainder and majority of this study to Milarepa's recurring humorous types.

The story of Milarepa's life is perhaps the most famous of the *namthar* (liberation stories), a literary genre that has played a central role in Tibetan culture, literature and identity. His story has been told and retold so many times that at some point, perhaps even during his own lifetime, Milarepa ceased to be merely a man and became a myth. His is a heroic story of redemption; he is the mass murderer who accepts responsibility for his wrongdoings and then, personifying the power of the 'new', recently imported Indian *tantra*s, not only redeems himself through rigorous *yoga*, but also attains Buddhahood. In the Tibetan Buddhist world, this is *the* grand narrative. Milarepa not only personifies the Tibetans' general narrative of transformation from warring tribes to peaceful inhabitants of a Buddhist land, but also holds out hope for anyone struggling to live up to this problematic ideal. No matter how bad you are, it says, you can reform, just like Milarepa.

Yet, Milarepa's story is not just about grand narratives. Through its retellings, first by people who knew him personally, his tale has also accrued a surprising focus on minutiae. His story records that he survived on nettles, wore cotton (gTsang 1999:116–31), had a gap between his two front teeth (gTsang 1999:121) and developed calluses on his backside (Karma-pa 1978:f497). He was also funny, and his storytellers relish his jokes. Milarepa, in short, is a very human myth.

Several years ago, Andrew Quintman (2006) put together a thorough and engaging study of the development of Milarepa's hagiography. It explains how his story started as brief accounts composed by his students, including Gampopa (1079–1153 CE) (bSod 1982), developed into literature in Gyalthangpa's 13th-century version as he became a symbol of power (Quintman 2006:120) and reached its full form in its most famous redaction by the 'Mad Saint of Tsang', Tsangnyön Heruka (1452–1507 CE), whose life became inextricably linked with Milarepa's story (Quintman 2006:252). He also notes the ways Milarepa's character is formed in these retellings. Gampopa's fragmented version presents a self-deprecating, caring teacher. As the narrative of his tale developed, he came to be seen as an exemplary model of a *yogi* (Quintman 2006:184), and, in Tsangnyön's famous redaction, he is a fully formed legend with a repertoire of adventures and jokes.

Although Quintman's study does not go beyond Tsangnyön's redaction, developments in Milarepa's story did develop beyond it. His tale continued to be reworked by professional bards in the Tibetan commentarial tradition[3] and has even travelled to other cultures and media. Milarepa's tale was one of the first Tibetan texts to be translated into English, in 1928 (Evans-Wentz 1928), and it has been in print in several European languages ever since. It was even published as a comic book (Van Dam 1991). In 1974, the Italian filmmaker Liliana Cavani adapted the story for the film *Milarepa,* which was selected for showing at the Cannes Film Festival. In recent years, two more film versions of the story have appeared. The first, a 'no-budget' film using the Tibetan script romanisation, *Mi la ras pa,* was made in Tibet by Sonam. The second, *Milarepa: Magician, Murderer, Saint,* is a low-budget film made in India by Bhutanese filmmaker and Buddhist teacher Neten Chokling for Western, Indian and Tibetan audiences.

As this brief survey indicates, even though there was most certainly an historical Milarepa,[4] this historical figure has been swamped by an inundation of storytelling. Milarepa's tale may be based on a true story and the songs sung in his name may be creative versions of his originals, but entangling man from myth would mean applying the incompatible paradigm of 'historical accuracy' to a historic culture that did not recognise it. Treating Milarepa as a literary character and then analysing this character is not only a more practical approach, but also enables those studying his tale to read it with varying emphases. Although most previous studies of Milarepa's story have chosen to focus on one or other particular aspect of his story (his poetry, symbolic path, 'madness', relationship with his teacher, saintliness, demons, conflicts, and perceived support of the patriarchy[5]), they have not only been somewhat ambivalent about their subject's historic or literary nature, but have also missed his humour, sometimes to their detriment. Perhaps the reason for this omission was the 'serious' nature of their work, in which the humorous aspects of his tale would have seemed out of place. It is interesting to note that most of the studies and translations undertaken by Tibetans do recognise and emphasise this humour.[6] This may imply a cultural bias in the appreciation of his humour, which should be investigated before I attempt its analysis.

While laughter and smiling may play a big role in many people's lives, they are not generally things that many people spend much time thinking about. Yet, undertaking an analysis of Milarepa's humour necessitates the distinctly unfunny task of examining laughter, humour and joy. To begin with, it is important to recognise that laughter and smiling do not necessarily express amusement or reflect joy. With perhaps the exceptions of grief and awe (Clarke 1987:242), we laugh or smile to convey almost any emotion. We also laugh or smile when other people laugh or smile, when we are embarrassed, hysterical, tickled, affectionate or inhaling nitrous oxide (Clarke 1987:240; Ruch 1993:605). Laughter and smiling can also be a reflection of a combination of joyful and sombre mental states, and it is perhaps in these intersections that they are at their most poignant.

Despite these qualifications, the most common cause of laughter and smiling is amusement, occurring usually when we find something humorous. We experience humour in our interactions with others, either spontaneously or through the aesthetic construction of comedy (Lee.1976: 240).[7] As well as causing us to laugh or smile, amusement also generates joy or happiness and, conversely, a cheerful state facilitates the experience of amusement, laughter and smiling (Ruch 1993:606). A cheerful state may also facilitate laughter and smiling that is not a response to external humour, but an expression of autonomous joy. As this joy is not dependent on external stimulus, it can be maintained and is a more reliable support for other positive emotions (Ruch 1993:612).

Over the centuries, Western theorists have developed three main ways of understanding humour, laughter and joy: the superiority theory; the psychological repression theory; and the incongruity theory. While the first two of the theories do not present a very helpful framework for understanding Milarepa's humour, their perspectives do offer interesting insights into the reasons why his humour has been overlooked by Western observers. The last theory, the incongruity theory, sits much better with Milarepa's humour and with Buddhist concepts of humour more generally.

The ancient Greeks developed the superiority theory. Humans only laugh, they explained, when they feel superior to someone else (Morreall 1989:244) and, as this superiority is a form of hostility, it is best avoided (Bremmer 1997:13). In ancient Greek writing, there is no mention of humour's use as a tool for social reform and improvement. Instead, in what Stephen Halliwell calls 'something of a Greek topos', they feared and restricted laughter because of its tendency to 'degenerate into more serious forms of discord or antipathy' (Halliwell 1991:284).

As restrictive as this idea of humour may seem now, the continuing veneration of the ancient Greeks by later European cultures meant that its influence outlived its cultural setting by two millennia (Palmer 2005:81). Indeed, those who wished to curtail humour's critical power—usually powerful states—have conveniently cited this distrustful approach to humour throughout the centuries, from medieval laws that banned jokes (Le Goff 1997:44) to Italian Prime Minister Silvio Berlusconi's 2002 legal injunction against five satirical television programs on grounds of 'national security' (Willan 2002).

British Orientalists also evoked this theory to assist in their curious transformation of the Buddha in the late 19th century. When the British scholars first discovered the Buddha, they were eager to present him as 'an Indian version of Martin Luther' (King 1999:144; Almond 1988:72) and highlighted his satirical criticism 'as a useful foil for the critique of Hindu religion in general and brahmanical priestcraft in particular' (King 1999:145). But with the rise of socialism in the 19th century, there were concerns that the Buddha's atheistic, reformist agenda would 'be perceived as early evidence of precisely those forms of socialism that were seen by many as a threat to the structure of English society from the 1880s onwards' (Almond 1988:75; King 1999:145).

In order to move the Buddha from left to right, he was remade in the image of 'an ideal Victorian gentleman' (Almond 1988:79) and particularly praised for 'the manly endeavour he made to arouse a true feeling of self-reliance amongst a people prone to lean for support upon others' (Medhurst 1840:215). His 'dangerous' satire disappeared from polite discourse, and his 'filial devotion' came to the fore (Almond 1988:80).

The Repression Theory has had a similar inhibiting affect on Western approaches to Milarepa's humour. Although it was brought to prominence by Sigmund Freud in his 1905 book *Jokes and their relation to the unconscious*, the social discourse that enabled it began much earlier. In the Christian Bible, Ephesians 5:4, for example, warns Christians to abandon 'jesting',[8] along with 'whoremongering' and 'filthiness'. Later, medieval Christianity viewed the *bodily* action of laughter with intense suspicion. Pope Gregory I (ca. 540–604 CE) defined the body as 'the abominable garment of the soul' (Le Goff 1997:46) and, through its association with this abomination, laughter became a 'great enemy' for many orders of Christian monks (Le Goff 1997:45). Even as late as 1690, the Bishop of Gent asked, 'How impertinent is the miserable worm who laughs in the presence of his God, the humiliated Christ?' (Verberckmoes 1997:77)

It was this suppression of laughter that led Bakhtin to develop his idea of 'carnival,' in which medieval society was divided into two distinct groups: the sombre ecclesiastical and aristocratic officials at the top, and the masses' 'culture of laughter' at the bottom (Bakhtin 1968: 88). The clearly divided, all-encompassing opposition that Bakhtin proposed does not withstand a thorough analysis. St Francis's injunction to maintain a *hilari vultu* (laughing face) alone disproves his point (Le Goff 1997:51; Gurevich 1997) and the stories of laughing mystics and holy fools further refute it. Yet, Bakhtin's theory does point to one well-established discourse in Western culture, a violent hierarchy between the serious and the humorous; anything that is considered important, is also considered serious.[9]

This violent hierarchy could not help but influence the perception of Buddhist laughter as it travelled between Indo-Tibetan Buddhist discourse and the modern West. As Lydia Liu has pointed out, 'translingual practice', the intersection between languages, often affords interesting insights into the influence of one culture on another (Liu 1995:4). The basis of much of this practice, she argues, are 'tropes of equivalence' that develop between cultures and languages. The translingual practice between Western and Buddhist discourses has thrown up many such tropes. English words, for example, tend to paint a theistic, faith-based picture of 'religion' (King 1999:37) and a belief in the otherness of redemption or damnation. Its vocabulary encourages two of the few emotions that stand in opposition to humour—awe and fear. These emotions are the main reason that, in Western religious traditions, the 'sacred can be identified as precisely that which may not be laughed at' (Sands 1996:502).

In contradistinction to this, in Buddhism, the cause of suffering is ignorance, not original sin, and the Buddha or *guru* is the teacher, not the ultimate judge. If Buddha-dharma and Christianity were separate, discrete discourses, scholars could note and dissect these differences with little or no violence to either dialogue, but things have not evolved this way. Instead, Christianity's vocabulary has been used to interpret Buddha-dharma and, in the process, to create the discursive space of 'Buddhism' (King 1999:143). In this conversation, words like 'religion', 'devotion', 'faith', 'prayer', 'truth', 'salvation', 'confession' and 'sin' have lent 'Buddhism' a judging solemnity that is foreign to Buddha-dharma.

Evans-Wentz's translation of Milarepa's life story contains a good example of this phenomenon. In Tibetan, the following extract is quite amusing. Milarepa teasingly tells some scholars that, if he ever learnt anything, he has forgotten and, making puns with their debate terminology, sings a song called 'The consequence of learning is forgetting'.[10] He continues teasing them and, to some extent, parodying himself by singing: 'I bow down at the translator Marpa's feet. Inspire me to stay away from [debaters'] jargon!'[11] Evans-Wentz's translation is as follows:

> I pray that thou wilt give ear to the song which I am about to sing, to show my reasons for forgetting book-learning...
>
> Obeisance to the honoured Feet of Marpa the Translator!
>
> May I be far removed from arguing creeds and dogmas (Evans-Wentz 1928:245).

The last Western theory to examine is the incongruity theory of humour, which is the latest to gain credibility and acceptance. Francis Hutcheson first explained it in his 1750 work *Reflections upon laughter*, but it was not until criticisms of Freud's work became numerous in the mid 20th century that it gained general acceptance. The incongruity theory broadened the scope of laughter. Instead of only laughing when we feel superior, it argues that we laugh when things do not meet our expectations. This is not to say, as Clarke has pointed out, that everything we find incongruous is necessarily funny. Rather, 'the formal object of humour' is 'perceived incongruence'. We may not find everything that is incongruous amusing, but everything we find amusing is in some way incongruous (Clarke 1987:239). There are some things that enhance the humour of the incongruous—its aesthetic quality, how safe we feel, and our affection for the object. There are others that inhibit it, such as the previously mentioned emotions, fear, awe and pity.

As John Morreall has noted, however, the general acceptance of the incongruity theory in recent times has thrown up a new objection to humour—that it is irrational (Morreall 1989:249). It is an objection, according to Morreall, based on the 'assumption usually made by Western philosophers—that rationality has some ultimate value' (Morreall 1989:254).

Philosophical reasoning may inhibit humour as Morreall has stated, but perhaps the most potent weapon against irrationality, and, therefore, against humour, is science. Based as it is on proving hypotheses, the scientific discourse is rational by necessity. In and of itself, this should not be a problem; science does not have to be funny. But the application of scientific 'rational analysis and sound empirical investigation'(King 1999:43) to studies in the humanities has made it difficult for this all-too-human of characteristics to be acknowledged. An example of the effect this can have on humour can be found in Herbert Guenther's translation of a song by one of Milarepa's Indian predecessors, Saraha. A translation of this verse that highlighted its humour could read like this:

> I recited the scripture's first line ('let there be success')
>
> Then I drank my beer and forgot it.
>
> Now I remember one of the letters,
>
> But sorry, friend, not its name.[12]

Guenther's translation, by contrast 'draw[s] heavily on what [he saw] as clear affinities between modern "process thinking" and the ancient Buddhist notion of the Way' (Guenther 1983:xvi):

> First I [was shown and] recited the four opening words [of life's lesson]
>
> But when I had imbibed the nectar [of the message]
>
> I became oblivious [to the words]. He who knows the
>
> One [resounding] letter
>
> No longer knows [or bothers about] words. (Guenther 1983:115–16, Interpolations are Guenther's)

There are also other, non-Western discourses that have the potential to inhibit Milarepa's humour. India, the culture in which Buddhism developed, has a great tradition of analysing laughter, usually within the study of aesthetics. In India, this form of analysis dates back to the *Nāṭyaśāstra* of Bharata (estimates range from 500 BCE to 500 CE) (Dace 1963:249).[13] Bharata's influence on Buddhist laughter and humour came through his division of laughter and smiling into six hierarchical categories. The first and second of these—*smita* (the slight smile, with no display of teeth) and *hasita* (the full, silent, toothy smile)—were appropriate, he said, for refined people. The third and fourth types—*vihasita* (sweet giggling sound) and *upahasita* (hearty laughter)—were appropriate for the middle orders. The fifth and six types—*apahasita* (roaring laughter with tears) and *atihasita* (convulsive, hysterical, screaming) of—were only ever appropriate for 'ill-bred and low disreputable characters' (Gnoli 1956:29; Siegel 1987:46; Rangacharya 1996: 58-59).

The hierarchical notion of this prescription is in some ways similar to the social structures that Bakhtin noted in his work on carnivals (Bakhtin 1968:270). Indian thought did not, however, base its hierarchical structure on the concepts of sin or sinlessness. Instead, it referred to the specific *dharma* of the castes—some things were appropriate behaviours for some castes and not for others.

Over time, Bharata's laughing proscriptions and the caste system grew in influence and authority on the sub-continent. By the fifth century CE, Buddhist scholars, such as Buddhadata, were proposing that even the heterodox Buddha had only engaged in the most refined *smita* (Hyers 1974:164). But in this, as in other areas, the traditional collection of the Buddha's instructions is ambiguous. On the one hand, he proscribes some forms of loud laughter. 'This is reckoned as childishness in the discipline of the (Noble Ones),' he said, 'namely immoderate laughter that displays the teeth... Enough for you, if you are pleased righteously, to smile just to show your pleasure' (Woodward 1979:239). Yet other *sūtra*s, as Hyers tells us, 'seem to suggest, if not state outright that on such and such an occasion the Buddha laughed'(Hyers 1989:268). Part of the problem seems to be that, since humour often relies on insider knowledge, we may not know what the Buddha's audience found funny. Despite these problems, two recent studies have assessed the Buddha's humour in the most unexpected of places, the *vinaya* (Schopen 2007; Clarke 2008), or writings on monastic vows.

Perhaps these contradictions come from the presumption that one person, one Buddha, is responsible for all the things that he is credited with saying, when Buddha-dharma, the teachings of the Buddha and his followers, is in fact a many-layered, liberative narrative. At its heart is the Buddha's story of suffering, its causes, its cessation and the path that leads there, but around this basic plot myriad explanatory stories have arisen. Like Milarepa, the Buddha is very much the main character of an oral and literary tradition, based on an historical person. As such, this enables him to be, like Milarepa, many things to many people, but also means he can appear contradictory.

As Buddhism developed, this contradictory nature manifested in many different ways. In relation to humour, this meant that, while some Buddhists rejected raucous laughter as unseemly, other groups appear to have revelled in it. Certainly, Milarepa's lineal predecessors, the Indian *siddha*s, were not averse to a chuckle. Milarepa's teacher Marpa travelled to India and apprenticed himself in the tradition of 'the accomplished ones' (*siddha*). The *siddha*s were famous for their flouting of societal rules—they purposely transgressed the laws of caste and lived outside of society's norms. Their songs, which are called *dohā*s and *caryāgītī,* reflect both their emphasis on naturalness and the play of the senses. They are humorous and, despite their venerability, very earthy. The *siddha*s most probably sang these songs at gatherings called *gaṇacakras* (*tsogi khorlo*) and they reflect their oral beginnings. They came from a tradition of storytelling, and 'employed forms of versification most closely allied with folk theatre [and] wandering poets' (Davidson 2002:237). Their rhythms and rhymes, along with the *rāga*s, or tunes, to which they were set, made them easy to remember and accessible to many more people than written poems (Davidson 2002:223).[14]

A thorough study of humour in the *siddha* tradition is beyond the scope of this chapter,[15] but a taste of their humour will at least convey something of Milarepa's humorous, lineal influences. The aforementioned *siddha,* Saraha, is said to have suggested, for example, that:

If nudity is liberation,

Then dogs and jackals are free.

If baldness is perfection,

Then girls' bottoms are perfect.[16]

Milarepa consciously aligned himself with the tradition of the *siddha*s, his lineal forebears, and their influence on his songs and humour is evident. Many of the *siddha*s, for example, play the role of the outcast clown who lives outside society's mainstream and is frequently portrayed as mad, drunk and naked. There is a lot of satire in their songs, particularly in Saraha's, and they became masters at expressing their joy. But Milarepa did not merely continue the tradition of the *dohā*s and *caryāgītī* in Tibet; there is too much discontinuity between the two traditions to argue this. What he did do was adapt the influences of the *siddha*s' songs, stories and humour to the Tibetan milieu. A closer analysis of his humour through the schema of these three humorous roles, to which I now turn, will hopefully bring out this network of ideas and influences.

The first of Milarepa's roles, that of outcast clown, highlights the counterculture nature of Milarepa's characters. 'Living on the edge,' he says, 'I have penetrated the centre'.[17] His character's clown credentials are also affirmed when he is described as 'mad'—sometimes remaining solitary and spending a lot of time naked. Although he is not portrayed as a 'holy fool', his storytellers do make reference to his foolishness. Yet, unlike his *siddha* antecedents, it is harder to *define* Milarepa by this category; he is, after all, also an ascetic who sometimes encourages monasticism (Jackson 1994:64–5), berates lascivious youths (gTsang 1999:340) and practises sexual morality.

Out of all his redactors, it is Tsangnyön Heruka who is most insistent on Milarepa's 'madness'. Indeed, the other tellers of his story rarely mention it. Given that Tsangnyön showed a predilection for lunacy in his own life, this is not surprising. As Quintman (2006:243) points out:

> The relationship between Mi La ras pa and Gtsang smyon Heruka was intimate—so close that the boundaries between biographical author and subject, the crafting of a Life and the telling of one's own life story, were effectively broken down.[18]

Tsangnyön's Milarepa was both his own reflection and his inspiration. It was a symbiotic relationship that produced the following lines:

I am mad, I laugh at death!

I have nothing, I want nothing.[19]

And:

Others say, 'Is the yogi Milarepa crazy?'

I have also thought, 'I may be crazy.'

I'll tell you about my madness.

The father, son and lineage are insane.

The lineage, great Vajradhara, is crazy.

Forefather Tilopa, the good sage, was crazy.

Forefather Nāropa, the great pandit, was crazy.

My old father Marpa, the translator, was crazy.

I, Mila, the cotton-clad one, am also crazy.[20]

Although there is this unevenness to the references to his madness, references to Milarepa's nudity are found throughout the retellings of his tale; even Gampopa's biography speaks of it (sGam 1982:f13). In one entertaining nude encounter in Tsangnyön's redaction, a young man runs into Milarepa at the side of the road. 'I saw a naked man resting,' he says, 'I thought, "Is he a mad *yogi* or a foolish joker, casually showing his stuff like that!"'.[21] Milarepa's reply is telling in its *siddha*-esque call to naturalness and its criticism of the young man's pretence.

> Hey! My good young man,
> You're ashamed when there is no shame.
> This is a self-arising penis!
> I know no shame of nature,
> But *you* don't shun the shameful—
> Debauched, degrading, pretentious,
> You're no guardian of modesty and morality![22]

Milarepa may not come across as a holy idiot, like some of his Indian predecessors, but sometimes, particularly in the earlier episodes of his story, he does foolish things. Gampopa relates an amusing, self-deprecating story that Milarepa once told him. In retreat in Marpa's compound, Milarepa said he fell asleep sitting up with a butter lamp on his head. When he awoke to see the room illuminated, he forgot about the light on his head and thought its luminosity was a sign of enlightenment (sGam 1982:30).

All this shows that the mask of the outcast clown re-appears throughout the retellings of Milarepa's tale, but it is not used as an end in itself. Unlike the use of this trope in some of the stories of the Indian *siddha*s' lives, its main function is to position Milarepa outside the mainstream of society—a position from which, as the satirical *guru*, he can more precisely aim his ridicule.

The satirical *guru* is another re-appearing humorous figure in Buddhist literature in general, and in the songs of Milarepa and his predecessors in particular. It points to the incongruence of conditioned existence, but is also tempered by compassion. Like most satirists, Milarepa uses this form of humour to criticise and transform. He pokes fun at hypocrisy, social norms, ritual, suffering and death, and regularly teases his students, particularly the wayward Rechungpa.

The most obvious of the satirist's targets, and a good place to begin, is hypocrisy. It is almost too easy to satirise hypocrisy, which is by its own nature almost satire. All the satirist has to do is point to it as fact, and satire emerges. The satirist's skill comes through the various ways they do this pointing. Milarepa uses a plethora of tools in his deconstruction of hypocrites; he alludes, puns, juxtaposes and parodies. In one song, addressed to a learned scholar and supposedly virtuous monk, he alludes to his addressee's hypocrisy in this way:

> The monastery's kitchen, behind the village,
> Is a beacon of frauds and ruination.
> Is this not so, my virtuous friend?
> You think about it.[23]

Unless it is assumed that this 'virtuous' monk was misbehaving in the kitchen, this verse does not make much sense. It is also, given the culture of the times, unlikely that learned monks would spend their time in a kitchen unless they were flouting their vows.

Milarepa also liked to make wordplays. These work particularly well in his encounters with intellectuals, as they point to the folly of words. In the following example, Milarepa plays on the similar sounding words 'tsöma', which means boiled vegetables, and 'tsema', which means valid cognition (*pramāṇa* in Sanskrit).

For words and the talk that births them, I have no time.

Validity or Vegetables—who can say,

So teacher, you win the debate today.[24]

In the song whose translation by Evans-Wentz was discussed earlier, Milarepa parodies the language of Buddhist debate, with its emphasis on consequences and causal relations.

I studied, but I didn't learn.

I knew, but I don't understand.

Listen as I sing you a song called

'The Consequence of learning is forgetting'.[25]

Like the *dohā* songs of the *siddha*s, Milarepa's songs also employ the parallel of 'if.... then....' sentences to juxtapose the expected and apparent. In the following example, taken from Gyalthangpa's hagiography, Milarepa exposes the pretence of the infamous Geshe Darlo. In Milarepa's hagiographies, this character is insistent, but unsuccessful, in his attempts to torment Milarepa; in this episode he has just kicked Milarepa in the head and thrown dust in his mouth. Milarepa replies with this song:

If you don't know your own mind,

Why bother learning about religion?

If you haven't calmed your mind-stream,

What use is great learning?

If you aren't hitting the head of 'self,'

Why are you hitting Mila?

If you aren't covering afflictions with dirt,

Why cover me with it?

If you are not paying attention to your mind,

Your vows are fake.[26]

If you aren't pure in body, speech and mind,

Your tidy robes are pretentious.

If you don't get rid of attachment, hatred and ignorance,

Your understanding of tenets is a sham.

I, the yogi Milarepa,

Thought there was nothing I hadn't eaten,

But now I've eaten dregs!

I thought there was nothing I hadn't meditated on,

But now I've meditated on dirt!

I thought there was nothing I hadn't rolled with,[27]

But now I've rolled with your kicks![28]

Another of his songs repeats two of the most common themes in Sanskrit satires—the holy man in the brothel and the man in women's clothing. This extract, which is taken from the Amdo and Kham oral traditions of his songs, is unusual in that it is the only time Milarepa uses indirect satire. In indirect satire, a person or character highlights their own incongruous state rather than having it pointed out to them. Milarepa uses this technique to lampoon 'Bön'[29] origins and to explain comically how its followers came to wear blue robes.

According to more modern sources,

A very clever Buddhist pandit

In the land of India,

Visited the house of a whore.

Arising before dawn, he dressed,

But by mistake wrapped himself

In the woman's skirt instead of his own (Kunga 1995:144).

The satire in Milarepa's songs also highlights the differences between his social milieu and the *siddha*'s milieu. Tibet was not, for example, a caste-based society; nor did it support vastly wealthy kingdoms. Instead, Tibetan clans, homelands and the normalisation of social inequalities become the stuff of Milarepa's satire. The physical setting also transformed the substance, if not the intent, of his songs. While the *siddha*s sang of rivers and boats, for example, Milarepa's songs contain frequent references to the cold, snow, warming tea, meat and thick clothing. A large part of the humour and social criticism in these songs comes from the unusual way he presents the substance of Tibetan's everyday lives. Things as ordinary as clothes, food, and work became metaphors for entrapment in *samsara*. In this next verse, which makes up in satirical insight for what it lacks in direct humour, he transforms social resistance to his nudity into a criticism of the position of women in his society

> We know we have male and female bodies,
>
> And everyone knows the signs of these.
>
> Protectors of real modesty and decency
>
> Don't thrive in our society.
>
> Real shame is a woman bought for a fee,
>
> Real shame is the son who takes her breasts.[30]

Milarepa also frequently comments on the plight of old people in his community. One major theme of these songs is, of course, impermanence, but they also contain criticism of their neglected state. In one song he converses with a grandmother about her situation. A recent commentator criticised this song as an example of patriarchal abuse (Campbell 2002:32), and it does indeed reflect patriarchal social constructs, but, at least in the original Tibetan, it is also hard to miss the scathing criticism it directs towards the grandmother's enforced, submissive position.

> When you first came to this house
>
> Did you think things would turn out like this?
>
> You get up early,
>
> You go to bed late,
>
> And in between, your work is endless.
>
> Take these three into account, Grandmother,
>
> And you are an unpaid servant.
>
> [In your home] the master of the house comes first,
>
> Or if there is none, then the taxes must be paid—
>
> If neither, capable sons and nephews are endowed.
>
> Take these three into account, Grandmother,
>
> And your bequest is negligible, you have nothing you need.[31]

Milarepa's attempt to convey his message in the simplest of forms meant that even something as ordinary as food became a re-occurring theme in his songs. In Tibet, however, the necessity of food did not place it beyond criticism. Tibetan Buddhist culture has a problem with its food; one of its fundamental tenets argues against killing, yet one of the plateau's primary food sources is meat. Milarepa points to this discrepancy when he sings:

> Since eating the food of concentration,
>
> Meat and beer deceive me.
>
> Nauseants like these are of little use.
>
> Why would I want the essence of pretence?[32]

Milarepa is also critical, as most satirists in most times are, of the rich hoarding their wealth. Among his many scathing remarks about miserliness is this one:

> Won't there be food and drink where we live in our next lives?
>
> Then why aren't landlords and ladies generous?[33]

While an entrenched caste system confronted the Indian *siddha*s, Milarepa's Tibetan audience was much more concerned with their clan affiliations and land. The word '*phayül*' (father land) has become a synonym for Tibet in modern parlance; its two syllables represent the two most-treasured and, in Milarepa's view, deceptive, elements of Tibetan culture—clans and property. In this next extract, Milarepa turns Tibetan notions of the value of land on their head by pointing at the incongruity between people's perception of their land and what land ownership actually entailed.

> Property, at first, is cosy and kind,
>
> Then it grinds away at body, speech and mind.
>
> How tiring—you plough and sow,
>
> You plant, but nothing grows.
>
> Your village becomes famine-stricken,
>
> A ghost town with no defences, barren,
>
> And in the end—
>
> You leave.
>
> Dwellings that degrade pain my mind,
>
> I don't want a temporary prison,
>
> I won't be your adopted son.[34]

The *phayül* and its clan also demanded allegiance. Milarepa's experience of this phenomenon was not pleasant; he had suffered the indignity of being ostracised and viewed it with suspicion. 'It is so stupid,' he said, 'to throw your life away fighting your enemies, those fading flowers'.[35]

This approach to land and clans stands in marked contrast to his teacher Marpa, who spent many years establishing his territory and influence. While Marpa built towers, Milarepa said, 'Busy landlords are like demented demons'.[36] The two men also had very different approaches to wealth; Marpa collected it, Milarepa practised poverty. 'If you are content you are rich',[37] he told one of his students. This next song, which Paltrul Rinpoche later quoted at length in his famous work *Kun bzang bla ma'i zhal lung* (The Words of My Perfect Teacher) (dPal 1968:133), illustrates this approach quite amusingly.

Wealth, at first, makes you happy and admired,

But however much you have, you're never satisfied.

Soon the demon of stinginess gets you in his vice,

And you cannot bear to do anything nice.

Wealth is a beacon for enemies and ghosts,

You collect it and it's spent by everyone else,

And in the end—

You die. [38]

Minding enemies' money pains my mind.

I have given up the fools' gold of *saṃsāra*. [39]

I don't want to be swindled by Māra.[40]

Intimate relationships are another favourite topic of Milarepa's satire. Given the primacy that Tibetan culture placed—and still places—on family life and abundant offspring, his decision not to settle down with a partner and have children seemed as strange to his compatriots as their compulsion to procreate was to him. He certainly composed some vivid descriptions of married life to defend his decision to satirise intimate relationships, such as the following verse:

A girlfriend, at first, is a smiling goddess,

You can't gaze at her face in excess.

Then she's a corpse-eyed shrew,

Say one thing, and she'll spit back two.

Pulling your hair, clawing at your leg,

She'll brandish a ladle if you swing a tent peg.

And in the end—

She is old and toothless.

Ogresses with hateful eyes pain my mind,

Brawling with hags—I've given up the fight,

So your young friend will bring me no delight.[41]

This only son of an only son also made some amusing comments about the large families his neighbours held in such high regard.

Parents of many children

Are like pieces of cooked meat in the hands of hungry men.[42]

And again:

Is there a fear that *samsara* will be emptied?

Then why do lay people want children so much?[43]

In Tsangnyön's version of his tale, Milarepa is also critical of monastic brotherhoods, although this is not always true of the earlier redactions. By comparing Tsangnyön's version with Gyalthangpa's telling, we even find an instance where Tsangnyon's slight changes have lent a verse an anti-monastic feel. The verse, as Gyalthangpa expounded it, said:

I have water and wood near me,

So I have little need of companions

Who are known to be crooked and deceptive.[44]

Tsangnyon's twist comes in the first line when he reads the two syllables '*chu*' (water) and '*shing*' (wood), to come up with the compound word '*chu shing*', which means driftwood. He also replaces a couple of resting syllables with '*dzom*' (to collect) and '*gön*' to indicate a monastery, and adds an extra line. The transformed verse is quite different:

In those collections of driftwood called monasteries,

Live those deceptive, so-called disciples.

Companions like this are of little use

All their spiteful rumours are depressing.[45]

While hypocrisy lends itself to wordplays and allusion, pointless ritual lends itself to parody, and Milarepa takes particular delight in using parody to lampoon followers of 'Bön'. Not only does he poke fun at their origins, as mentioned earlier, but he also parodies a Bön ritual (a whole chapter of Tsangnyön's *rNal 'byor gyi dbang phyug chen po Mi la ras pa'i rnams mgur* [100,000 Songs] (gTsang 1999: 399-415) is dedicated to this parody). The detail of this parody is intriguing; he not only refers to Bön liturgies, but also their costume and dance.

The following extract comes from the stage in the ritual at which the Bön priest would normally 'throw a *mo*,' or perform a divination.

> According to the divination,
>
> There is bad news about your health—
>
> You were born, so you will die!
>
> There is bad news about your household—
>
> All meetings must break up!
>
> There is bad news about your finances—
>
> Whatever you save will run out!
>
> There is bad news about your enemies—
>
> You've got them all wrong!
>
> To stop all this coming to pass,
>
> Let's do another Bön ritual![46]

The crone or the old woman was also a 'conventional figure in Sanskrit satire' (Siegel 1987:109) and we meet her again in Milarepa's songs. Milarepa's conversation with the grandmother is a clear example of this. In this next extract, Milarepa has moved on from elucidating her social plight and is now discussing her body. While it may seem insulting, this song is still popular in Tibetan society today, where elderly, and not-so-elderly, Tibetans often recite its first verse, giggling, as they lift themselves up or lower themselves down.

> Standing up is like extracting a tethering pole.
>
> Walking, you clamber along like a chicken.
>
> Sitting down, you drop like a bag of dirt.
>
> Take these three into account, Grandmother,
>
> And your decrepit body must make you depressed.
>
> Outside your skin is nought but wrinkles.
>
> Inside your bones poke through shrunken flesh.
>
> In between, you are stupid, dumb, deaf, blind, senile and tottering.
>
> Take these three into account, Grandmother,
>
> And your wrathful, repulsive face will grimace.
>
> Your food and drink are cold and dirty.
>
> There in the dung is your worn-out coat.

In your bed, the bridegroom aged.[47]

Take these three into account, Grandmother,

And you are only part human, and part bitch.[48]

These frequent reminders of suffering, old age and death are something of an innovation in the songs of his lineage. While the *siddha*s sang many songs about *sahaja*, bliss and the foolishness of *samsara*, curiously they rarely ruminate on death.[49] Milarepa, on the other hand, seems to have a particular fondness for this subject and sings of it frequently. His songs about death are often striking in their imagery and potent in their descriptions of impermanence. Curiously, they are also sometimes amusing. In the compilation of Milarepa's songs attributed to the Third Karmapa, Rangjung Dorje for example, there is the following verse.

Death!

It hurts, it hurts, it hurts,

Ouch, ouch, ouch,

It's coming, it's coming, it's coming—

You're gone![50]

There are also several songs in which he used the imagery of a decrepit house to convey the collapse of death. The similarity of imagery in these songs suggests either that they developed from one song or that Milarepa used similar imagery in different songs. The following is the most completely developed song of this:[51]

Your body, this old house, is going to collapse.

It has been raining day and night,

And the months, the years of drips and leaks have eroded it.

Your body, this old house, will definitely collapse.

The corroding trickles of death have accumulated.

The end is like the shadow of an old sun,

You run, run, and still it comes, comes –

I haven't seen anyone escape yet.

When Buddhists see death,

It is as a teacher that goads them to goodness.

Look to see if anyone seeks out amusement as they die.[52]

This song also points to an interesting distinction that Milarepa's songs repeatedly stress—the difference he sees between seeking amusement and being amused. In line with his calls to practice contentment, he encourages laughter, joy and amusement. But he also warns against the pursuit of or attachment to this very same experience. His next song about death is a perfect example of this distinction; it criticises those who would seek alternative amusement in the face of death, but is itself amusing.

> When the body's warmth is only a spark[53]
>
> And the end is closing in,
>
> Some practice astrology
>
> Others scream with pain,
>
> And yet others focus on their stores and jewels.
>
> 'Everyone else will spend my savings!'
>
> However much you love, you have to go on alone.[54]

Further satire is also evidenced in Milarepa's relationship with his students. Perhaps this is something he learnt from his own teacher, who insisted on calling him 'The Great Magician' (Abo Thuchen), despite his disastrous stint in that occupation. At one point Marpa even quipped, 'What are you doing with that fire, are you trying to demolish my house too?' (gTsang 1999:61). As Gyalthangpa tells it, Milarepa continued the trend, teasing his students at one stage that he had invited 80 *siddha*s to a *ganacakra* communal ceremony so they had 'better go and find some more offerings!' Later, as the story goes, when they were running around in a panic, he said, 'I'm just joking, this is fine'.[55]

The usual recipient of this teasing, however, was his much-loved but disobedient student, Rechungpa. In some ways, Milarepa's relationship with Rechungpa resembled that of a parent and child; Rechungpa was exasperating and Milarepa often responded with gentle humour. There is, for example, the time he said to Rechungpa:

> You managed to give up your jewels and beautiful girlfriends,
>
> Even though it depressed you a little,
>
> But you are never going to give up your soft, comfortable, warm bed, are you?
>
> Give up corpse-like sleep too, Rechungpa![56]

His hagiographies also evidence his frustration with Rechungpa's intellectualism. Rechungpa became embarrassed when his teacher could not defeat some learned men in a debate and did not even show an interest in the contest, so he studied dialectics with various learned individuals in Tibet and India.[57] Milarepa responded to Rechungpa's endeavours with the song:

> Rechungpa, whom I have nurtured since childhood,
>
> I sent you to [India to] get instructions
>
> Now with all this philosophical writing
>
> You are in danger of becoming a scholar!
>
> Do you want to burst your meditator's cushion?
>
> With all your new scholarly talk,
>
> You are in danger of becoming a 'great teacher'
>
> And too big for your boots.[58]

The last of Milarepa's humorous types, the smiling Buddha, is familiar from its many visual representations. It differs from the previous two in that it is a manifestation of laughter in its most subdued form, rather than its encouragement. Milarepa repeatedly expressed his happiness. He sings songs of joy about contentment, his meditations, the arising of his *caṇḍalī* (mystic heat), and even beer. '*Yogi*s who've turned desire around,' he tells us, 'See all as illusion and are always happy'.[59]

Some of the most compelling manifestations of the smiling Buddha in Milarepa's songs are those that deal with contentment. Contentment, after all, smiles by its nature. It is true joy that makes the best of whatever happens—a smile that does not rely on humour. According to his hagiographies, Milarepa had this in abundance and expressed it directly in this song:

> Whatever. I have no goals.
>
> I am a beggar with no food,
>
> I am a nude with no clothes,
>
> I am destitute with no possessions.
>
> I don't think about outcomes.
>
> I am here, but I don't live here.
>
> I have mastered the *yoga*s;
>
> I am crazy. I laugh at death.
>
> I have nothing. I want nothing.[60]

Milarepa also sang many songs reflecting the sheer exuberance of his joy. There are, for example, six songs in Tsangnyön Heruka's hagiography that include the words '*de*' (joy) or '*kyibo*' (happiness) in their titles.[61] In the redactions made by Gyalthangpa and Tsangnyön Heruka, but curiously not in Rangjung Dorje's work, there are also many songs that end a line with the syllable '*de*', which not only indicates joy but also provides a convenient end rhyme. Gyalthangpa often adds the grammatical particle '*o*' (here translated as 'what bliss!') to this syllable, while Tsangnyön's leaves it unadorned. Here is an example from Gyalthangpa's redaction:

> Experience is pleasure,
>
> Mind is delightful,
>
> Body is illusory—what bliss!
>
> I can go, I can stay,
>
> But either way,
>
> I have no notion of 'I'—what bliss!
>
> The discipline of yoga
>
> Doesn't get me down—what bliss!
>
> I see no duality—what bliss!
>
> I meditate without tension or daze—what bliss!.[62]

Another important aspect of Milarepa's smiling-Buddha persona was his mastery of *tummo yoga*, or *caṇḍalī*. This practice developed in India (Samuel 1993:240) and is similar to *kuṇḍalinī yoga* in that the practitioner encourages dormant energy to rise through successive *cakra*s (energy centres). The *siddha*s treasured these exercises for the experiences of bliss they created (Bhayani 1997:103). In Tibet, however, it was one of their side effects that brought them to prominence—they generate warmth. As a metaphor for bliss in 'the land of snows', as Tibet was and is known, heat was also, obviously, a much more evocative image than it was on the stifling plains of India. Indeed, it was because of *caṇḍalī* that Mila was able to be a *repa* (cotton-clad one), and he mentions it many times in his songs. For Milarepa its mastery meant freedom from the encumbering clothes that define life for most on the plateau, as he tells us here:

> Since firing up *caṇḍalī*'s heat,
>
> Woollen clothes deceive me.
>
> Baggage like this is of little use;
>
> Why would [I] want a lice farm?[63]

For those who had not managed to 'fire up' *caṇḍalī*, another way to stay warm was to drink. While the *siddha*s sang songs about wine and played at drunkenness, the Tibetans' intoxicant of choice is barley beer, *chang*. Milarepa used this common experience and the common image of beer as a metaphor for bliss on quite a few occasions. Once, for example, he sang:

Concerned about thirst, I sought drink;

Now my drink is the ambrosial beer of mindfulness,

And I don't worry about thirst.[64]

On another occasion he used it as a metaphor for the 'leaping over' practice (*thögal*) of the Dzogchen tradition.

Everyone drunk on the beer of actuality

Leaping over [the path's stages], lets play!

Influenced by both let's each sing a song

And nurture inspiring experiences![65]

These examples of humour are not isolated incidents in Milarepa's poems, but are representative of patterns of humour that are found throughout the tradition of his songs and life story. Neither are they an isolated example of humour being lost in translation; for many reasons, humour is often one of translation's first casualties. Sometimes, especially when it is based on the structure of words, it simply does not translate. At other times, an insider's status is necessary to 'get' a joke. But humour is also lost when readers assume either that it should not be there or that it is not important. Indeed, many of scholarship's ingrained discourses insist that 'seriousness', said to be humour's antithesis, is a prerequisite for quality. The development of these discourses obviously had its reasons. There is no point, for example, spending much time and effort researching and writing about a topic if the scholar does not think that she is going to be taken seriously. Yet, humour and laughter are such an important part of collective experience that sidelining them means partitioning off a whole area of communication, knowledge and empathy. Milarepa's stories and songs are one example of this, but there are many others in the translation of Indo-Tibetan Buddhism and religious texts more generally.

Notes

1. I have chosen to use this colloquial expression because the Tibetan (gTsang 1999:866) says '*gas bas bzhad pa*', which means, literally, 'to crack with laughter'.
2. The inspiration for these three humorous types comes from Hyers (1970. 1974. 1989), who discusses the mode of Zen humour and decides that it has three main types: the simple laughter of the child; the more sophisticated laughter of the critic; and the higher humour of a Buddha. I recognise the similar types in the story of Milarepa, but not the pejorative terms he has given them or what he essentialised as the 'oriental' nature of these images. I will, instead approach these characters as 're-appearing masks' in what Michel Foucault (1991:94) called 'the great carnival of time'.
3. Another interesting reading of Milarepa was by the early 20th-century Gelug teacher, Pabongkha Rinpoche, who recast Milarepa as a mind-training (*lojong*) practitioner, who had completed the graduated path (*lamrim*) practices in an earlier life as the Kadampa Geshe Chag Trichog, a student of Atiśa. Establishing that Milarepa performed these practices is imperative for the Gelug tradition, as their doctrine insists that all beings must perfect these practices before attaining awakening. Pabongkha does not explain, however, the problematic chronological logistics that would allow Milarepa to be the reincarnation of a member of an order that was not founded for years after his birth (Pha bong kha & Khri byang 2003:182).
4. No manuscripts signed by him survive, but his existence can be established by references to him in contemporary manuscripts and, particularly, by the version of his life story written by his student Gampopa only a short while after his death. The tower he reportedly built for Marpa still stands in southern Tibet near the Bhutanese border. Wylie (1964:284) says that it is 'on the banks of the *gsas* river in *lho-brag*'. There is even general agreement on his dates; according to most sources he was born in 1040 and died in 1123 CE (see, for example, 'Gos 1996:427, 437). However, gTsang smyon (1999:19) writes that he was born in the water dragon year and, therefore, in 1052.
5. See, for example, Don (1985); Urubshurow (1984); Goss (1993); Garvey (1988); Tiso (1989); Berghash and Jillson (2001); Powers (1992); Campbell (2002).
6. This is particularly true of both recent movies, but Lhalungpa's earlier translation of Milarepa's story (Lhalungpa 1997) succeeds in emphasising his humour.
7. In their combination of comic constructions and the recordings of conversations, Milarepa's songs contain not only the comic but also other forms of humour.
8. This is the King James version's translation of the Greek word *eutrapelia*, which has also been rendered as 'wit' and 'puns'(Bremmer 1997:22).
9. In Tibetan and Indic languages, the correlation between seriousness and importance is much less clear. The Tibetan word used to reflect importance is *gal chen po*, which originally meant 'to have a greater share of produce'. Many other Tibetan words also reflect a correlation between importance and wealth; a teacher is a *rin po che* (great jewel), for example. A link is also apparent in Indic languages too in words such as *ratna* and *maṇi*, which both mean jewel. Along with wealth, several other metaphors are used to express a thing's import. In Tibet height was also used to

designate importance—*bla ma*, for example, indicates either the 'high mother', or 'none higher'. In India, weight came to take on importance, in words like *alugha* (not light) and *guru* (heavy).

10 The Tibetan text reads, 'ngas bslabs kyang ma bslabs. Shes kyang mi shes. shes rung brjed de thal ba'i rgyu mtshan gyi glu 'di nyon cig' (gTsang 1999:folio 457). For an alternative translation, see Lhalungpa 1997:153).

11 The Tibetan text reads, 'sgra sgyur mar pa'i zhabs la 'dud. tha snyad bral bar byin gyi rlobs' (gTsang 1999:814)

12 Versions of the text translated here can be found in Jackson (2004:104 no90); Shahidullah (1928:159 no92); Snellgrove (1954:236 no90); Schaeffer (2005:165 nos441–4). The Apabraṃśa text reads, 'siddhir atthu mai paḍame paḍiau. maṇḍa pivanteṃ visaraa e maiu. akkharamekka ettha maiu. akkharamekka ettha mai jāṇiu. tāhara ṇāma jāṇami e saiu'. The Tibetan text reads, 'sgrub yig bzhi la dang po dbag gis ston. khu ba 'thungs pas nga ni brjed par gyur. gang gis yi shes cig shes pa. de yis ming ni mi shes so'. In Shahidullah (1928), the Tibetan reads 'sgrub yig bzhi la' and not 'gzhi la', as Schaeffer seems to have read it. This fits well with Jackson's (2004:104) comment on the Apabraṃśa text that *siddir atthu* refers to 'The four-syllable phrase that is the traditional opening to many Hindu treatises; in Sanskrit, it is: *Siddhir astu*'

13 Bharata's theory of aesthetics is based on the idea that there are 'eight principal feelings of human nature (*stāyibhāva*),' and that in the arts we experience a taste (Sanskrit: *rasa*) of these. It is because the arts only afford us a taste of our everyday experiences, he argued, that we can enjoy in them feelings we would usually avoid. Among the everyday experiences is laughter or *hāsa*, and in the arts we taste it as *hāsya* or the comic (Gnoli 1956:29).

14 For the different *rāgas*, see Kværne (2010).

15 In relation to the humour of the *tantras* in general, see Davidson (2002:277–90). As far as I know, there has not been a thorough study of the *siddha*'s humour.

16 My own translation; alternative translations can be found in Jackson (2004:56 no7); Bhayani (1997:3 no7); Shahidullah (1928:127 no7); Snellgrove (1954:225 no7) and Schaeffer (2005:135 nos23–36).

17 The Tibetan text reads, 'mtha' ru bsdad pas dbus su tshud' (gTsang 1999:698). Given the nature of this work and the time that has elapsed since their original translation by Chang (1962), I have chosen to retranslate many of the extracts from Tsangnyön Heruka's work referred to here.

18 As noted by Quintman (p. 253) and Smith (1969:3) Tsangnyön Heruka's identification with Milarepa was so strong that he saw himself as the Repa's reincarnation.

19 The Tibetan text reads, 'nga ni smyon pa shi skyid mkhan. nga ni cang med dgos med mkhan' (gTsang 1999:248).

20 The Tibetan text reads, 'rnal 'byor mi la ras pa la. gzhan yang smyo'am zer. rang yang smyo'am smyam pa byung. smyo ba'i smyo lugs bshad tsa na. pha smyo bu smyo rgyud smyo. rgyud pa rdo rje 'chang, chen smyo. yang mes tee lo she bzang smyo. mes po nā ro pan chen smyo. pha rgan mar pa lo tsā ba smyo. nga rang mi la ras pa smyo' (gTsang 1999:758). There is a similar song recorded in Kunga Rinpoche

(1995:85): 'Afflicted by the devil of ignorance / Most beings of the six realms are crazy. / Having realized appearances to be illusory / Milarepa especially is crazy. / With supernormal knowledge of other's minds / Old father Marpa Lotsawa is crazy. / With courage in hardships for the sake of Dharma. / Grandfather, great pandit Nāropa, is crazy. / With inconceivable powers of transformation / Great-grandfather Tilo Sherab Sangpo is crazy.'

21   The Tibetan text reads 'gcer nyal byed pa'i mi zhig mthong. 'o na rnal 'byor smyon pa zhig. spyod pa tho co byed pa zhig. cha lugs gang dgar ston pa zhig' (gTsang 1999:345–6); for an alternative translation, see Chang (1962:179).

22   The Tibetan text reads, "o na khye'u chung skyes legs po. khyed ngo mi tsha la ngo tshar byed. 'di ni rang byung pho rtags yin. bcos ma'i ngo tsha ngas mi shes. ngo tsha ba rnams la khyed mi 'dzem. ngan spyod sdig dang gyo sgyu la. khrel ngo tsha bsrung ba khyed la med' (gTsang 1999:342); for an lternative translation, see Chang (1962:176).

23   The Tibetan text reads, 'grong ltag dgon pa'i ja thab de. mgo gyogs phung gzhi'i gyab mo 'dra. de e 'dra dge ba'i bshes rang soms' (gTsang 1999:319); for an alternative translation, see Chang (1962:155).

24   The Tibetan text reads, 'tshig la tshig skyes lab mi khom. tshad ma'i tshod ma ngas mi shes. da res kyi rtsod pa ston pa rgyal' (gTsang 1999:539).

25   The Tibetan text reads, 'ngas bslabs kyang ma bslabs. Shes kyang mi shes. shes rung brjed de thal ba'i rgyu mtshan gyi glu 'di nyon cig' (gTsang 1999:814); for an alternative translation, see Lhalungpa (1997:153).

26   Here I have translated the Tibetan word *cad* as 'fake'.

27   Literally *dril ba* means 'to roll'. This verb can also imply a more metaphorical 'essentialising' or a phenomenon. If I took out its active aspect, however, the song would lose its very evident physicality.

28   The Tibetan text reads, 'khyod rang sems kyi ngo bo'i mi shes pa'i dam chos shes pas cing zhig phan. byed rang rgyud zhi zhing ma thul ba'i. thos pa che nas ci zhig bya. khyed da bdag gi mgo bo mi brdung bar. nga mid la rdungs pas ci zhig phan. khyed nyon mongs thal bas mi gyog par. nga thal bas gyogs pas ci zhig phan. khyed shes rgyud bad dang mi ldan pa'i. tshul chos sdom pa yod nas ced khyed lus ngag yig sum mi btsun pa'i. thang sham chos gos gyon nas ced. khyod chags sdang rmongs gsum ma spangs pa'i. grub mtha'i dbye bshag mkhas nas ced. rnal 'byor mid la ras pa ngas. sngad ma zos pa gcig med pa la. zag pa zos da res tsam. nga ma 'goms pa gcig med pa la. thal ba 'goms pa da res tsam. ngas ma dril ba gcig med pa la. rdog pas dril pa da res tsam' (rGyal 1973:247–8); for an alternative translation, see Tiso (1989:410).

29   It is unlikely that Milarepa, or his interpreters, were referring to practitioners of the *bon* religion as it exists today. It is much more likely, as Davidson (2002:13) has noted, that this term refers to practitioners of ritual, which would make them ideal foils for a parody of ritual.

30   The Tibetan text reads, 'lus pho mor grub pa shes zin nas. mtshan ma yod pa sus kyang shes. khred dang ngo tsha bsrung ba rnams. 'jig rtan phal la mi 'dug ste. ngo

tsha'i bu mo rin gyi nyos. ngo tsha'i bu pho pang du blangs' (gTsang 1999:179); for an alternative translation, see Lhalhungpa (1997:140).

31   The Tibetan text reads, 'khyod dang po khyim la btang dus na. 'di 'dra ma zhig e byung soms. snga dro ldang ba'i snga ma dang gcig. dgong mo nyal ba'i phyi ma dang gnyis. zin pa med pa'i bya las dang gsum. dzum de gdum 'dzoms 'ai dus tshod na. a phyi gla lto med pa'i bran khol ma...gal po che yi bza' dpon dang cig. med kyang dgos pa'i khral sdud dang gnyis. med mi rung gi bu tsha dang gsum. gsum de gsum 'dzoms pa'i dus tshod na. a phyi gal chung rang la dgos pa'i skal med ma' (gTsang 1999:303); for an alternative translation, seeChang (1962:137).

32   The Tibetan text reads, 'da ni mi la'i rdzun drug 'chad...ting 'dzin zas su zos tsa na. sha chang, zer ba rdzun du gda'. ngan skyug rgyu de dgos pa chung. gyo skol byed snying nga mi 'dod' (gTsang 1999:522).

33   The Tibetan text reads, 'tshe phyi ma'i yul na bza' btung yod dam. yon bdag pho mo tsho sbyin pa mi gtong gda' ba' (gTsang 1999:693).

34   The Tibetan text reads, 'yul dang po nyams dga' skyid kyid po. lus ngag yid gsum 'brad pa'i seg rdar yin. bar du rmo rko 'o re bryal. sa bon phar btab tshur mi 'byung. yul ngan mu ge'i grong khyer de. mgon med dri ze'i gnas dang 'dra. tha mar bskyur nas 'gro rgyu yin. sdig gsog gi gnas khang sems la gzan. gnas skabs kyi btson dong nga mi 'dod. khyed kyi bu dod nga mi byed' (gTsang 1999:286–7); for an alternative translation, see Chang (1962:119).

35   The Tibetan text reads, 'sdang dgra me tog bzhin du yal rgyu la. 'thab mos rang srog skyel ba shin tu glen' (gTsang 1999:226); for an alternative translation, see Chang (1962:33).

36   The text refers to a specific type of demon, the *dkor bdag srung ma*. The Tibetan text reads, 'spyad pa mang po'i bdag po de. Lta log dkor bdag srung ma 'dra' (gTsang 1999:688); for an alternative translation, see Chang (1962:535).

37   The Tibetan text reads, 'nor chog shes yod na phyug po yin. dpa' rang tshod zin na rang srog brtan' (gTsang 1999:699).

38   Literally, 'the māras that attack the life force come' (*srog gi bdud du 'ong*), which is another way of saying 'you die'.

39   Literally, 'false rock' (*bslu rdo*), which means the same as the English expression 'fool's gold'.

40   The Tibetan text reads, 'nor dang po bdag skyid gzhan smon po. ci tsam yod kyang chog shes med. bar du ser sna'i mdud pas 'ching. dge ba'i phogs su gtong mi phod. dgra 'dre gnyis kyi gyab mo yin. rang gis bsogs pa mi yis spyod. tha mar srog gi bdud du 'ong. dgra ba'i nor gnyer sems la gzan. 'khor ba'i bslu rdo spangs pa yin. bdud kyi mgo skor de nga mi 'dod' (gTsang 1999:289); for an alternative translation, see Chang (1962:121).

41   The Tibetan text reads, 'grogs dang po lha mo bzhad kha ma. blta ba'i gdong la chog rgyu med. bar du srin mo ro mig ma. phar gcig lab na tshur gnyis rgol. skra la 'chang, na sgyid par 'ju. dbyug pa brgyab na gzar bu 'phyar. tha mar ba rgan so med ma. srin mo'i sdang mig sems la gzan. bdud mo'i 'thab a spangs pa yin. khyed kyi gzhon grogs mi 'dod' (gTsang 1999:287); for an alternative translation, see Chang (1962:120).

42 The Tibetan texts reads, 'bu phrag mang po'i pha ma de. khrel med lag gi sha btson 'dra'(gTsang 1999:688; for an alternative translation, see Chang (1962:535).

43 The Tibetan text reads, "khor ba 'di stongs kyis dogs pa lags sam. skya btsun med bu slog rem zhing gda' ba' (gTsang 1999:693).

44 The Tibetan text reads, 'chu shing gam na yod rtsa na. gyog po zer dang rdzun du gda'. za rogs 'dis dang dgos ched chung' (rGyal 1973:238); for an alternative translation, see Tiso (1989:397).

45 The Tibetan text reads, 'chu shing 'dzoms pa'i dgon pa na. nye gnas zer yang rdzun du gda'. za grogs 'di kyang dgos rgu chung. Gtam ngan mang po rna ba tsha' (gTsang 1999:522).

46 The Tibetan text reads, 'skyes nas 'chi bas srog cha ngan. 'dus nas 'bral bas khyim cha ngan. bsog nas 'dzad pas nor cha ngan. rang snang log pas dgra cha ngan. mo ngan bzlog phyir bon zhig byed' (gTsang 1999:406). This verse lends even greater credence to the idea that Milarepa's use of the word bon refers to ritualists rather than practitioners of any particular religion, because mos are performed by many Buddhists as well.

47 Literally, 'performed the activity of the fourth' (*bzhi sbyor ba*). Das, Sandberg and Heyde (1988:1084) refer to 'the fourth stage of life' (*bzhi gnas skabs*) as being old age. As this fits the context, I have translated it as such.

48 The Tibetan text reads, 'brtod phur 'don pa'i ldang lugs dang gcig. cha la 'jab pa'i 'gro lugs dang gnyis. sa do chad pa'i sdod lugs dang gsum. gsum de gsum 'dzoms pa'i dus tshod na a phyi sgyu lus rgud pa'i yid pham ma. xx de rjes 'di 'dra e byung soms. phyi pags pa 'dus pa'i gnyer ma dang gcig. nang sha khrag zad pa'i rus 'bor dang gnyis. bar glen lkugs o'n long thom yor dang gsum. gsum de gsum 'dzoms pa'i dus tshod na. a phyi mi sdug ston pa'i khro gnyer ma. xx da lta 'di 'dra e 'dug soms. grang la nyog pa'i bza' btung dang gcig. lci la hril ba'i dug po dang gnyis. pag po bzhi sbyor gyi mal sa dang gsum. gsum de gsum 'dzoms pa'i dus tshod na. a phyi mis 'gom khyi 'gom gyi rtogs ldan ma' (gTsang 1999:304); for an alternative translation, see Chang (1962:138).

49 Most mentions of death in the work either use metaphors, such as 'dying of thirst on the plane of the commentaries', or, sometimes, refer to it as another practice; see Jackson (2004:91) for other examples.

50 The Tibetan text reads, "chi ba. dug ge dug ge dug ge. sa na sa na sa na. 'ong ngo 'ong ngo 'ong ngo. chid' (Karma-pa 1978:497). This verse reflects a tendency in Rang byung's redaction, which is not as evident in other versions, to use humorous sounds and onomatopoeia.

51 Another example of this kind of song is to be found in Tsangnyon's redaction. The translation reads, ' For months it's been raining / On this battered house, my body / The drips have eroded it over the years / Now this illusory dwelling is collapsing / Better to save the dripping and die. / Sinful men don't think of death / Rechung, you and I should go to the snows of Lachi'. The Tibetan text reads, 'sgyu ma lus kyi khang hrul la. zhag dang za ma'i char bab abs. lo dang zla ba'i thigs pas brdungs. sgyu ma'i khang hrul 'jig las che. 'chi brod kyi thigs tshogs byed re ran. mi sdig

can la 'chi ba yong snyom med. rang re ras chung gnyis la phyi gangs la gshegs' (gTsang 1999:717); for an alternative translation, see Chang (1962:568).

52 The Tibetan text reads, 'sgyu ma lus kyi khang rul la. zhag dang za ma'i char bab abs. lo dang zla ba'i thigs pas gdungs. sgyu lus kyi khang rul nges par 'jig. 'chi brod kyi thigs tshogs byed re ran. dpe ni nyi rgas grib so bzhin. phar phar bros kyang tshur tshur sleb. bros pas thar par ngas ma mthong. chos pa 'chi bam thong tsa na. dge la bskul ba'i slob dpon yin. de la dga' spro ci 'dug blta yang blta' (gTsang 1999:398); for an alternative translation, see Chang (1962: 237).

53 The expression 'drod me stag tsam' proved a little difficult to translate. As the expression *stag chas* can refer to tinderboxes (Das, Sandberg and Heyde 1988:547), it makes sense to translate it as referring to the spark from a tinderbox.

54 The Tibetan text reads, 'drod me stag tsam de mtha' nas sdud. la la gza' dang skar ma brtsi. la la sdug bsngal 'o dod 'bod. la la zas dang nor la sgom. rang gis bsogs pa gzhan gyi spyod sems brtse ba mang yang gcig pur 'gro' (gTsang 1999:707); for an alternative translation, see Chang (1962: 556).

55 The Tibetan text reads, 'rje btsun gyi gsung nas. ngas bla ma grub thob brgyad po spyan drangs la 'ong gis. khyed rang tshogs 'khor sogs gcig gsung. de la ji tsam 'tshal zhus pas. mad dang ku re yin 'di kas chog gis gsung nas' (rGyal 1973:254).

56 The Tibetan text reads, 'mchor po'i rgyal dang mdzes ma'i grogs. spangs na 'phangs tsam gda' lags te. mal bde dro 'jam 'di la 'phongs dus med. gti mug ro nyal spangs shing ras chung pa' (gTsang 1999:450); for an alternative translation, see Chang (1962:450).

57 Considering that Rechungpa later become the rallying point for many of the Kagyu's anti-intellectual movements, including the *sMyon pas*, this is rather ironic.

58 Literally, 'who burst their boots' (*lham rdol*). The Tibetan text reads, 'bu chung nas bsyangs pa'i ras chung pa. khyod gdams ngag len du btang ba la. rtsod yig 'di yi mang lugs kyis. gzhung bshad mkhan zhig byung gis dogs. khyod sgom chen stan rdol re ba la. bshad pa 'di yi mang lugs kyis. ston chen lham rdol byung gis dogs' (gTsang 1999:609); for an alternative translation, see Chang (1962:453).

59 The Tibetan text reads, 'zhen pa nang nas log nas thams cad sgyu mar rtogs pa'i rnal 'byor nam yang bde' (gTsang 1999:616–17).

60 The Tibetan text reads: 'nga ni gang byung gtad med mkhan. nga ni zas med ldum bu pa. nga ni gos med gcer by pa. nga ni nor med slong mo pa. nga ni phyi tshis bsam med mkhan. nga ni 'dir sdod 'dir gnas med. nga ni spyod pa byung rgyal mkhan. nga ni smyon pa shi skyid mkhan. nga ni cang med dgos med mkhan' (gTsang 1999:248); for an alternative translation, see Chang (1962:63).

61 The names of the songs are:—'skyid pa ngo mtshar brgyad kyi mgur [Eight amazing joys]' (gTsang 1999:668); 'rnal 'byor bde ba bcu gnyis mgur [Twelve happy yogas] (gTsang 1999:388); 'The Growth of joyfulness' (Chang 1962:339); 'How to gain happiness and avoid suffering' (Chang 1962:459); 'The Eight wondrous joys' (Chang 1962:508); 'The Six positive joys of the mind' (Chang 1962:608).

62 The Tibetan text reads, 'nyams dga' blo bde sgyu lus bde 'o. nga 'dzin chags med ba'i 'gro 'dug bde 'o. zhum pa med pa'i rtul shugs bde 'o. bnyis su med pa'i lta ba

bde'o. bying rgod med pa'i gsam gtan bde'o' (rGyal 1973:225); for an alternative translation, see Tiso (1989:379).

63 The Tibetan text reads, 'lus la gtum mo 'bar tsa na. snam phrug zer ba rdzun du gda'. khres po 'dis kyang dgos rgyu chung. shig sro'i gnas tshang nga mi 'dod' (gTsang 1999:522); for an alternative translation, see Chang (1962:363).

64 The Tibetan text reads, 'ngas skom gyi dogs nas btung ba btsal. btung bad ran shes bdud rtsi'i chang. da skom gyi dogs pa ngal la med' (gTsang 1999:263); for an alternative translation, see Chang (1962:84).

65 The Tibetan text reads, 'chos nyid chang, gi tshams cad bzi. thod rgal nyams kyi rtsed mo rste. gnyis dbang glu chung rtse re re. nyams len byin rlabs thul lu lu' (gTsang 1999:413) ; for an alternative translation, see Chang (1962:256).

glossary

Spelling of Tibetan terms and names

In the text	Wylie
Abo Thuchen	*a bo mthu chen*
aku	*a khu*
Amdo	*a mdo*
Beri	*be ri*
Bökhor depa	*bod skor sde pa*
bön	*bon*
bumpa	*bum pa*
chabsee	*chab srid*
Chador Namgyal	*phyag rdor rnam rgyal*
Chamdo	*chab mdo*
Chana Dorje	*phyag na rdo rje*
chang	*chang*
Chatring	*cha phreng*
Chenrezig	*spyan ras gzigs*
chösi	*chos srid*
chu	*chu*
Chubori	*chu bo ri*
Chuzhi Gangdrug	*chu bzhi sgang drug/ chu bzhi gangs drug*
Dartsedo	*dar rtse mdo*
de	*bde*
Dégé	*sde dge*

Dekyi	*bde skyid*
Demojong	*'bras mo ljongs*
Denjong	*'bras ljongs*
Denjong Dzogchen	*'bras ljongs rdzogs chen*
Depa	*sde pa*
Derge Dzogchen	*sde dge rdzogs chen*
Desi	*sde srid*
Dokham	*mdo khams*
Dora Karmo	*rdo ra dkar mo*
Dorje Shugden	*rdo rje shugs ldan*
Dorje Tashi	*rdo rje bkra shis*
draché	*drwa phyed / dra phyed*
Dragmag	*drag dmag*
Drakyab	*brag gyab*
Drakpa Gyaltsen	*grags pa rgyal mtshan*
drama	*dra ma / khra ma*
drawa	*dra ba / drwa ba*
Drepung	*'bras spungs*
Drölma	*sgrol ma*
Drukpa Kagyü	*'brug pa bka' brgyud*
Drugu	*dru gu*
Drugu Chögyal	*dru gu chos rgyal*
Drugu Ladrag	*gru gu lha brag*
Dubdi	*bdub bdi*
dubtop	*grub thob*
dükhang	*'du khang*
dungrab	*gdung rabs*
Dzemay Rinpoche	*dze smad rin po che*
Dzogchen	*rdzog(s) chen*

dzom	*'dzom*
Dzongsar	*rdzong gsar*
Galdan Phodrang	*dga' ldan pho 'brang*
Gampopa	*sgam po pa*
Ganden Podrang	*dga' ldan pho 'brang*
Ganzi	*mkhar mdzes / dkar mdzes*
Gelug	*dge lugs*
Gelugpa	*dge lugs pa*
Geshe Chag Trichog	*dge bshes phyag khri mchog*
Geshe Darlo	*dge bshes dar blo*
golay	*sgo klad*
Golden Stūpa	*gser kyi mchod rten*
gomba	*sgom pa*
gön	*dgon*
Gonpo Namgyal	*mgon po rnam ryal*
Gonpo Tashi Angdrugtsang	*mgon po bkra shis a'brug tshang*
go ra	*sgo ra*
gothö dzégyen	*sgo thod mdzes rgyan*
Guru Rinpoche	*gu ru rin po che*
gyalön	*rgyal blon*
gyalpo	*rgyal po*
gyalrab	*rgyal rabs*
Gyalthangpa	*rgyal thang pa*
gyang	*gyang*
gyelpo	*rgyal po*
Gyurmé Namgyal	*'gyur med rnam rgyal*
Hor	*hor*
Jalse Rinpoche	*rgyal sras rin po che*
Jambayang	*'jam dpal dbyangs*

Jonang	*jo nang*
Kadampa	*bka' gdams pa*
Kalön Lama	*bka' blon bla ma*
Kangchejunga	*gangs can mdzod lnga*
Kargyüd / Kargyüdpa	*bka' brgyud / bka' brgyud pa*
Karmapa	*ka rma pa*
Karmapa Rangjung Dorje	*karma pa rang byung rdo rje*
Karma Tenkyong	*ka rma bstan skyong*
Karma Tensrung	*ka rma bstan srung*
Katen dang Sergi chagje	*bka' bstan dang gser gyi phyag rjes*
Kham	*khams*
Khampa	*khams pa*
Kharnang depa	*mkhar nang sde pa*
khatag	*kha btags*
khenpo	*mkhan po*
Khenpo Dorje Tashi	*mkhan po rdo rje bkra shis*
Khenpo Jigme Phuntsog	*mkhan po 'jigs med phun tshogs*
Khenpo Zhara Chudrak	*mkhan po rtsa ra chos grags*
khyamra	*khyams rwa*
korpo	*'khor po*
Kuntuzangpo	*kun tu bzang po*
kyibo	*skyi bo*
Labrang	*bla brang*
lama	*bla ma*
lami	*lha mi*
lamrim	*lam rim*
Lepcha	*mon pa*
Lhadag Pema Yang Dzong	*lha brag pad ma yang rdzong*
Lhagang	*lha sgang*

lhakhang	*lha khang*
Lhasa	*lha sa*
Lhathog	*lha thog*
Lhathog may	*lha thog smad*
Lhathog tö	*lha thog stod*
Lhathothori Nyen Tsen	*lha tho tho ri gnyan btsan*
Lhatsen	*lha btsan*
Lhatsün Namka Jigmé	*lha bstun nam mkha 'jigs med*
Lhomontsongsum	*lho mon tshong gsum*
Lhopo	*lho po*
Lhorong	*lho rong*
Lithang	*li thang*
Lo	*glo*
lojong	*blo sbyong*
loong pai chos	*lung pa'i chos*
Maṇi khang	*ma ṇi khang*
Maṇi Lakhang	*ma ṇi lha khang*
Markham	*smar khams*
Marpa	*mar pa*
Metok Yul	*me tog yul*
Milarepa	*mi la ras pa*
Minyag Dora Karmo	*mi nyag rdo ra dkar mo*
mo	*mo*
Mön	*mon*
namgyal	*rnam rgyal*
namthar	*rnam (par) thar (pa)*
Nangchen	*nang chen*
Narthang	*snar thang*
ngag	*sngags*
Nyatri Tsenpo	*gnya' khri btsan po*

Nyima Yangtso	*nyi ma gyang mtsho*
Nyingma	*rnying ma*
Nyingmapa	*rnying ma pa*
o	*'o*
Pabongkha Rinpoche	*pha bong kha rin po che*
Paltrul Rinpoche	*dpal sprul rin po che*
Paltrul Urgyen Jigme Chos Kyi Wangpo	*dpal sprul o rgyan 'jigs med chos kyi dbang po*
Panchen Drakpa Gyaltsen	*paṇ chen grags pa rgyal mtshan*
Panchen Lama	*paṇ chen bla ma*
Pelma Tsewang	*dpal ma tshe dbang*
Pemayangtse	*pad ma dbyang brtse*
phayül	*pha yul*
Phüntsokling	*phun tshogs gling*
Phüntsog Namgyal	*phun tshogs rnam rgyal*
pön	*dpon*
rakor	*ra skor*
Rangit	*rang gyit*
Rangjung Dorje	*rang byung rdo rje*
Ratung	*ra tung*
rawa	*ra ba*
raypa	*ras pa*
Rebkong	*reb gong*
Rechungpa	*ras chung pa*
répa	*ras pa*
Rigsum Gonpo	*rigs gsum mgon po*
Rinchen Dorje	*rin chen rdo rje*
Rinpoche	*rin po che*
Rohtang	*ro thang*
Rongwo (Gönchen)	*rong bo (dgon chen)*

Sakya	*sa skya*
Samduptse	*bsam grub rtse*
Samgyé	*bsam rgyas*
sang	*bsangs*
Saqi Dewa	*sa dkyil sde pa*
senge	*seng ge*
Sengeshong	*seng ge gshong*
Sengeshong yago	*seng ge gshong ya mgo*
Sergichöten	*gser gyi mchod rten*
Sertha	*gser mtha'*
Sherab	*shes rab*
Sherab Sangpo	*shes rab bzang po*
Shigatse	*gshis ka rtse*
shing	*shing*
sok trel	*srog 'brel*
Sonam Gyaltsen	*bsod nams rgyal mtshan*
Sonam Gyatso	*bsod nams rgya mtsho*
Tai Situ Rinpoche	*ta'i si tu rin po che*
tanka	*thang ka / thang kha*
Tapontsang (possibly)	*rta pho tshang /rta dpon tshang*
tatsang	*grwa tshang*
tensrung	*bstan srung*
Tensrung Dragmag	*bstan srung drag dmag*
ter	*gter*
tertön	*gter ston*
thanka	*thang ga*
thawa	*mtha' ba*
thempa	*them pa*
thögal	*thod rgal*

Thowakya	*tho 'a kya*
Tingkyé	*gting skyes*
Trijang Rinpoche	*khri byang rin po che*
Trisrong Detsen	*khri srong lde 'u btsan*
trulku	*sprul sku*
Trulku Druga	*sprul sku 'grug dga'*
tsampa	*rtsam pa*
Tsang	*gtsang*
Tsangnyön Heruka	*gtsang smyon he ru ka*
tsema	*tshad ma*
Tsenpo	*btsan po*
Tshompa Lo Washul Tsering Geleg	*rtsom pa lo wa shul tshe ring dge legs*
Tshong	*tshong*
tsipatra	*tsi pa tra*
tsog	*tshogs*
Tsogi khorlo	*tshogs kyi 'khor lo*
Tsongkhapa	*tsong kha pa*
Tsopa Dorlo rinpoché	*khros pa rdo lo rin po che*
Tsö	*gtsos*
Tsögon Geden Chöling	*gtsos dgon dge ldan chos gling*
tsöma	*tshod ma*
tummo	*gtum mo*
Ü	*dbus*
yab	*gyab*
Yarlung	*yar klung / yar lung*
Zhara	*bzhag bra*
Zhaypa Dorje	*bzhad pa rdo rje*

bibliography

Al-Jazeera 2008, 'The Dalai Lama: the devil within', *People and Power*, Aljazeera.net, 1 October, http://english.aljazeera.net/programmes/peopleandpower/2008/09/200893014344405483.html, viewed 10.5.2010.

Almond, PC 1988, *The British discovery of Buddhism*, Cambridge University Press, Cambridge.

Anderson, Benedict 1991, *Imagined communities*, Verso, London.

Angdrugtsang, GT 1973, *Four rivers, six ranges: reminiscences of the resistance movement in Tibet*, Information and Publicity Office of HH the Dalai Lama, Dharamsala.

Appadurai, A 1986, 'Introduction' in *The social life of things: commodities in cultural perspective*, Cambridge University Press, Cambridge.

Aris, Michael 1979, *Bhutan: the early history of a Himalayan kingdom*, Aris & Phillips, Warminster.

Arora, Vibha 2006, 'Changes in the perception of Tibetan identities in contemporary Sikkim, India' in Klieger, Christiaan (ed), *Tibetan borderlands: proceedings of the Xth International Association of Tibetan Studies*, Brill, Leiden.

Ashcroft, Bill 2001, *Post-colonial transformation*, Routledge, London and New York.

Assmann, Jan and Czaplicka, John 1995, 'Collective memory and cultural identity', *New German Critique*, 65.

Backman, Michael 2008, 'Selling Tibet to the world', the *Age*, 5 June.

Bajpai, SC 2000, *Lahaul-Spiti: a forbidden land in the Himalayas*, 4th ed, Indus, New Delhi.

Bakhtin, MM 1968, *Rabelais and his world*, translated by Hélène Iswolsky, MIT Press, Cambridge.

Bakshi, PM 2006, *The Constitution of India: selective comments*, Universal Law Publishing, Delhi.

Batchelor, Stephen 1998, 'Letting daylight into magic: the life and times of Dorje Shugden', *Tricycle: The Buddhist Review* 7(3).

Berghash, R and K Jillson 2001, 'Milarepa and demons: aids to spiritual and psychological growth' in *Journal of Religion and Health* 40(3).

Bernis, Ursula 1999, *Condemned to silence: a Tibetan identity crisis*, www.shugdensociety.info/pdfs/BernisResearch.pdf, viewed 12.5.2010.

Beverley, John 2004, *Testimonio: on the politics of truth*, University of Minnesota Press, Minneapolis and London.

Bhabha, Homi K 1994, *The location of culture*, Routledge, London and New York.

Bhayani, HC 1997, *Dohā-Gīti-Kosa of Saraha-Pāda and Caryā Gīiti Kosa*, Prakrit Text Society, Ahmedabad.

Bhutia, Kalzang Dorjee 2009, 'The Monastery as a Sign of Nation: the role of Pad ma dbyang brtse Monastery as part of an ideal Buddhist nation in Mthu stobs rnam rgyal and Ye she sgrol ma's *The History of Sikkim* (*'Bras ljongs rgyal rabs*)', MPhil thesis, University of Delhi.

Bishop, Peter 1989, *The myth of Shangri-la. Tibet, travel writing and the Western creation of a sacred landscape*, University of California Press, Berkeley.

BJGR = HRH Mthu stobs Rnam rgyal the Chos rgyal of Sikkim and HRH The Maharani Rgyal mo Ye shes sgrol ma 1908 [2003], *'Bras ljongs rgyal rabs*, The Tsuklhakhang Trust, Gangtok.

Boot, DP 1996, *Monasteries in Sikkim: a geographical study*, Centre for Himalayan Studies, North Bengal University, Raja Rammohunpur.

Bourdieu, P 1984, *Distinction: a social critique of the judgement of taste*, Routledge and Kegan Paul, London.

Bremmer, J 1997 'Jokes in ancient Greek culture' in Bremmer, Jan and Herman Roodenburg (eds), *A cultural history of humour*, Polity Press, Cambridge.

Brockmeier, J 2002, 'Remembering and forgetting: narrative as cultural memory', *Culture & Psychology* 8(1).

bSod (nams rin chen sGam po pa) 1982, *sGam po pa'i gsung 'bum*, Kargyud Sungrab Nyamso Khang, Darjeeling.

BYGY1 = 1972, *Sbas yul 'bras mo ljongs 'og min rnam dag pad ma drwa can gyi gnas yig lung bstan gsol 'debs smon lam gter srung gsol mchod bcas bzhugs. Collection of visionary texts revealed by Lha bstun Nam mkha'i 'jigs med and Bde chen rdo rje gling pa*, Publisher unknown, Gangtok.

BYGY2 = Rgod kyi ldem 'phru can and Sangs rgyas rdo rje 2003, *Sbas yul spyi dang bye brag yol mo gangs ra'i gnas yig,* Khenpo Nyima Dondup at Lusha Press, Kathmandu.

Campbell, J 2002, *Traveller in space: in search of female identity in Tibetan Buddhism*, Continuum International Publishing Group, London.

Carrasco, Pedro 1959, *Land and polity in Tibet*, University of Washington Press, Seattle.

Chang, GCC 1962, *The hundred thousand songs of Milarepa*, University Books, Secaucus.

Clarke, M 1987, 'Humour, laughter and the structure of thought', *British Journal of Aesthetics* 27(3).

Clarke, S 2008, 'Locating humour in Indian Buddhist monastic law codes: a comparitive approach', *Journal of Indian Philosophy* 37(4).

Clifford, James 1997, *Routes: travel and translation in the late twentieth century*, Harvard University Press, Cambridge and London.

Coleman, William M 2002, 'The uprising at Batang: Khams and its significance in Chinese and Tibetan history' in Epstein, Lawrence (ed), *Khams pa histories: visions of people, place and authority. PIATS 2000: Tibetan Studies: proceedings of the Ninth Seminar of the International Association for Tibetan Studies, Leiden 2000*, Brill, Leiden.

Cowan, HJ and PR Smith 1998, *Dictionary of architectural and building technology*, 3rd ed., Spon Press, London.

Dace, W 1963, 'The concept of 'rasa' in Sanskrit dramatic theory', *Educational Theatre Journal* 15(3).

Das, SC, G. Sandberg and AW Heyde 1988, *A Tibetan-English dictionary, with Sanskrit synonyms*, Rinsen, Kyoto.

Datta-Ray, Sunanda K 1984, *Smash and Grab: the Annexation of Sikkim*, Vikas Publishing, Delhi.

Davidson R 2002, *Indian esoteric Buddhism: a social history of the tantric movement*, Columbia University Press, New York.

Davis, RH 1997, *Lives of Indian images*, Princeton University Press, Princeton.

Derrida, Jacques 1979, 'Living on: border lines' in Bloom, Harold et al, *Deconstruction and criticism*, Routledge and Kegan Paul, London.

Dickie, J 1985, 'The Mughal garden: gateway to paradise' in Grabar, Oleg (ed), *Muqarnas III: an annual on Islamic art and architecture*, EJ Brill, Leiden.

Diehl, Keila 1997, 'When Tibetan refugees rock, paradigms roll' in Korom, Frank J (ed), *Constructing Tibetan culture: contemporary perspectives*, World Heritage Press, St Hyacinthe.

Diemberger, Hildegard 2007, *When a woman becomes a religious dynasty: the Samding Dorje Phagmo of Tibet*, Columbia University Press, New York.

Don (Grub rGyal) 1985, *Bod kyi mgur glu byung 'phel gyi lo rgyus dang khyad chos bsdud par ston pa rig pa'i khye'u rnam par rtsen pa'i skyed tshal: mgur glu'i lo rgyus dang khyad chos,* Mi rigs dpe skrun khang, Lhasa.

Dotson, B 2009, *Contemporary visions in Tibetan studies*, Serindia Publications, Chicago.

dPal (sprul, O rgyan 'jigs med chos kyi dbang po) 1968, *Kun bzang bla ma'i zhal lung: sNying thig sngon 'gro'i khrid yig*, Karmapa'i Chos sGar, Rum btegs.

Dreyfus, Georges 1999, 'The Shuk-den affair: the origins of a controversy', http://www.nktworld.org/Dreyfus.pdf, viewed 12.5.2010.

Duara, Prasenjit 1988, *Culture, power and the state: rural north China, 1900–1942*, Stanford University Press, Stanford.

Duncan, James and Derek Gregory 1999, *Writes of passage: reading travel writing*, Routledge, London and New York.

Dutton, Lee S 1999, *Anthropological resources: a guide to archival, library, and museum collections* (Library-Anthropology Resource Group, Chicago), Garland, New York.

Dye, Daniel S 1949, *A grammar of Chinese lattice* (Harvard-Yenching Institute monograph series Vol. V–VI), Harvard University Press, Cambridge.

Ekvall, Robert B 1964, 'Law and the individual among the Tibetan nomads', *American Anthropologist* 66(5).

——1968, *Fields on the hoof: nexus of Tibetan nomadic pastoralism*, Holt, Rinehart and Winston, New York.

Ellis, Bill 2005, 'Legend/anti-legend: humor as an integral part of the contemporary legend process' in Fine, Gary Alan, Véronique Campion-Vincent and Chip Heath (eds), *Rumor mills: the social impact of rumor and legend*, Aldine Transaction, New Brunswick.

Emberley, Julia 1993, *Thresholds of difference: feminist critique, native women's writings, postcolonial theory*, University of Toronto Press, Toronto.

Evans-Wentz, WY (ed) 1928, *Tibet's great yogi, Milarepa: a biography from the Tibetan,* Oxford University Press, London.

Fan Jialai 2005, *Zhongguo chuantong chuangling* [Traditional Chinese window lattices], Renmin meishu, Beijing.

Featherstone, Mike 1996, 'Localism, globalism, and cultural identity' in Wilson, Rob and Wimal Dissanayake (eds), *Global/local: cultural production and the transnational imaginary*, Duke University Press, Durham and London.

Focus on Tibet 2008, 'Signed article exposes autocratic nature of Dalai clique's theocracy', 12 December, http://news.xinhuanet.com/english/2008-12/12/content_10494330.htm, viewed 10.5.2010.

Foucault, M 1991, 'Nietzsche, genealogy, history' in Rabinov, P (ed), *The Foucault Reader*, Penguin Books, London.

Fraser, Robert 2000, *Lifting the Sentence: a poetics of postcolonial fiction*, Manchester University Press, Manchester.

Frembgen, Jürgen W 2005, 'Traditional art and architecture in Hunza' in Bianca, Stefano (ed), *Karakoram: hidden treasures in the northern areas of Pakistan*. Umberto Allemandi for the Aga Khan Trust for Culture, Torino.

Garvey, MT 1988, 'The guru-disciple relationship as exemplified in the life and songs of Milarepa', unpublished Masters Degree, dissertation, University of Colorado.

Germano, David 1998, 'Re-membering the dismembered body of Tibet: contemporary Tibetan visionary movements in the People's Republic of China' in Goldstein, Melvyn C and Matthew T Kapstein (eds), *Buddhism in contemporary Tibet: religious revival and cultural identity*, University of California Press, Berkeley.

Getty Research Institute 2009, 'Lattices' in *Art & Architecture Thesaurus Online*, Getty Research Institute, Los Angeles. www.getty.edu/research/conducting_research/vocabularies/aat/, viewed 28.4.2010.

GGLG (Nor dpon a: dkar) 1988, 'Gru gu'i lo rgyus/ gna' gtam 'bab chu'i zegs ma' in LBPYDY.

Ghosh, TK 2002, *A profile of the Himalayan Lahaula*, Anthropological Survey of India, Kolkata.

Gnoli, R 1956, *The aesthetic experience according to Abhinavagupta*, Istituto Italiano Per Il Medio Ed Estremo Oriente, Roma.

Goffman, Erving 1959, *The presentation of self in everyday life*, Doubleday, Garden City.

Goldstein, M, Ben Jiao and Tanzen Lhundrup 2009, *On the Cultural Revolution in Tibet: the Nyemo incident of 1969*, University of California Press, Berkeley.

'Gos (lo tsā ba gZhon nu dpal) 1996, *The blue annals*, translated by George N Roerich, Motilal Banarsidass Publishers, Delhi.

Goss, R 1993, 'The hermeneutics of madness (Mila rNam Thar)', unpublished PhD. Dissertation, Harvard University.

gTsang (smyon He Ru Ka) 1999, *rNal 'byor gyi dbang phyug chen po Mi la ras pa'i rnams mgur*, Sherig Parkhang, Delhi.

Guenther, HV 1983, *Ecstatic spontaneity: Saraha's three cycles of Dohā*, Asian Humanities Press, Berkeley.

Gurevich, A 1997, 'Bakhtin and his theory of carnival' in Bremmer, Jan and Herman Roodenburg (eds), *A cultural history of humour*, Polity Press, Cambridge..

Hall, Stuart 1990, 'Cultural identity and diaspora' in Rutherford, Jonathan (ed), *Identity: community, culture, difference*, Lawrence & Wishart, London.

Halliwell, S 1991, 'The uses of laughter in Greek culture', *Classical Quarterly* 41(2).

Harcourt, AFP 1972 [1871], *The Himalayan districts of Kooloo, Lahoul and Spiti*, Vivek Publishing House, Delhi.

Harlow, Barbara 1987, *Resistance literature*, Methuen, New York.

Hirsch, Marianne and Leo Spitzer 2007, '*Testimonia*l objects. Memory, gender and transmission' in Baronian, Marie-Aude, Stephan Besser and Yolande Jansen (eds), *Diaspora and memory. Figures of displacement in contemporary literature, arts and politics,* Rodopi, Amsterdam.

Hitchens, Christopher 1998, 'His Material Highness', *Salon Newsreal*, 13 July, www.salon.com/news/1998/07/13news.html, viewed 10.5.2010.

HOS = HRH Mthu stobs Rnam rgyal the Chos rgyal of Sikkim and HRH The Maharani Rgyal mo Ye shes sgrol ma 1908, *'Bras ljongs rgyal rabs*, translated by Kazi Dawa Samdup as *History of Sikkim*. Unpublished MS from the British India Office Library. Mss. Eur. E78. (Microfiche copy at the Menzies Library, Australian National University, Canberra, Australia.)

Huber, Toni 2001, 'Shangri-la in exile: representations of Tibetan identity and transnational culture' in Dodin, Thierry and Heinz Räther (eds), *Imagining Tibet: perceptions, projections and fantasies*, Wisdom Publications, Somerville.

Huggan, Graham 2001, *The post-colonial exotic: marketing the margins*, Routledge, New York and London.

Hyers, C 1970, 'The ancient Zen master as clown-figure and comic midwife', *Philosophy East and West* 20(1).

—— 1974, *Zen and the comic spirit*, Rider and Company, London.

—— 1989, 'Humor in Zen: comic midwifery', *Philosophy East and West* 39(3).

Ibbetson, Sir Denzil 1980 [1919], *Glossary of the tribes and castes of the Punjab and North-West frontier province, based on the census report for the Punjab, 1883, by the late Sir Denzil Ibbetson, KCSI, and the census report for the Punjab, 1892, by Sir Edward Maclagan, KCIE, CSI*, vol. 3, Amar Prakashan, New Delhi.

I-Tsing 1998 [1896], *A record of the Buddhist religion as practised in India and the Malaya Archipelago (A.D. 671–695),* translated by J Takakusu, Munshiram Manoharlal, New Delhi.

Jackson, D 1994, *Enlightenment by a single means: Tibetan controversies on the 'self sufficient white remedy' (dkar po chig thub)*, Österreichischen Akademie der Wissenschaften, Wien.

Jackson, R 2004, *Tantric treasures: three collections of mystical verse from Buddhist India*, Oxford University Press, New York.

Jacobson, Calla 2004, 'Spirituality, harmony, and peace: situating contemporary images of Tibet', *Himalaya. The Journal of the Association for Nepal and Himalayan Studies* 24(1–2).

Kaplan, Caren 1988, 'Michael Arlen's fictions of exile: the subject of ethnic autobiography', *A/B: Auto/Biography Studies* 4(2).

—— 1992, 'Resisting autobiography' in Smith, Sidonie and Julia Watson (eds), *De/colonizing the subject. The politics of gender in women's autobiography*, University of Minnesota, Minneapolis.

Kapstein, Matthew 2006, *The Tibetans*, Wiley-Blackwell, Oxford.

Karma-pa III Rang byung rdo rje 1978, *rNal byor gyi dbang phyug Mi la bshad pa rdo rje'i gsung mgur mdzod nag ma: the life and songs of realization of Mi-la-ras pa*, Damchoe Sangpo, Dalhousie.

King, R 1999, *Orientalism and religion: postcolonial theory, India and 'the mystic East'*, Routledge, London.

Klieger, Christiaan P 1989, *Accomplishing Tibetan identity: the constitution of a national consciousness*, PhD thesis, University of Hawai'i.

Klimburg, Max 2005, 'Traditional art and architecture in Baltistan' in Bianca, Stefano (ed), *Karakoram: hidden treasures in the northern areas of Pakistan*. Umberto Allemandi for the Aga Khan Trust for Culture, Torino.

Kunga Rinpoche, Lama 1995, *Drinking the mountain stream: songs of Tibet's beloved saint, Milarepa: eighteen selections from the rare collection,* translated by Lama Kunga Rimpoche and Brian Cutillo, Wisdom Publications, Boston.

Kværne, Per, 2010 *An anthology of Buddhist tantric songs: a study of the caryāgīti*, Orchid Press, Bangkok.

Latour, B and P Weibel 2005, *Making things public: atmospheres of democracy*, MIT Press, Cambridge.

LBPYDY 1988, *Khams gru gu lha brag ye brdzu gnyan po'i chos skor bzhugs so*, Library of Tibetan Works and Archives, Dharamsala.

Le Goff, J 1997, 'Laughter in the Middle Ages' in Bremmer, Jan and Herman Roodenburg (eds), *A cultural history of humour*, Polity Press, Cambridge.

Lee, KJ 1976, 'The philosophic significance of the comic', *Philosophy East and West* 26(2).

Lefebvre, H 1991 [1974], *The production of space*, translated by Donald Nicholson-Smith, Blackwell, Oxford.

Lhalungpa, L 1997, *The life of Milarepa,* Book Faith India, Varanasi.

Lindholm, Charles 2003, 'Culture, charisma and consciousness: the case of the Rajneeshee', *Ethos* 30(4).

Liu, LH 1995, *Translingual practice: literature, national culture, and translated modernity: China, 1900–1937*, Stanford University Press, Stanford, California.

LNJSB = Lha bstun Nam mkha' 'jigs med, 1974, *The Collected Works of Lha-bstun Nam-mkha'i 'Jigs-med,* 4 vols, Jurme Drakpa, New Delhi.

Lopez, Donald 1999, *Prisoners of Shangri-La. Tibetan Buddhism and the West*, Chicago University Press, Chicago and London.

LTDR1 ('Gyur med rnam rgyal) 1984, *Rgyal rigs shing sa la chen po lta bu Lhathog dpon gyi gdung rabs deb ther legs par bshad pa chos srid sgo brgya 'byed pa'i lde'u mig*, Library of Tibetan Works and Archives, Dharamsala. (Martin 387B)

LTDR2 (Rtsom pa lo wa shul tshe ring dge legs) 2006, *Mdo Khams Lhathog gi rgyal rabs mdo tsam gleng ba gangs ljongs skye bo'i rna rgyan*, publisher and place of publication unknown.

Mahajan, Uma Singh 2002, 'A separate reality: trance possession and exorcism in the magico-religious system of the Ravi River valley of Chamba, Himachal Pradesh' in Thakur, Laxman S (ed), *Where mortals and mountain gods meet: society and culture in Himachal Pradesh,* Indian Institute of Advanced Study, Shimla.

Marcus, G 1995, 'Ethnography in/of the world system: the emergence of multi-sited ethnography', *Annual Review of Anthropology* 24.

McCarthy, RE 1997, *Tears of the lotus: accounts of Tibetan resistance to the Chinese invasion, 1950–1962*, McFarland & Company, Jefferson.

McGranahan C 2005, 'Truth, fear, and lies: exile politics and arrested histories of the Tibetan resistance', *Cultural Anthropology* 20(4).

—— 2006, 'Tibet's Cold War: the CIA and the Chushi Gandrug resistance, 1956–1974', *Journal of Cold War Studies* 8(3).

McLagan, Margaret 1996, *Mobilizing for Tibet: transnational politics and diaspora culture in the post-Cold War era*, PhD thesis, New York University.

McMillin, Laurie Hovell 2001, *English in Tibet, Tibet in English: self-presentation in Tibet and the diaspora,* Palgrave, New York.

McNeil, Kent 2001, *Emerging Justice?: Essays on Indigenous Rights in Canada and Australia*, Native Law Centre, University of Saskatchewan, Saskatoon.

Medhurst, WH 1840, *China: its state and prospects, with especial reference to the spread of the Gospel, containing allusions to the antiquity, extent, population, civilization, literature, and religion of the Chinese*, J Snow, London.

Morreall, J 1989, 'The rejection of humor in Western thought', *Philosophy East and West* 39(3).

Mumford, Stan Royal (1989), *Himalayan dialogue: Tibetan lamas and Gurung shamans in Nepal,* University of Wisconsin Press, Madison.

Orange, Claudia 1987, *The Treaty of Waitangi*, Allen & Unwin, Wellington.

Ortner, Sherry 1989, *High religion: a cultural and political history of Sherpa Buddhism*, Princeton University Press, Princeton.

Palmer, J 2005, 'Parody and decorum: permission to mock' in Lockyer, S and M Pickering (eds), *Beyond a joke: the limits of humour*, Palgrave Macmillan, Basingstoke.

Panchen 1969 [c1612], *The autobiography of the First Panchen Lama Blo-bzang-chos-kyi-rgyal-mtshan*, Ngawang Gelek Demo (ed), Gedan Sungrab Minyam Gyunphel Series, New Delhi.

PDDEC = Phyad rdor Rnam rgyal's statement (believed to have been edited c.1901 by Srid skyong rnam rgyal), Unpublished manuscript, 1952–1953.

Pha bong kha, Rinpoche and Khri byang, Rinpoche 2003, *Rnam grol lag bcang*. Delhi: Ser re rje dpe skrun khang.

Phull, Archana 1998, 'Spies' links with Shugden activists suspected', *Indian Express*, 23 September.

Powers, John 1992, 'Conflict and resolution in the biography of Milarepa', *The Tibet Journal* XVII (1).

—— 2004, *History as propaganda: Tibetan exiles versus the People's Republic of China*, Oxford University Press, Oxford.

Prost, Audrey 2006, 'The problem with "rich refugees": sponsorship, capital, and the informal economy of Tibetan refugees', *Modern Asian Studies* 40(1).

Pu Wencheng 1990, *Gan-Qing Zangchuan fojiao siyuan* [The Tibetan Buddhist monasteries of Gansu and Qinghai], Qinghai renmin, Xining.

Quintman, AH 2006, *Mi la ras pa's many lives: Anatomy of a Tibetan biographical corpus*, unpublished Ph.D. thesis, University of Michigan.

Rangacharya, Adya 1996, *The nāṭyaśāstra: English translation with critical notes*, Mushiram Manoharlal Publishers, New Delhi.

rGyal thang pa bde chen rdo rje 1973, *Dkar brgyud gser 'phreng*, Sungrab Nyamso Gyunphel Parkhang, Palampur, HP.

Risley, HH 1894, *The gazetteer of Sikkim,* Bengal Secretariat Press, Calcutta.

Ruch, W 1993, 'Exhilaration and humor' in Lewis, M and JM Haviland-Jones (eds), *The Handbook of Emotions,* Guilford Press, New York.

RZSG = Lha bstun Nam mkha' 'jigs med, 2000, *Rig 'dzin srog sgrub,* 5 vols, Chos spyod dpar skrun khang, Delhi.

Said, Edward W 2000, *Reflections on exile and other essays*, Harvard University Press, Cambridge.

Samuel, Geoffrey 1982, 'Tibet as a stateless society and some Islamic parallels', *Journal of Asian Studies* 41(2).

—— 1993, *Civilized shamans: Buddhism in Tibetan societies*, Smithsonian Institution, Washington.

—— 1995 [1993], *Civilized shamans: Buddhism in Tibetan societies*, Mandala Book Point, Kathmandu.

Sands, KM 1996, 'Ifs, ands, and butts: theological reflections on humor', *Journal of the American Academy of Religion* 64(3).

Schaeffer, K 2005, *Dreaming the great Brahmin: Tibetan traditions of the Buddhist poet-saint Saraha*. Oxford University Press, New York.

Schopen, G 1997, *Bones, stones and Buddhist monks: collected papers on the archaeology, epigraphy, and texts of monastic Buddhism in India*, University of Hawai'i Press, Honolulu.

Schopen, G 2007, 'The learned monk as a comic figure: on reading a Buddhist Vinaya as Indian literature', *Journal of Indian Philosophy* 35(3).

Schultheis, Alexandra W 2006, 'Subjectivity politics in *Sorrow mountain:* transnational feminism and Tibetan autobiography', *Gender Journal* 44.

Scott, James C 2009, *The art of not being governed: an anarchist history of upland Southeast Asia*, Yale University Press, New Haven and London.

sGam po pa 1982, *sGam po pa'i gsung 'bum*, Kargyud Sungrab Syamso Khang, Darjeeling.

Shahidullah, M1928, *Les chants mystiques de Kāṇha et de Saraha: les Dohā-koṣa et les Caryā,* Adrien-Maisonneuve, Paris.

Sharma, Mahesh 2001, *The realm of faith: subversion, appropriation and dominance in the western Himalaya*, Indian Institute of Advanced Study, Shimla.

Shugden Society 2008, 'Outcast society emerging among Tibetans', Dorje Shugden Devotee's Charitable & Religious Society, www.shugdensociety.info/outcastSocietyEN.html, viewed 10.5.2010.

Siegel, L 1987, *Laughing matters: comic tradition in India,* University of Chicago Press, Chicago.

Sinha, Veer Bahadur 2006a, interview with the author, Triloknāth, 29 June.

—— 2006b, interview with the author, Triloknāth, 20 August.

Smith, EG 1969, 'Preface to the Life of the Saint of Gtsang' in Chandra, Lokesh (ed), *The Life of the Saint of gTsang by rGyod tshang ras pa sna tshogs rang grol*, Satapitaka Series, New Delhi.

Smith, W 2008, *China's Tibet? Autonomy or assimilation*, Rowman and Littlefield, Lanham.

Snellgrove, David 1954, 'Saraha's treasury of songs' in Conze, E (ed), *Buddhist texts through the ages*, Harper and Row, New York.

—— 1987, *Indo-Tibetan Buddhism: Indian Buddhists and their Tibetan successors*, Serindia Publications, London.

Sommer, Doris 1999, 'No secrets' in Gugelberger, Georg M (ed), *The real thing: testimonial discourse and Latin America*, Duke University Press, Durham and London.

Spivak, Gayatri Chakravorty 1988a, 'Can the subaltern speak?' in Nelson, Cary and Lawrence Grossberg (eds), *Marxism and the interpretation of culture*, Macmillan Education, Basingstoke.

—— 1988b, *In other worlds: essays in cultural politics*, Routledge, London and New York.

Stutchbury, EA 1991, *Rediscovering western Tibet: Gonpa, Chorten and the continuity of practice with a Tibetan Buddhist community in the Indian Himalaya*, PhD thesis, Australian National University, Canberra.

Tapontsang, Adhe 1997, *Ama Adhe: the voice that remembers*, as told to Joy Blakeslee, Wisdom Publications, Somerville, Mass.

Tāranātha 2000 [1633], *rgyal khams pa tā ra nā thas bdag nyid kyi rnam thar nges par brjod pa'i deb gter shin tu zhib mo ma bcos lhug pa'i rtogs brjod* in Dzamthang, *rJe btsun Tā ra nā tha'i gsung 'bum*, volume 1, Tibetan Buddhist Resource Centre, Cambridge.

Teichman, Eric 2000 [1922], *Travels of a consular officer in eastern Tibet, together with a history of relations between China, Tibet and India*, Pilgrims Publishing House, Kathmandu.

Templeman, David 2008, *Becoming Indian: A study of the life of the 16–17th century Tibetan lama, Tāranātha*, PhD thesis, Monash University.

Thargyal, Rinzin 2007, *Nomads in eastern Tibet: social organization and economy of a pastoral estate in the Kingdom of Dege*, Brill, Leiden.

Tiso, FV 1989, 'A study of the Buddhist saint in relation to the biographical tradition of Milarepa, unpublished PhD. dissertation, Columbia University.

Tsering, Tashi 1985, 'Ngag rong mgon po rnam rgyal: a 19th century Khams pa warrior' in Aziz, Barbara N and Matthew Kapstein (eds), *Soundings in Tibetan civilization*, Manohar, New Delhi.

Tucci, Giuseppe 2000 [1978], *The religions of Tibet*, Kegan Paul, London.

Turner, Victor 1967, *The forest of symbols: aspects of Ndembu ritual*, Cornell University Press, Ithaca.

Urubshurow, VK 1984, 'Symbolic process on the Buddhist path: spiritual development in the biographical tradition of Milarepa', unpublished PhD. dissertation, University of Chicago.

Van Dam, E 1991, *Magic life of Milarepa,* Shambhala, Boston.

Verberckmoes, J 1997, 'The comic and the Counter-Reformation in the Spanish Netherlands' in Bremmer, Jan and Herman Roodenburg (eds), *A cultural history of humour*, Polity Press, Cambridge.

Vogel, JP 1972 [1926], *Indian serpent lore, or the Nagas in Hindu legend and art*, Indological Book House, Varanasi.

Waring, Wendy 1995, 'Is this your book? Wrapping postcolonial fiction for the market', *Canadian Review of Comparative Literature* 22(3/4).

Weber, Max 1991 [1948], *From Max Weber: essays in sociology*, Routledge, New York.

White, JC 1986 [1909], *Sikkim and Bhutan: Twenty one years on the north-east frontier 1887–1908,* Manas Publishing, Delhi.

Willan, P 2002, 'State TV pulls plug on Berlusconi satire', the *Guardian* 11October, www.guardian.co.uk/international/story/0,3604,809664,00, viewed 25.9.2006.

Woodward, FL 1979, *The book of the gradual sayings (Anguttara nikaya)*, Pali Text Society, London.

Woodward, Kenneth L 1998, 'A scratch in the teflon Lama: a rift over a Buddhist deity reveals that the Tibetan religion isn't such a Shangri-La after all', *Newsweek,* 11 May.

Wylie, TV 1964, 'Mar-Pa's Tower: notes on local hegemons in Tibet', *History of Religions* 3(2).

Xue Yu 2005, *Buddhism, war, and nationalism: Chinese monks in the struggle against Japanese aggressions, 1931–1945*, Routledge, New York.

Yim Seock Jae 2005. *Floral lattices, columns and pavilions: a study of Korean architecture*, translated by Lee Jean Young, Ewha Woman's University Press, Seoul.

Yudru, Tsomu 2006, *Local aspirations and national constraints: a case study of Nyarong Gonpo Namgyel and his rise to power in Kham (1836–1865)*, PhD thesis, Harvard University, Cambridge.

Zongtse, CT (rDzong rtse byams pa thub bstan) 1977, *dga' ldan phun tshogs gling gi thog mtha' bar gsum gyi byung ba yid la dran byed kun khyab snyan pa'i rnga sgra zhes bya ba* [History of the monastic university dGa' ldan Phun tshogs gliṅ], Veröffentlichungen des Seminars für Indologie und Buddhismuskunde der Universität Göttingen, Göttingen.

—— 1994, *gtsang myang smad bsam 'grub rtse'i sde srid gtsang pa rim byung gi mnga' thang 'byor rgud kyi lo rgyus* [History of bSam-grub rtse Fort: the rise and Fall of the sDe pa gTsang pa rulers], Library of Tibetan Works and Archives, Dharamsala.

BIBLIOGRAPHY